Understanding Ka

Kant's ethical thought remains one of the most influential, yet notoriously challenging, systems in the history of philosophy. This volume provides a sympathetic but critical reconstruction of the main strands of Kant's ethics, focusing on the most commonly read of Kant's ethical works, the *Groundwork of the Metaphysics of Morals*. Part I outlines Kant's arguments in defense of his Categorical Imperative, as well as elaborating Kant's understanding of dignity and human freedom. Part II addresses the most common objections to Kant's ethics, including challenges to the Formula of Universal Law; Kant's controversial ethical stances on suicide, sex and marriage, and non-human animals; and the place of reason, sentiment, and happiness in Kant's ethics. For scholars and specialists alike, the volume offers a clear and accessible account of what Kantian morality both offers us and asks of us.

MICHAEL CHOLBI is Professor of Philosophy at California State Polytechnic University, Pomona.

Understanding Kant's Ethics

Michael Cholbi
California State Polytechnic University, Pomona

CAMBRIDGE
UNIVERSITY PRESS

CAMBRIDGE
UNIVERSITY PRESS

University Printing House, Cambridge CB2 8BS, United Kingdom

Cambridge University Press is part of the University of Cambridge.

It furthers the University's mission by disseminating knowledge in the pursuit of education, learning, and research at the highest international levels of excellence.

www.cambridge.org
Information on this title: www.cambridge.org/9781107163461

First published 2016

Printed in the United Kingdom by Clays, St Ives plc

A catalogue record for this publication is available from the British Library.

Library of Congress Cataloging-in-Publication Data
Cholbi, Michael, author.
Understanding Kant's ethics / Michael Cholbi, California State
Polytechnic University, Pomona.
New York : Cambridge University Press, 2016. | Includes index.
LCCN 2016016320 | ISBN 9781107163461
LCSH: Kant, Immanuel, 1724–1804. | Ethics.
LCC B2799.E8 C53 2016 | DDC 170.92–dc23
LC record available at http://lccn.loc.gov/2016016320

ISBN 978-1-107-16346-1 Hardback
ISBN 978-1-316-61522-5 Paperback

For my wife and children,
my Kingdom of Ends in miniature

Contents

Contents

Preface

Many others had a hand in making *Understanding Kant's Ethics* possible. A special debt is owed to those who had the patience and courage to try to teach me about Kant's ethics: Richard Eldridge, Kathleen Wright, Talbot Brewer, and, most especially, John Marshall. His encouragement during my graduate studies was invaluable in persuading me that I had a contribution to make to the world's understanding of Kant's ethics. David Kaspar, Chris Naticchia, and Rivka Weinberg read and provided extensive comments upon drafts of this work. Many colleagues have served as my interlocutors regarding Kant's ethics over the years. These include David Adams, Matthew Altman, Carl Cranor, John Davis, Paul Hurley, Robert Johnson, Sharon Lloyd, James Mahon, Herbert Morris, Stephen Munzer, and Maura Priest. No doubt I have inadvertently omitted some, for which I apologize. My wife, Wendy, offered a crucial non-philosopher's perspective throughout the writing of this book. Some of the claims defended here were first developed as part of a project sponsored by the Research, Scholarship, and Creative Activities program at the California State University. Thanks lastly to all those students to whom I've had the pleasure of teaching Kant's ethics; you helped me see the need for this book and motivated me to bring it to fruition.

Abbreviations

A note regarding references to Kant's works: because there are many editions and printings of Kant's writings, as well as many translations, the philosophical community now employs a standardized reference system for Kant's works. In this reference system, volume and page references refer to the German edition of Kant's works, Kant's Gesammelte Schriften, edited by the Royal German Academy of Sciences (Berlin: deGruyter, 1900–). In this book, I have used parenthetical references with abbreviations referring to Kant's specific works, followed by the volume and page references to Royal German Academy text. So, for instance, G 4:424 refers to Kant's Groundwork, found in volume 4 of the Royal German Academy text, p. 424. The list of abbreviations I have used are as follows:

C2	Critique of Practical Reason (aka, the 'second Critique')
G	Groundwork of the Metaphysics of Morals
LE	Lectures on Ethics
MM	Metaphysics of Morals
R	Religion Within the Limits of Reason Alone
SRL	"On a Supposed Right to Lie from Philanthropy"
TP	"On the Common Saying, 'That May Be True in Theory but Is of No Use in Practice'"

All English translations are by Mary Gregor, printed in the Cambridge Edition of the Works of Immanuel Kant (Cambridge, 1996).

Introduction

Over the past two decades, I have had the good fortune of encountering Kant's writings on ethics from three distinct perspectives: as a student, both undergraduate and graduate; as a teacher of Kant's ethics; and as a philosophical scholar attracted to Kant's ethics but also genuinely troubled by the objections that are raised against it.

This book is intended to serve readers who come from each of these perspectives. In particular, I hope that this book will fill a long-standing gap in the literature on Kant's ethics. In addition to Kant's own voluminous writings on ethics, there is now an even more voluminous body of scholarly literature on Kant's ethics, written in German, English, and other languages, comprised of hundreds of books and thousands of published articles. In one way, this large body of scholarly literature is a blessing to students, teachers, and scholars. Kant's philosophy is notoriously difficult to penetrate, packed full of obscure jargon, cryptically organized, and informed by assumptions Kant often does not bother to highlight. Fair to say, then, that Kant achieved his greatness as a philosopher despite, rather than because of, the style and presentation of his works. And since his moral philosophy is no exception to this overall tendency, this large body of scholarly literature (we might hope) should help readers of Kant's ethics to grasp at least the main ideas and insights that Kant offers.

Regrettably, the existing scholarly literature does not altogether fulfill this hope. For one, much of this literature succumbs to gross oversimplification. Introductory textbooks on ethical theory, for example, often reduce or distort core Kantian ideas, depicting it as a morality focused on 'good intentions' or acting on the basis of broad, exceptionless rules. On the other hand, much of the literature is unhelpful to newcomers to Kant's ethics in particular because it sticks too close to Kant's own language and presentation. I firmly believe that getting a foothold in Kant's ethics requires us to acknowledge Kant's shortcomings as a philosophical stylist, seeing Kant's style not as a feature of his philosophy to be admired but as an obstacle we need to work around. Unfortunately, much of the scholarly literature does not take this difficulty seriously enough, and, as a result, does not help newcomers to Kant's ethical works ascertain the assumptions and motivations that drive Kant's writings on ethics. Hence, those who read this literature often leave it with no deeper understanding of Kant's ethics than they could glean from their own reasonably careful reading of Kant's own ethical texts. As a result, there is not, in my estimation and in the estimation of many philosophers I know, a piece of secondary literature to assist readers, particularly those new to Kant or to moral philosophy, in grasping the main claims and overall significance of Kant's ethics.

This book aims to fill that role. However, I have striven to give readers more than an acquaintance with, or conceptual mastery of, the main claims or arguments Kant makes. I have written the book to try to help readers perceive why Kant's ethics is viewed as a viable candidate for the true (or the best) philosophical theory of morality. The book is therefore best described as an opinionated analytical introduction: opinionated, in that I try to present Kant's moral theory not in a neutral way, but to defend the theory in a sympathetic way; analytical, because it seeks to relate the various components of Kant's ethics to one another and to his moral theory as a whole; and an introduction, because it presupposes little if any familiarity with Kant's ethics. As will emerge in these pages, Kant was hardly infallible in his thinking about morality. Nevertheless, he articulated and integrated insights about morality that many thoughtful, reflective people can recognize and embrace.

This book thus differs from other secondary literature on Kant's ethics in some crucial respects. First, it is not a 'big book' on Kant's moral philosophy that tries to offer a careful, textually based interpretation of all the elements of Kant's moral philosophy. Hence, there is a substantial portion of Kant's writings on ethics and related areas that I will not touch upon. I will have fairly little to say, for instance, about Kant's anthropology, philosophy of religion, political philosophy, or philosophy of history, all of which inform his theory of morality.

Second, Kant was a deeply systematic philosopher. He did not theorize about ethics in isolation from his theorizing about metaphysics, human knowledge, cognition, nature, etc. No doubt a thorough grasp of Kant's ethics demands a thorough grasp of the other elements of his philosophical system. However, this book assumes that readers know little about Kant's philosophical enterprise as a whole and thus attempts to outline and motivate his ethics with minimal reference to non-ethical texts or ideas. Admittedly, this complicates the task of understanding Kant's ethics, and there are certain topics (for example, Kant's discussion of freedom of the will) where claims from elsewhere in Kant's philosophy cannot be avoided. Still, my aim has been, to the extent possible, to present Kant's ethics as a freestanding theory.

Third, a book such as this must confront the fact that the work through which virtually everyone is introduced to Kant's ethics is his Groundwork of the Metaphysics of Morals. The Groundwork sets the agenda of the early portions of this book inasmuch its early chapters are oriented around the Groundwork's central project: identifying and establishing the supreme principle of morality. That said, this book is not intended to be a commentary on the Groundwork, and it presents Kant's ethical thinking in ways that diverge significantly from their presentation in the Groundwork. Most notably, in the Groundwork, the first version of his supreme principle of morality that Kant presents is the Formula of Universal Law. Here, the first version I present of that principle is the Formula of Humanity. This deviation from Kant's own approach in the Groundwork is nevertheless warranted. The Formula of Humanity plays a larger role in texts besides the Groundwork, tends to be less technical and abstract than the Formula of Universal Law, and provides a roadmap for Kant's account of our moral duties.

Furthermore, while the Groundwork is indispensable to understanding Kant's moral philosophy, it is likely to give an incomplete, if not outright misleading, picture of Kant's ethical thought when read in isolation. It is therefore unfortunate that many never engage at all with Kant's other ethical texts, for there are important components of his ethical thought that Kant does not discuss in the Groundwork. That text says little, for instance, about moral psychology, the details of our moral duties, or key institutions such as marriage or punishment. The Groundwork has the advantage of being relatively brief and directed at core questions in Kant's ethics. Still, it is a work of limited aims or scope, and therefore readers whose sole understanding of Kant's ethics comes from that work get a similarly limited understanding of Kant's ethics. Thus, when (in my estimation) a central Kantian claim or insight can be articulated solely by reference to the Groundwork, I refer to that text alone. However, I make liberal use of other Kantian texts when the Groundwork is either silent or sketchy concerning the matter at hand. Especially important here will be Kant's Metaphysics of Morals, the work for which the Groundwork was intended as preparatory. (Kant's Critique of Practical Reason plays a prominent role in Chapter 5 and in Section 8.8.) My hope is that readers familiar with the Groundwork will thereby come to a more thorough understanding of Kant's ethics without having to plow through the entirety of Kant's ethical writings. That said, I also hope that readers will be inspired to see the value of reading outside the Groundwork in order to understand Kant's ethics.

For instructors responsible for teaching Kant's ethics, especially those who are not scholars of Kant's ethics, this book provides a way to organize one's thinking about Kant's ethics, and, by extension, a way to organize the teaching of Kant's ethics. Many students come to Kant's ethics with little or no background in Kant's philosophy or in philosophical ethics. They thus understandably struggle to get a toehold on Kant's ethics and often become overly reliant on their instructor's exposition of Kant's texts. There is of course no substitute for students' grappling with those texts. Still, Kant's idiosyncratic style, need for systematicity, etc., are a recipe for frustration, and this book is intended to ameliorate that frustration without replacing the experience of reading Kant's texts directly. Students should also benefit from the fact that I have attempted to draw contrasts with other ethical theories with which students may be familiar (utilitarianism, virtue ethics, intuitionism, etc.).

The book is divided into two parts. Part I consists of five chapters that begin with Kant's stated aim in the Groundwork: to identify and defend the supreme principle of morality. One puzzling feature of the Groundwork is that though its first two sections have the same general aim – to identify and defend the Categorical Imperative as the supreme principle of morality – Kant deploys very different argumentative strategies in those sections. Hence, Chapter 1 sets the stage for the first two sections of the Groundwork by setting out the criteria Kant believed this supreme principle must satisfy. We then turn in Chapters 2 and 3 to the two aforementioned versions of Kant's supreme principle, the Categorical Imperative. Chapter 2 addresses the Formula of Humanity and Chapter 3 the Formula of Universal Law. Throughout Part I, I articulate an understanding of Kant's theory of value and how this theory of value provides the underpinning for Kant's Categorical Imperative. As I see it, *rational agency* is the central value for Kant, and his Formula of Humanity and Formula of Universal Law represent or express two distinct ways in which rational agency ought to be valued. Chapter 4 outlines an important moral concept Kant introduces in the Groundwork: dignity. Appeals to dignity have become popular recently in ethics, but Kant's contributions to these contemporary discussions are sometimes obscure. Chapter 5 takes up perhaps the most vexing issues in Kant's ethics: namely, how Kant understands human freedom and its relationship to morality and to the Categorical Imperative.

In Part II, the emphasis turns from exegesis to defense. Over the past two centuries, Kant's ethics has been subject to innumerable criticisms, more than I can answer here. However, there seem to be certain criticisms that recur and trouble even those otherwise sympathetic to Kant's ethics. Part II groups these objections into three broad categories and gives a spirited but (I hope) fair-minded defense of Kant's ethics against these objections. The first chapter of this section (Chapter 6) addresses three objections concerning the Formula of Universal Law: first, that because we are unable to determine what principles a person acts upon, we cannot determine whether her actions are morally permissible; second, that the Formula of Universal Law gives us implausible verdicts about particular actions; and third, that it implies an implausible sort of absolutism where acts of a given kind (for example, lying) are always wrong. Addressing these objections will also help answer a vexed question in Kantian ethics, namely, the relations among the different formulations of the Categorical Imperative and their supposed equivalence. Chapter 7 addresses three areas where Kant's ethical views have been seen as having problematic implications: sexual conduct, suicide, and our treatment of non-human animals. The final chapter, Chapter 8, answers three criticisms resting on the claim that Kant's ethics assigns reason too prominent a place at the expense of sympathy or other sentiments: first, that Kant's ethics rests on an unrealistic or unattractive moral psychology, wherein we should strive to expunge all sentiment or emotion from our moral deliberation and strive to be motivated purely by austere rational considerations; second, that Kantian ethics does not take due account of the special moral significance we ascribe to our relationships with our friends, family, and loved ones; and third, that Kant's ethics fails to offer a defensible model of a happy or well-lived human life and the role of morality in such a life. Answering this latter objection leads to a brief discussion of another of Kant's central moral ideals, the Kingdom of Ends, as well as a consideration of Kant's 'practical postulates.'

For philosophers and scholars of Kant's ethics, there is obviously a great deal here that is familiar and (I expect) uncontroversial. Nevertheless, they too stand to benefit inasmuch as few books attempt to make the case for Kant's ethics, or at least its central claims or principles, in a direct and compact way. I do defend certain interpretive claims that may strike some scholars as novel, though, in the end, I hope that such scholars will find these interpretations both provocative and plausible. Of particular interest to scholars are my criterial approach to the supreme principle of morality, my emphasis on Kant as a theorist of value, my analysis of respect as the attitude underlying the Formula of Humanity, and my 'rational contradiction' interpretation of the Formula of Universal Law.

In the end, I do not expect readers of this book to conclude that Kant's ethics is unproblematic. Rather, I hope this will function as the book I wish I could have had when I first encountered Kant's ethics: a book that does not attempt to indoctrinate, but attempts to make the case for Kant's ethical theory being worthy of study and appreciation as much as it makes the case for the correctness of the theory itself. Philosophy students in particular need to know not only *what* Kant said about morality and *why*. They also need to better appreciate *why what he said matters* – why, for example, philosophers as estimable as John Rawls admired it, or why historically prominent philosophers such as Hegel or Mill saw Kant's ethics as worth criticizing. As I have learned through teaching Kant's ethics – to date, I have taught Kant's ethics, in lesser or greater depth, in about forty academic courses over a fifteen year span – understanding Kant's ethics and understanding its value or importance are inextricably linked.

****

Let me conclude this preface with some guidance about how best to read this book.

Although the book as a whole functions as an argumentative brief on behalf of Kantian ethics, I have tried, to the extent possible, to make each chapter sufficiently free standing that it can be read (or re-read) without referring to material earlier or later in the book. Hence, those wanting insight about certain topics (for example, the Formula of Humanity) should be able to consult the relevant chapter (Chapter 2, in this case) without having to read from cover to cover.

Each chapter concludes with a list of recommended 'Further Readings.' These were selected not only for their quality, but also to give readers the opportunity to explore perspectives on Kant's ethics different from my own.

Further Reading

Among the more useful introductions to Kant's ethics are Bruce Aune's Kant's Theory of Morals (Princeton, 1979) and Roger Sullivan's An Introduction to Kant's Ethics (Cambridge, 1994). Jennifer Uleman's An Introduction to Kant's Moral Philosophy (Cambridge, 2010) emphasizes Kant's theory of the will and moral psychology. More advanced overviews of Kant's ethics can be found in Allen Wood's Kant's Ethical Thought (Cambridge, 1999) and Kantian Ethics (Cambridge, 2007). Readers interested in placing Kant's ethics in historical context will profit from the chapters on Kant's ethics in John Rawls' Lectures on the History of Moral Philosophy (Harvard, 2000). Some shorter, essay-length introductions to Kant's ethics include chapter 7 of Mark Timmons' Moral Theory (Rowman & Littlefield, 2002); David Velleman's "Reading Kant's Groundwork," in G. Sher (ed.), Ethics: Essential Readings in Moral Theory (Routledge, 2012); Christine Korsgaard's 'Introduction' to the Groundwork in the Cambridge Texts in the History of Philosophy series (Cambridge, 2012); and Andrews Reath, "Contemporary Kantian ethics," in J. Skorupski (ed.), Routledge Companion to Ethics (Routledge, 2012). Marcia Baron's contribution ("Kantian ethics") to Three Methods of Ethics (Wiley-Blackwell, 1997), pp. 3–91, is a useful argumentative defense of Kantian ethics that engages with its chief theoretical rivals: consequentialism and virtue ethics. J.B. Schneewind's "Autonomy, obligation, and virtue: An overview of Kant's moral philosophy," in P. Guyer (ed.), Cambridge Companion to Kant (Cambridge, 1992) is an introduction to Kant's moral philosophy emphasizing autonomy and virtue. Arnulf Zweig, "Reflections on the enduring value of Kant's ethics," in T.E. Hill (ed.), Blackwell Guide to Kant's Ethics (Wiley-Blackwell, 2009) helps readers see the many threads that intertwine in Kant's ethical theorizing. Readers seeking more line-by-line commentary on Kant's Groundwork can consult Paul Guyer, Kant's *Groundwork for the Metaphysics of Morals*: A Critical Guide (Continuum, 2007); Jens Timmermann, Kant's *Groundwork for the Metaphysics of Morals*: A Commentary (Cambridge,

2010); and Henry Allison, Kant's *Groundwork for the Metaphysics of Morals*: A Commentary (Oxford, 2011). Sally Sedgwick's Kant's *Groundwork of the Metaphysics of Morals*: An Introduction (Cambridge, 2008) is an especially useful introduction to that work that helps situate Kant's ethics within his larger philosophical enterprise.

Part I

1 Kant's Pursuit of the Supreme Principle of Morality

In the preface to the Groundwork, Kant announces that the book's aim is "nothing more than the search for and the establishment of the *supreme principle of morality*" (G 4:392). Kant is hardly the only historically important philosopher to attempt to identify the most basic or fundamental principle that underlies morality. But Kant brings to this search certain assumptions and expectations, many of which are not stated directly and only become apparent later in the course of his arguments (and, to judge by the experience of most of Kant's readers, after multiple encounters with the text). The purpose of this chapter is to explain these assumptions and expectations. The principle that Kant ends up identifying as the supreme principle of morality is the Categorical Imperative. By explaining the assumptions and expectations that Kant brings to his search for morality's supreme principle, we will be better positioned to understand why Kant concludes that the Categorical Imperative is the supreme principle of morality. We will also be better positioned to understand (in Chapters 2 and 3) how the different versions of the Categorical Imperative reflect Kant's distinctive theory of moral value.

1.1 Morality Grounded in a Supreme Principle

One assumption that Kant makes right from the outset is easy to overlook, but nevertheless merits comment. Kant assumes that the demands of morality can be captured in rules or principles – in fact, that they can be captured in a single *supreme* principle. While many philosophers share this assumption, some do not. In recent moral philosophy, a view called *particularism* has been ascendant. Most closely associated with Jonathan Dancy, particularism downplays the role of principles in moral thought and justification. Particularists allow that we sometimes make moral decisions by referring to principles. During a water shortage, we might, for instance, decide that a fair way of limiting water use would be to let households with even-numbered street addresses engage in water-intensive activities, such as laundry and watering of lawns, on even-numbered dates, and let households with odd-numbered street addresses engage in water-intensive activities on odd-numbered dates. Particularists do not think we should never appeal to principles in moral decision making or that principles never explain what makes an act right (or wrong). But they tend, on the whole, to be skeptical of moral principles. Principles will always admit of exceptions, particularists argue, and because many moral situations are complex, we should not necessarily expect all such situations to be addressed by the same principle. Indeed, as particularists see it, many moral situations can only be adjudicated by deciding among multiple principles, each of which is applicable to those situations. Particularists would therefore be very hesitant about Kant's search for a single supreme principle of morality.

Another group of philosophers who would reject Kant's assumption are the *pluralists*, such as the twentieth-century British philosopher W.D. Ross. Pluralists hold that the demands of morality can only be captured in *multiple* principles. According to Ross, we are subject to a number of what he called "*prima facie* duties," each of which corresponds to a moral principle such as *keep one's promises*, *express gratitude to those who assist us*, *avoid harming others*, and so on. But Ross denied that there is a supreme principle – i.e., a single basic or fundamental principle – that would explain these principles or adjudicate whenever a conflict between them arises. As we will see later in our discussion of the role played by maxims in Kant's ethics (Section 3.1), there is a sense in which Kant agreed with Ross that there are basic duties that can be captured in principles. However, Kant departs from Ross in assuming that a basic or fundamental principle underlies these various subsidiary principles. On Kant's view, if, for example, it would be wrong to break a promise that one has made, then while the wrongness of breaking the promise could be explained by referring to the principle *keep one's promises*, there is a more fundamental principle – the supreme principle of morality – that provides a still more basic explanation for what makes breaking that promise wrong.

Thus, in embarking on a search for the supreme principle of morality, Kant undertakes an ambitious task – too ambitious, in the eyes of some. I shall not defend directly Kant's assumption that there is a supreme principle of morality. Instead, I propose that the best test of the plausibility of this assumption is the success (or failure) of Kant's search. So, for now, our approach will be to set aside the general philosophical question of whether morality can be captured in a single basic principle and give Kant the benefit of the doubt. If Kant persuades us that the Categorical Imperative is the supreme principle of morality, then his assumption that there is a supreme principle of morality will have been vindicated. If he fails to persuade us of this, then we face two options: we can look to other candidates for the supreme principle of morality (we will briefly discuss one candidate, the utilitarian principle of morality, in Chapter 2), or we can follow the pluralists and the particularists in denying that there is a supreme principle of morality.

1.2 Common Sense Morality

Initially, however, we may be at a loss when we try to envision what the supreme principle of morality will turn out to be. Not only might it be hard even to identify candidates for this principle, it might be hard to ascertain what we are looking for. One of the most distinctive – and, in my estimation, most brilliant – of Kant's contributions to moral philosophy is the *method* he deploys in his search for morality's supreme principle. Rather than simply considering different principles that might fulfill this role, Kant proceeds to single out certain *criteria* that a principle would have to satisfy in order to be morality's supreme principle. Kant does this by implicitly asking his reader: "If there is a supreme principle of morality, what would it be like?" The answer to this question tells us what criteria the supreme principle of morality will need to meet. Any principle that meets these criteria will be an outstanding candidate for the supreme principle.

What, according to Kant, are the criteria that a supreme principle of morality has to meet? One criterion can be extracted from Kant's remarks about the relationship between his own inquiries into ethics and "common sense moral thinking" (G 4:406, 4:411). As he states in the preface to the Groundwork, Kant understands his ethics as a reconstruction or elaboration of 'common sense' moral thinking (G 4:389, 4:391). For the most part, Kant thought that the difficulties morality poses for us human beings stem primarily from the challenge of living up to morality's requirements, rather than from figuring out what those requirements are. For Kant, moral knowledge is not obscure or elusive. Philosophy needs a 'metaphysics of morals' to purify the muddled moral thinking that can arise when we are ignorant of morality's supreme principle, but there is "no need of science and philosophy to know what one has to do in order to be honest and good, and even wise and virtuous" (G 4:404). Indeed, once Kant has identified the supreme principle of morality, he will assert that this principle has been implicit in our moral thinking all along. It is the principle we actually have before our eyes when we engage in moral deliberation, even if we do not recognize it in so abstract a form (G 4:403–404).

These remarks suggest that, for Kant, one aim of a philosophical theory of ethics should be to vindicate 'common sense' beliefs regarding the *content* of morality. A viable ethical theory should demonstrate that much of what we already believe about our moral obligations – that it is usually obligatory to keep our promises, usually forbidden to lie or cause other physical harm, etc. – is on the right track, even if those beliefs would benefit from greater precision or systematization. This does not mean that a viable ethical theory can never have surprising implications or suggest that widely shared moral beliefs are false. As we will see in Chapter 7, Kant often reaches conclusions about specific moral questions that are surprising, even unlikely. But, at the very least, a viable ethical theory should begin from the assumption that our existing moral beliefs contain a crucial grain of truth, and so should not be radically revisionary in its implications regarding our moral obligations. It should instead provide plausible explanations of moral beliefs that we largely take for granted (and, to Kant's mind, that we are *entitled* to take for granted).

We have identified, then, one of the criteria that, in Kant's estimation, the supreme principle of morality must satisfy. It must

[1] provide plausible explanations of moral obligations we already recognize.

1.3 Imperatives, Hypothetical vs. Categorical

A second criterion for the supreme principle of morality is that the supreme principle will have to be a particular sort of *imperative*. Here is Kant's explanation of what he means by an imperative:

> The representation of an objective principle, insofar as it is necessitating for a will, is called a command (of reason), and the formula of the command is called an **imperative.** (G 4:413)

As we will see many times in this book, Kant rarely does his reader the favor of translating his often baroque philosophical vocabulary into accessible language. So, we will frequently have to parse Kant's statements carefully in order to extract his meaning. Here Kant says that a principle that is "necessitating for a will" is a "command (of reason.)" We will have much more to say about Kant's understanding of the will in Chapter 5, but for now, we only need to grasp that to have a will is to have a capacity for choice, on Kant's view. You have a will, and so do I. The supreme principle of morality must, we might say, *address* our wills: That principle will generate demands or 'commands' that we, by virtue of having wills, can obey or disregard. Morality's supreme principle therefore must express a command rather than declare some fact.

Indeed, it would be difficult to envision how morality could be based on anything other than an imperative. Morality asks us to do things: to perform certain actions, to adopt certain attitudes, to treat certain considerations or facts as important in our deliberations about what to do. Hence, if there is a supreme principle of morality – a principle that asks us to perform certain actions, etc. – that principle can be expressed as a command. A principle that was not an imperative, or, to put it in more contemporary terms, a principle that was not *normative*, would not be a candidate for the supreme principle of morality.

In this passage, Kant states that an imperative expresses a principle that is "necessitating for a will." Here Kant seems to mean a principle that it is necessary for a will to adopt. Furthermore, it is necessary because it is a "command (of reason)." That is, a principle can be such that it is *rationally necessary* for a will to adopt it inasmuch as it would be irrational for a will *not* to adopt such a principle. The "formula" of a rationally necessary principle is its expression in terms of an imperative. So, to say that the supreme principle of morality must be an imperative is to say that it must be expressible in terms of a principle that it is rationally necessary for a will to adopt. We human beings, who are also rational agents in Kant's view, therefore grasp that morality's demands are rationally *necessary* – as demands the non-satisfaction of which entails that we are choosing or acting *irrationally*. And because it is an imperative, the supreme principle of morality will not be a principle that merely suggests, recommends, or advises us to perform certain actions, etc. It will be a principle that *requires* us to perform certain actions. It will, in short, be a principle that delineates our moral *obligations*.

An obvious question arises at this point: In what way (or ways) can a principle be rationally necessary for us? Here Kant introduces his famous distinction between *hypothetical* and *categorical* imperatives:

> all imperatives command either *hypothetically* or *categorically*. The former represent the practical necessity of a possible action as a means to achieving something else that one wills (or that it is at least possible for one to will). The categorical imperative would be that which represented an action as objectively necessary of itself, without reference to another end. . . . if the action would be good merely as means *to something else* the imperative is *hypothetical*; if the action is represented as *in itself good*, hence as necessary in a will in itself conforming to reason, as its principle, *then it is categorical.* (G4:414)

As it turns out, Kant will argue that the supreme principle of morality must

[2] be a rationally necessary command, that is, a categorical imperative.

To see why, we need a better handle on what distinguishes hypothetical and categorical imperatives.

Recall that an imperative expresses a rational command. Kant's distinction between hypothetical and categorical imperatives rests on a difference in *how* an imperative can serve as a rational command. A hypothetical imperative, Kant says, justifies an action "as a means to achieving something else that one wills." Here Kant elaborates his *means–ends* view of action. On this view, when we act voluntarily, our actions are means to our ends – that is, by acting we strive to bring about certain states of affairs or ends (MM 6:385, C2 5:34). Our ends provide us the reasons for performing the actions that realize those ends.

Here are some illustrations of Kant's means–ends view of action.

- A woman wanting to vacation in Mexico buys a plane ticket. Her buying the ticket is a means to her end of vacationing in Mexico, and this end provides her reason for buying the ticket.
- A restaurateur hoping to increase lunchtime sales offers a two-for-one special. Offering the special is the means to his end of increasing lunchtime sales and the end of increasing lunchtime sales provides him a reason to offer the special.
- A student desiring a career in medicine enrolls in biology courses, knowing that medical schools require them as prerequisites for admission. Enrolling in the biology courses is her means to the end of pursuing a medical career, and this end provides her a reason to enroll in them.

In each of these cases, a person has willed a particular end, and her chosen course of action is the means she has chosen in order to achieve that end. Willing an end is not the same as simply desiring it or wishing it to be the case. To will an end is to make a rational commitment to realize that end through one's actions. And in each of these examples, the action is *rational* to the extent that it advances or realizes the end that the person has willed – that is, that she has endorsed or approved of. The vacationer acts rationally in buying the ticket only because she has willed the end of vacationing in Mexico. The restaurateur acts rationally in offering the lunch special only because he has willed the end of increasing his sales. The student acts rationally in enrolling in biology courses only because she has willed the end of attending medical school. Of course, any given means can be a means to multiple possible ends, and, as a result, individuals can have other reasons to will these same actions as means. A student might enroll in a biology course not in order to pursue a medical career but simply because her university requires her to do so in order to earn a degree. In that case, the means in question serve a different end (earning the degree rather than a medical career). But the important point here is that, with respect to hypothetical imperatives, the ends a person has antecedently willed are what render acting on that imperative rational.

Hypothetical imperatives, then, are *contingent* rational commands, for their status as imperatives or rational commands depends upon the ends one has willed, or, in less Kantian terms, upon the desires or purposes that the action in question would serve. Hypothetical imperatives can thus be represented in the following general form:

- If you will end E, then do act A (as a means to E).

Note that the hypothetical imperatives suggested in our previous three examples can all be captured according to this general form:

- If you will to vacation in Mexico, then buy a plane ticket to get there.
- If you will to increase your restaurant's profits, then offer a lunch special.
- If you will to attend medical school, then enroll in biology courses.

Again, in each of these cases the actions in question are means to the individuals' chosen ends, and the actions are rational on the condition that the individuals will the ends for which these actions serve as means. Notice that we need not assume that a given means is *uniquely* suited to a given end. There are other means by which to reach Mexico, increase your restaurant's profits, or ready yourself for a career in medicine. And many other considerations enter into our deliberations about which means are best suited to our ends, including the availability of various means, their cost or burdensomeness, how various means fit into our plans for pursuing other ends, and so on. Hence, *how* rational it is to choose a particular means to an end one has willed depends on factors independent of those means. Nevertheless, these observations underscore that in order for a particular means to be minimally rational in light of one's ends, that means need not be necessary to the achievement of that end, nor need it be uniquely well-suited to the achievement of that end. The means need only be sufficient for achieving the end in question.

Furthermore, acting on these various hypothetical imperatives may not *actually* be rational. For instance, the restaurateur may be making a poor management decision in offering the lunch specials. Perhaps the specials will not be popular and so will fail to increase profits. Or perhaps there is some alternative business strategy that would increase the restaurant's profits much more. So notice that there will be *irrational* hypothetical imperatives: imperatives which, if acted upon, will not result in the individual achieving the end she has willed. But Kant's point is not that every hypothetical imperative is in fact rational. Rather, his point concerns the *source* of a hypothetical imperative's functioning as a rational command: A given hypothetical imperative is rational for an individual only due to its serving to realize the end that the individual has willed. *If* a hypothetical imperative is rational, this is because acting upon it serves a person's rationally willed ends.

Now, in saying that the supreme principle of morality is a categorical imperative, instead of a hypothetical imperative, Kant is not being dismissive of hypothetical imperatives. Novice readers of Kant sometimes misunderstand him to be claiming that we ought not to act on hypothetical imperatives – that there is something defective or deficient about hypothetical imperatives, since they cannot serve as the supreme principle of morality. This impression is erroneous though. As we will see, Kant sees morality as putting constraints on how we pursue our ends – or, put differently, morality constrains which hypothetical imperatives it is permissible for us to act upon. But in general Kant has no beef with our acting in order to achieve our chosen ends. Kant recognized that we humans are creatures with needs and wants. It will thus inevitably be the case that we have to figure out how to satisfy these needs and wants, and Kant is thus very willing to allow that an important dimension of our practical lives consists in willing, and acting upon, hypothetical imperatives.

1.4 The Supreme Principle Must Be Categorical

Nevertheless, Kant is clear that only a categorical imperative can serve as morality's supreme principle. Why? One important clue arises from the fact that, as we noted, hypothetical imperatives are contingent rational commands. For a particular individual, the rational force of a hypothetical imperative depends on his or her ends. If I have no desire to vacation in Mexico – i.e., if I have not willed this as one of my ends – then the hypothetical imperative

> If you will to vacation in Mexico, then buy a plane ticket to get there

has no rational force for me.

But this sort of rational force – force dependent on one's ends, desires, or purposes – does not seem like the kind of rational force that a moral demand has. A moral demand has rational force – i.e., we ought to fulfill the demand even if doing so would not serve our particular ends, desires, or purposes. In fact, it will often be true that *not* fulfilling a moral demand better serves our ends than fulfilling it. Presumably, a merchant who programs her store's electronic product scanners to charge customers higher prices than those listed on the shelf acts wrongly. But the merchant's ends, especially the end of maximizing profits, may well be better served by dishonest pricing than by honest pricing. Again, that will depend on an array of different factors: how high the scanned mark-up is, whether customers notice and complain, etc. Yet the important point, from Kant's point of view, is that even *if* dishonest pricing serves the merchant's ends better than honest pricing, this fact is essentially irrelevant to the moral justifiability of her actions. It would certainly not be a valid *excuse* for a merchant accused of such dishonest pricing to proclaim, "Yes, I overcharged my customers, but that served my end of maximizing my profits!" In effect, the merchant mistakenly treats the moral demand to honestly charge her customers as a hypothetical imperative, as a command whose rational force depends upon how well fulfilling that command serves her particular ends. But that seems implausible on its face: The rational force of this moral demand is instead independent of her particular ends.

Recall that Kant is after a principle of morality that will account for our obligations. Whatever the supreme principle of morality turns out to be, it will have to be a principle that generates moral obligations, moral 'musts.' If the supreme principle were a hypothetical imperative, then it would not generate 'musts'; it would generate *options* based on what one wills as an end. But a supreme principle of morality that gives moral agents an 'out' any time satisfying the principle would not serve their ends is, by Kant's lights, not a principle of morality at all.

This claim – that any candidate for the supreme principle of morality resting on a hypothetical imperative does not account for how moral obligations are rationally binding independent of our ends – becomes clearer when we consider a moral principle that rests on a hypothetical imperative. Suppose that the following principle, similar to one articulated by Plato in Book I of his famous dialogue the *Republic*, were the supreme principle of morality:

> If you want to maintain a good reputation within the community, help your friends and harm your enemies.

Note that this principle expresses a hypothetical imperative. It asserts that one ought to pursue a particular policy (helping one's friends and harming one's enemies) *if* one has willed an end of maintaining a good reputation within the community. One obvious worry about this as a candidate for morality's supreme principle is that it seems to have counterintuitive implications. As Plato had Socrates argue, the idea that we should intentionally harm anyone, even our enemies, is morally dubious. But Kant would offer a second diagnosis for why this principle is inadequate. What if someone simply doesn't care about his or her reputation within the community? A person with a strong belief in self-reliance might be indifferent to his reputation in the community. Or someone influenced by Stoicism might believe that all that matters in life is one's inner state of virtue, and hence we should not give any heed to 'external' goods such as one's reputation. Yet the demands of morality would still apply to such individuals even though they do not much care about their reputations. Again, a hypothetical imperative, because it makes the rational force of an imperative depend upon the particular ends, desires, or purposes that individuals will for themselves, cannot fully capture the apparently inescapable or unavoidable rational force of morality's demands.

So, Kant believed that the supreme principle of morality must be a categorical imperative because a merely hypothetical imperative would not capture the rational force that underlies moral obligation. Only a categorical imperative can explain the *nature* of moral normativity. But Kant had a second reason for concluding that the supreme principle of morality must be a categorical imperative, relating to the *scope* of morality's demands. If there is a supreme principle of morality, who is subject to its demands? Here is Kant's answer.

> unless we want to deny to the concept of morality any truth and any relation to some possible object, we cannot dispute that its law is so extensive in its import that it must hold not only for human beings but for all *rational beings as such*, not merely under contingent conditions and with exceptions but with *absolute necessity*. (G 4:408)

The supreme principle of morality, Kant says, holds not just for human beings but for all rational beings as such. Now, Kant's moral philosophy is clearly directed *at* human beings. When he makes claims about what moral obligations there are, etc., he is making claims about what *we human beings* are obligated to do. But he implies in this passage that if there are non-human beings who are also rational beings, then they too would be subject to moral obligations. Perhaps Kant would grant that an intelligent extraterrestrial species, or an especially sophisticated non-human animal species (such as dolphins or chimpanzees), may possess the requisite capacities to qualify as "rational beings." (We will explore what Kant thought characterized rational beings in Chapter 2 and later in Chapter 6.) But the more crucial claim, for our present purposes, is that morality must hold for rational beings "as such." Here Kant is claiming that we are subject to morality because we are rational beings.

This claim provides Kant his second reason for concluding that the supreme principle of morality must be a categorical imperative. Let us follow Kant in assuming that all (or almost all) human agents have some set of capacities that render them rational beings. Furthermore, let us also assume that morality's commands apply to all such human agents. We then ask: On the basis of what facts about those human agents do the commands of morality apply to them? If the supreme principle of morality were a hypothetical imperative, then the answer would be their *particular* ends, purposes, or desires. If the supreme principle of morality, the principle that is supposed to ground our moral obligations, were based on a hypothetical imperative – a principle of the form 'if you will end E, then do act A (as a means to E)' – then it would apply *only* to those rational agents who will E, whatever E happens to be. But there doesn't seem to be any end E that all rational agents will simply as a matter of course. So, if morality's supreme principle were a hypothetical imperative, then there would be rational agents who, because they do not will the end incorporated in that hypothetical imperative, would be exempt from moral requirements. This reasoning shows, in Kant's mind, that the supreme principle of morality must rest on something common to rational beings as such: their rational nature.

Kant thus argues that only if morality's supreme principle is a categorical imperative will morality turn out to have both the rational necessity and universality that defines it. Now, Kant would grant that, in a very broad sense, there is a hypothetical imperative that universally applies to us: All rational agents will their own happiness. Happiness, on Kant's view, consists of our "needs and inclinations" being fully satisfied (G 4:405) so that everything proceeds in accordance with our "wish or will" (C2 5:124). Kant recognized that we vary in our inclinations, or in what we wish or will for ourselves. We vary in our ends, purposes, or desires. Some of us desire fame, others wealth. Some pursue urban life, others are more reclusive. Even despite this diversity, happiness is an end all rational beings will. It would thus seem possible to ground morality's supreme principle in a hypothetical imperative somehow rooted in the pursuit of happiness. Indeed, this is arguably what philosophers such as Aristotle and utilitarians have done, claiming that, in the end, our moral obligations rest on an imperative to promote happiness.

But Kant rejects happiness as a possible basis for morality's supreme principle. (This is not to say that Kant is 'anti-happiness,' as we shall investigate in Chapter 8.) In part, this is because Kant believed that happiness can never be the basis for morality because this would undermine the freedom necessary for morality. I will set this argument aside, as it will be addressed in Chapter 5. Kant also rejected happiness as the basis of morality for reasons developed by David Hume, whose work influenced Kant enormously. A first problem with grounding morality in a hypothetical imperative based on happiness as a universal end is that the "empirical" generalization *all rational agents will their own happiness* can never be demonstrated. This statement is "empirical" in that our evidence for it is drawn from sensory experience. But sensory experience can only tell us that all rational agents *we have observed* so far will their own happiness. So long as the possibility exists that some rational agents (perhaps rational agents we have not yet encountered) do *not* will their own happiness,[1] this statement expresses a principle but not, as Kant would say, a moral 'law.' Hence, grounding morality in a hypothetical imperative directing us to promote happiness would fall short of being genuinely universal. Furthermore, such a hypothetical imperative could not provide morality's supreme principle the sort of rational necessity Kant believed it had to have. Even if that empirical generalization were found to be universally true of all rational agents, that would still not show that it is necessarily true (in the way that, for example, laws of logic such as 'A=A' are necessarily true).[2]

To Kant's mind, we can only arrive at the supreme principle of morality through a priori reasoning, reasoning that does not draw upon sensory experience. For only a principle known a priori can have the universality and necessity characteristic of the supreme principle. Kant reasons, then, that this principle can only be based on considerations not derived from sensory experience, including facts about human nature and the circumstances in which we live out our lives. "Everyone must grant that a law, if it is to hold morally, that is, as a ground of obligation, must carry with it absolute necessity," Kant declares (G 4:389). As a result, the basis for a law such as the supreme principle of morality

[1] I will propose in Section 7.2 that some suicidal individuals do not will their own happiness.

[2] Sally Sedgwick, *Kant's Groundwork of the Metaphysics of Morals: An Introduction* (Cambridge, 2008), pp. 14–18, provides a very helpful elaboration of Kant's thinking on these issues.

must not be sought in the nature of the human being or in the circumstances of the world in which he is placed, but a priori simply in concepts of pure reason; and that any other precept, which is based on principles of mere experience – even if it is universal in a certain respect – insofar as it rests in the least part on empirical grounds . . . can indeed be called a practical rule but never a moral law. (G 4:389)

Thus, only principles that apply to all rational beings 'as such' – that is, solely because they are rational beings – are candidates for the supreme principle of morality (G 4:389. See also G 4:442, C2 5:12). Any such principle must be a categorical imperative in order to capture both the nature of morality (its special rational force) and its scope (its necessary applicability to all rational agents).

1.5 Forestalling a Confusion: A Categorical Imperative Versus the Categorical Imperative

We have established why Kant thinks the supreme principle of morality must be a categorical imperative. It is nonetheless crucial that we distinguish *a* categorical imperative from what Kant will call *the* Categorical Imperative. (Note the capitalization I am deploying.) The Categorical Imperative will turn out to be the supreme principle of morality, according to Kant. (As we will see, whether Kant is correct about this is complicated by the fact that he puts forth several different versions or 'formulas' of the Categorical Imperative.) In section II of the Groundwork, Kant argues (1) that the supreme principle of morality must be a categorical imperative, and (2) the Categorical Imperative is the only possible categorical imperative, and must therefore be the supreme principle of morality. In other words, Kant argues that by analyzing the *concept* of a categorical imperative, we will arrive at *the* Categorical Imperative: "we want first to inquire whether the mere concept of a categorical imperative may not also provide its formula containing the proposition which alone can be a categorical imperative" (G 4:420). The important point, in terms of Kant's method in identifying the supreme principle of morality, is that Kant is imposing a logical condition or criterion on the supreme principle of morality: that it be a categorical imperative. Confusingly, Kant ends up calling the principle that satisfies this condition the Categorical Imperative.

At this point, though, we have said little about the Categorical Imperative or how Kant argues that it uniquely qualifies as the supreme principle of morality. But the central aim of this chapter has been to set the stage for these arguments by identifying the criteria that Kant believes the supreme principle of morality must meet. Without understanding these criteria, we are at a loss to understand, much less appraise, Kant's attempt to vindicate the Categorical Imperative as the supreme principle of morality. We have already encountered what is arguably the most central criterion: that the supreme principle of morality must be a categorical imperative. We now turn to two other criteria that Kant imposes on this principle.

1.6 The Supreme Principle of Morality as the Good Will's Principle

The opening paragraphs of section I of the Groundwork are among the most influential – and most befuddling – remarks ever made by a moral philosopher. There Kant makes crucial claims about the supreme principle of morality that we will need to keep track of. The section begins:

> It is impossible to think of anything at all in the world . . . that could be considered good without limitation except a good will. Understanding, wit, judgement, and the like, whatever such *talents* of mind may be called, or courage, resolution, and perseverance in one's plans, as qualities of *temperament*, are undoubtedly good and desirable for many purposes, but they can also be extremely evil and harmful if the will which is to make use of these gifts of nature, and whose distinctive constitution is therefore called *character*, is not good. (G 4:393)

Let us dissect this passage with care.

Kant describes here a contrast between one good and another broad class of goods: on the one hand, the good will, and on the other, an array of capacities, talents, or virtues. The former, Kant says, is the only good that is good without limitation, or, as many commentators put it, the sole *unconditioned* good. Implicit in Kant's remarks is that all other goods, including these capacities, talents, and virtues, while good, are only *conditioned* goods. How, according to Kant, are conditioned goods distinct from the good will, the sole unconditioned good? Let us focus on one of the conditioned goods Kant mentions: courage.

Is courage good? Philosophers have long praised courage and called it a virtue. Notice that Kant does not appear to condemn courage as such. He is not claiming courage is *bad*. It is, Kant says, "undoubtedly good and desirable for many purposes." But courage still carries a moral blemish, as Kant sees it. Why? In moral terms, a courageous act is not necessarily praiseworthy and may even be wrong. After all, terrorism takes courage, but that fact hardly seems to be a good moral argument for terrorism. Brazen dishonesty can require courage, since there is always a risk of being found out. But that counts as no defense of brazen dishonesty. Some of history's great heroes (Lincoln, Gandhi) had courage. But so too did some of history's greatest villains (Stalin). Acting courageously has, at best, a contingent connection to acting rightly. Courage can enable us to achieve our chosen ends, but when allied with a morally bad will, it becomes "extremely evil and harmful." What is needed to make courage good, Kant claims, is a morally good will.

And the same goes, Kant says, for any of these other capacities, virtues, or talents. They can be good or praiseworthy, but only when allied with a morally good will:

> Moderation in affects and passions, self-control, and calm reflection are not only good for all sorts of purposes but even seem to constitute a part of the *inner* worth of a person; but they lack much that would be required to declare them good without limitation ... for, without the basic principles of a good will they can become extremely evil. (G 4:394)

Again, Kant argues that these other goods are often usefully deployed in the service of morally good purposes. But they need not be: A calculating, clever person, capable of great self-discipline, can nevertheless make use of these virtues for evil purposes.

Here we see an important contrast between Kant and some of his philosophical predecessors. Kant is offering a critique of the tradition known as *virtue ethics*. But it is easy to misunderstand the nature of Kant's critique. Philosophers in this tradition, such as Aristotle and Aquinas, believed that in acting rightly, individuals exemplify particular character traits: the virtues. Indeed, many of the traits Kant lists here, including not only courage but also good judgment, self-control, and moderation in one's emotions, are precisely the traits that Aristotle believed are on display when a person performs a morally right action. As we shall see in Chapter 8, Kant did not entirely disagree: He held that those who have morally good wills need to have traits such as sympathy in order to reliably act rightly. However, he splits with virtue ethicists in denying that the presence or absence of a character trait (or traits) helps explain what makes acts right or wrong. Right and wrong turn, as Kant says, on the *principle* of a person's will. What Stalin, terrorists, and the like lack is not a trait such as courage. They fail to act from morally defensible principles, according to Kant. Of course, virtue ethicists may respond that Stalin and his ilk are not *really* courageous in their actions; truly courageous action requires something further, perhaps that overarching virtue of practical decision that Aristotle called *phronesis*. This is a bit of philosophical finger crossing, in my estimation. Virtue ethicists are certainly free to define courage (or any other virtue) such that it is not exemplified when a person performs a wrongful act. But this stipulation seems at odds with fact: It takes nerve, guts, audacity, the overcoming of fear, etc., to engage in violence toward others that also poses risk to oneself, as terrorists do. Yet this seems rather to demonstrate Kant's point: Having good character traits is insufficient for right action. Something more – the right sort of moral *judgment* – is necessary as well.

In any event, Kant then proceeds to extend this analysis of the value of virtues and other traits to a number of other goods, including happiness:

It is the same with *gifts of fortune*. Power, riches, honor, even health, and that complete well-being and satisfaction with one's condition called *happiness*, produce boldness and thereby often arrogance as well unless a good will is present which corrects the influence of these on the mind and, in so doing, also corrects the whole principle of action. (G 4:394)

Wealth and good health are instrumental to achieving our ends, and in that respect, they contribute to happiness. But there is no assurance that wealth or good health will be exercised in the service of morally good ends or be allied with a morally good will. Even happiness itself, Kant argues, can make us arrogant or indifferent to morally good ends.

So it is only a morally good will that ensures that these conditioned goods are good. Hence, the morally good will is the sole unconditioned good, and all other goods derive their moral goodness from their relationship to the morally good will. The good will is unique in having no condition for its moral goodness. There is thus a fundamental asymmetry between the good will and all other goods: All other goods must be accompanied by, or governed by, the morally good will in order to be good. But the good will needs no other goods in order to be morally good.

All the same, a measure of frustration at this point would be understandable. Kant has told us something important *about* the good will – that its goodness is unconditioned. In this respect, the good will is *not* good in the way other goods are. In addition, he has assigned the good will an important role in our moral psychology. It "corrects" the unfortunate influence that other goods can have on our choices and is thus the condition under which the various conditioned goods are good. But Kant has not told us what the good will is or what its "basic principles" are. Yet residing behind Kant's discussion of this distinction is an unstated assumption essential to understanding the arguments of the Groundwork, particularly section I. We arrive at this assumption by returning to Kant's stated purpose in the Groundwork: to identify and defend the supreme principle of morality. Why is Kant bothering to discuss the good will and argue for its unconditional goodness? The direction of Kant's arguments becomes clearer when we recognize that one of his implicit criteria for the supreme principle of morality is that it must

[3] be **whatever** principle governs the choices of the morally good will.

Unfortunately, Kant does not signal his endorsement of this criterion when he first introduces the notion of a good will in Groundwork section I, thereby obscuring his argumentative strategy. He only makes this connection between the supreme principle and the principle that governs the choices of the morally good will later on, stating that the principle of an "absolutely good will," a "will which cannot be evil" is the "supreme law" of morality (G 4:437. See also G 4: 413–414). However, the reasoning of section I makes sense only if this criterion is treated as an unstated premise of Kant's reasoning. For immediately after arguing for the unconditioned goodness of the good will, Kant begins to identify the criteria the satisfaction of which make the good will good. He then uses these criteria to narrow in on the Categorical Imperative, which (we know) Kant believes is the supreme principle of morality. This set of moves is coherent only if Kant assumes that whatever principle governs the good will's choices is the supreme principle of morality.

We must not misconstrue the purpose of Kant's search for the principle that would govern the choices of the morally good will. In particular, we must not assume that Kant is proposing that only those with a morally good will can act *rightly*. A crucial distinction here is Kant's contrast between action from duty and action (merely) in conformity with duty. Here is an example Kant uses to articulate this contrast:

> it certainly conforms with duty that a shopkeeper not overcharge an inexperienced customer, and where there is a good deal of trade a prudent merchant does not overcharge but keeps a fixed general price for everyone, so that a child can buy from him as well as everyone else. People are thus served *honestly*; but this is not nearly enough for us to believe that the merchant acted in this way from duty and basic principles of honesty; his advantage required it; it cannot be assumed here that he had, besides an immediate inclination toward his customers, so as from love, as it were, to give no one preference over another in the matter of price. Thus the action was neither from duty nor from immediate inclination but merely for purposes of self-interest. (G 4:397)

By establishing uniform prices for all his customers, including children and the "inexperienced," the shopkeeper thereby "conforms with duty," according to Kant. Ultimately, what motivates the shopkeeper's uniform pricing scheme is his enlightened "self-interest" or "advantage." The shopkeeper thus seems to lack the motivation characteristic of a morally good will. He lacks, as Kant says, the motivation to charge uniform prices *because* doing so is honest. The shopkeeper thereby acts rightly (i.e., his act "conforms with duty"), but he does not act on morally admirable motivations or "from duty," as Kant says.

Unlike the shopkeeper, the morally good will fulfills its moral obligations not simply in deed but in spirit too. The morally good will does what it morally ought to do from a recognition that it morally ought to do it. The morally good will's choices are thus "in conformity with duty" – that is, the morally good will fulfills its moral obligations. But the morally good will also necessarily chooses "from duty" – that is, fulfills its obligations *because* those are its obligations (G 3:397–398. See also G 4:390). The *goodness* of the morally good will consists in its being motivated by considerations of duty. So Kant's purpose in offering criterion [3] is not to argue that only action from duty is right. Rather, his strategy seems to be that, given that the morally good will's will is good, it will also choose and act rightly. Hence, we can infer from the motivational structure of the morally good will what the supreme principle of morality is. The supreme principle of morality will be whatever principle governs the choices of the morally good will not because of its goodness, its being motivated solely by or "from duty." Rather, because the morally good will, in light of the fact that it is necessarily motivated to act from duty, will also necessarily act rightly or in accordance with duty. Christine Korsgaard explains that the key assumption behind Kant's method here is

> that the reason why a good-willed person does an action, and the reason why the action is right, are the same. The good willed person does the right thing because it is the right thing, so if we can discover why the good-willed person does it, we will have *ipso facto* discovered why it is the right thing.[3]

This means that Kant is not suggesting, as many readers interpret him, that an action is only right if accompanied by a morally good will. Because the morally good will necessarily acts rightly, the principle governing its choices will be an infallible guide to right action. But *we* need not be motivated as the morally good will is (from duty) in order to act rightly. Nor is Kant suggesting that we are to strive to be a "pure" or morally good will (C2 5:55). In fact, we will see that Kant is in some ways skeptical that we human agents can achieve the moral rectitude represented by the good will.

1.7 The Supreme Principle of Morality Is Non-consequentialist

So what makes the good will good? (G 4:394) The most daring and controversial claim Kant makes about the good will is found in the following passage:

> A good will is not good because of what it effects or accomplishes, because of its fitness to attain some proposed end, but only because of its volition, that is, it is good in itself . . . Even if, by a special disfavour of fortune or by the niggardly provision of a stepmotherly nature, this will should wholly lack the capacity to carry out its purpose – if with its greatest efforts it should yet achieve nothing and only the good will were left. . . – then, like a jewel, it would shine by itself, as something that has full worth in itself. Usefulness or fruitfulness can neither add anything to this worth nor take anything away from it. (G 4:394)

Here Kant shows his credentials as a *non-consequentialist* moral philosopher. 'Consequentialism' is a popular view within philosophical ethics, but the meaning of the term can be difficult to pin down. Many consequentialists believe that the rightness or wrongness of actions depends upon which acts have the *best* consequences. Other consequentialists believe that rightness or wrongness depends upon acts having *good enough* consequences or having the best consequences *from a particular point of view.* There are also significant disagreements among consequentialists about which facts or outcomes count as

[3] "Kant's analysis of obligation: The argument of Groundwork I," *The Monist* 72 (1989): 328.

morally relevant consequences: whether the relevant consequences concern pleasure and pain, well-being more generally, or other goods; whether the relevant consequences must be understood from a strictly impersonal perspective; and whether the relevant consequences are the actual consequences of someone's actions or merely the consequences that could reasonably be expected to result from an action. (We will further examine the most prominent consequentialist moral theory, utilitarianism, in the next chapter.)

These nuances are not of interest to Kant, however. For on his view, a morally good will is defined by the *principle* on which such a will acts, not the consequences, actual, expected, or otherwise, of acting on that principle. These features will become clearer in Chapter 2 and even more so in Chapter 3, when we investigate Kant's notion of a maxim. As we will see, 'consequences' have a role to play in Kant's ethics insofar as our actions, and hence our maxims, seek to realize our ends. Yet Kant seems to want no part of the consequentialist thesis that right and wrong turn on how good or valuable an act's consequences are. The consequentialist would say, against Kant, that the good will is good precisely *because* "of what it effects or accomplishes" or *because* of its capacity "to attain some proposed end." In contrast, Kant claims that the good will's goodness is "good in itself" and would remain so even if the good will does not actually succeed in carrying out the purpose or end it seeks to achieve in acting. Even then, Kant claims, the good will nevertheless shines "like a jewel," despite its actions not achieving their intended end. And since whatever principle governs the choices of a good will is also the supreme principle of morality, the supreme principle of morality (the principle that grounds our moral obligations) cannot be a consequentialist principle.

Hence, in the famous "shine like a jewel" passage, Kant adds an additional criterion for the supreme principle of morality. It must

[4] be a **non-consequentialist** principle, i.e., it must not make the rightness or wrongness of actions depend on the value of actions' consequences.

Elsewhere, Kant makes his non-consequentialism more obvious: "The objectives we may have in acting, and also our actions' effects considered as ends and what motivates our volition, can give to actions no unconditional or moral worth," Kant declares. Such worth "can be found nowhere but in the principle of the will, irrespective of the ends that can be brought about by such action" (G 4:400. See also G 4:415–416).

But what is Kant's justification for [4]? Unfortunately, Kant does not really provide us a direct argument as to why the good will's principle, and therefore the supreme principle of morality, must be non-consequentialist. Nevertheless, we get a clue in this passage as to the basis of Kant's non-consequentialist leanings.

Kant states that even if the good will should fail to achieve the purpose it pursues in its actions, it still has "full worth in itself." Why might a good will fail to achieve its purpose? In a word, *luck*. A person with a morally good will may act but suffer a "special disfavour of fortune" that prevents her from achieving (or fully achieving) her purpose. Suppose that a natural disaster occurs in the area where you live. Local charities issue desperate calls for donations of money and essential goods. Unfortunately, you just moved to the area from a distant locale, and in the process of moving, you gave away nearly everything you own. On top of that, the disaster occurs at the very end of a month, and because you are paid your meager salary on a monthly basis, you have no funds to donate to the local charities. Yet you sincerely want to help those stricken by the disaster, so you donate the few dollars left in your bank account. The donation hardly makes a dent in the overall need, and, in a sense, you fall short of achieving your purpose – namely, to provide substantial aid to the disaster victims. Yet no one would deny that your conduct, and the moral quality of your will, is praiseworthy. Your inability to provide significant aid is a matter of bad luck, not a morally bad will. Or consider examples involving taking care not to harm others. A careful driver, with no history of accidents and a sincere desire not to harm others, can nevertheless suffer bad luck that results in bad outcomes. Careful drivers sometimes collide with and injure pedestrians because the pedestrians themselves are inattentive. It would be unreasonable, and unfair, to blame such drivers for the injuries to which their actions causally contribute. In Kant's terms, a careful driver has a good will that is fully worthy "in itself" even if, due to misfortune, his acting with such good will nevertheless ends up harming others. Conversely, many inattentive or careless drivers, those who are indifferent to whether they injure others, enjoy the good fortune never to harm or injure others while driving. And while we are doubtless glad that they do not harm or injure others, their careless driving, insofar as it reflects the bad moral quality of their will, merits moral criticism.

These are examples where either (a) the "special disfavour of fortune" – that is, facts about the circumstances of an action – intervene in the actions of a person with a good will, resulting in bad (or less than optimal) outcomes, or (b) fortune smiles on the actions of a person with a bad will, resulting in good (or at least neutral) outcomes. But what of the other explanation Kant offers for why a good will may fail to achieve its purpose: that it has a "stepmotherly nature"? Kant's sexist expression notwithstanding, in what ways might deficiencies in a good-willed person's "nature" inhibit their capacity to achieve their purposes? The clearest example is someone who has low intellectual capabilities despite having a morally admirable will. A famous literary example is Lennie Small, from Steinbeck's Of Mice and Men. Lennie is mentally disabled but physically stout, with simple aspirations: to live off the land and raise rabbits. His affection for soft fur and fabrics proves to be his downfall, as he accidentally kills the wife of a ranch owner after she offers to let him stroke her hair. Lennie's friend George later kills him to save Lennie from a lynch mob. Throughout the novel, Lennie is depicted as morally innocent, even simple, averse to harming others. He poses a danger to others not because of moral vice but because of his physical strength and his difficulties in glossing the implied meanings of his interactions with others.

Lennie is an unusually stark example of someone whose moral goodness is counteracted by deficiencies in his nature. Yet we human beings are not powerless, nor are we omnipotent, and, as a consequence, there are innumerable ways in which our natures, both individual and collective, can stand in the way of achieving our chosen ends even when we have morally good wills. Our unrecognized fears, poor ability to forecast the future, tendency toward miscommunication, ignorance of causal relations – these are just some of the myriad explanations for why good-willed individuals can fail to achieve their chosen ends.

We must be careful not to exaggerate Kant's claims here. Kantian morality is sometimes characterized as a morality of 'good intentions.' But this interpretation is clearly misleading. For one, a person's intentions (or as we have been putting it, one's will) must really be good, not simply believed to be good. Moreover, Kant is not denying that it matters morally whether good-willed individuals achieve their ends or purposes. Nor is he suggesting that so long as we have morally good wills, we may as well be indifferent as to whether our actions achieve their morally desirable ends or purposes. On the contrary, Kant believed that we have moral duties to develop our talents precisely so that we are more likely to achieve our ends or purposes.

Nevertheless, the notion that moral goodness does not depend on luck is one of Kant's most fundamental philosophical commitments. Kant's moral philosophy was profoundly egalitarian and anti-elitist in this regard. If moral goodness depended on consequences one could not control, or required some special dispensation of divine grace, or was available only to a fortunate few with the proper upbringing or temperament, then, in Kant's eyes, morality would have a certain kind of injustice built into it. Hence, "Kant's moral picture is strictly egalitarian; the moral life is open to all, equally, at any time or their lives and under any circumstances."[4]

These considerations about luck and the possibility of moral goodness lead Kant to another constraint on the supreme principle of morality. Our ability to conform to morality's supreme principle must not be a matter of luck. This line of thought implies that whatever Kant intends by having a morally good will, it

[4] Nafsika Athanassoulis, *Morality, Moral Luck, and Responsibility* (Palgrave Macmillan, 2005), p. 132.

must be something that *is* within our power to have. But what could Kant have in mind as the fact or capacity that is within our power but is immune to the kinds of luck we have been discussing? All moral agents – that is, all individuals who can rightfully be held morally responsible for their choices and actions – possess *reason*, and in particular, practical reason, the powers associated with choice and action. In saying that our ability to conform to morality's supreme principle depends on our being practically rational, Kant is not claiming that every human being is practically rational. He would certainly grant that newborns, for example, lack the powers associated with rational choice and action. Nor is he claiming that those possessing practical reason always choose or act rationally in the sense that they choose or act on the best reasons or on the basis of sound rational deliberation. Kant is instead making the more modest claim that conforming to morality's supreme principle requires *nothing more than* a capacity to choose and act rationally. A person can act rightly without possessing particular traits of personality, resources, etc., and without its being true that her actions necessarily work out in the way that she intends. The supreme principle of morality must therefore

[5] be a principle conformity to which requires only that we are practically rational beings.

Again, Kant has not answered the question, 'what *makes* a good will good?' But he is building the path toward an answer and toward identifying the supreme principle of morality.

That the supreme principle of morality must be a non-consequentialist principle also reinforces Kant's earlier claim that it must be a categorical imperative. Kant is among the best examples of a *rationalist* in moral philosophy: He believes that morality's requirements are requirements of rationality. Because of this belief, he follows Aristotle in thinking that moral virtue, or moral goodness, is a kind of rational excellence. But unlike Aristotle, Kant thought of moral virtue as an excellence of "volition" – that is, an excellence of choice. Moral virtue is thus a property of the will, "the moral strength of a *human being's* will in fulfilling his *duty*" (MM 6:405). If the rational excellence that made us morally virtuous were a capacity to fulfill our ends or purposes, then the supreme principle of morality would be a hypothetical imperative. For a hypothetical imperative's rational force – the sense in which it tells us what we have a reason to do – rests on our willing the end contained in a hypothetical imperative. But since the rational excellence in question is an excellence in what we will, not of our capacity to achieve what we will, the supreme principle of morality must be a categorical, rather than a hypothetical, imperative.

1.8 Looking Ahead

Let's take stock of what we have learned about Kant's pursuit of the supreme principle of morality.

This chapter has identified five criteria that Kant believed the supreme principle of morality must meet. The supreme principle must:

[1] provide plausible explanations of moral obligations we already recognize,

[2] be an imperative that it is rationally necessary for us to adopt, that is, a categorical imperative,

[3] be whatever principle governs the choices of the morally good will,

[4] be a non-consequentialist principle, i.e., it must not make the rightness or wrongness of actions depend on the value of actions' consequences, and

[5] be a principle conformity to which requires only that we are practically rational beings.

What distinguishes Kant's method in searching for the supreme principle of morality is that he first tries to identify the features such a principle would have, and in particular, the kind of rational force it must have for us. As the Kantian moral philosopher Robert Johnson has put it, Kant's "account of the content of moral requirements and the nature of moral reasoning is based on his analysis of the unique force moral considerations have as reasons to act."[5]

Here I have sought to give the most direct and persuasive account possible of *why* Kant believed that any candidate for the supreme principle of morality must meet these criteria. Perhaps Kant (and I) have failed to persuade you that these are appropriate criteria for the supreme principle of morality. But this possibility should not obscure the insight and fruitfulness of Kant's method. If one rejects Kant's criteria for the supreme principle of morality, then one bears the burden of providing alternative criteria along with a rationale for why *those* are the appropriate criteria by which to appraise candidates for the supreme principle of morality.

Of course, even if Kant has identified the correct criteria, we do not yet know what the Categorical Imperative – the principle that, according to Kant, *uniquely* satisfies these criteria – is, nor do we know why Kant believed that the Categorical Imperative uniquely satisfies these criteria. Those are the tasks of the remainder of the Groundwork and the remaining chapters of Part I of this book. Of these five criteria, [5] will turn out to merit special attention. Criteria

[5] "Kant's moral philosophy," *Stanford Encyclopedia of Philosophy* (http://plato.stanford.edu/entries/kant-moral/), section 3, revised version published 2008.

[1]–[4] all concern the content of the supreme principle of morality. They tell us what the supreme principle of morality will have to look like. In Kant's terms, they set the agenda for the 'analytical' task of ethics, the identification of that principle. Criterion [5], on the other hand, does not concern the content of the supreme principle. It also concerns, well, us: Are we the kinds of beings who are capable of doing as morality directs us? Are we practically rational in the ways necessary to enable us (at least sometimes) to fulfill the supreme principle of morality? Whereas criteria [1]–[4] are straightforwardly ethical, [5] resides at the intersection of the ethical and the metaphysical. As such, criterion [5] needs to be treated separately. In Chapters 2 and 3, I will therefore only offer a tentative defense of the claim that Kant's Categorical Imperative satisfies [5]. A fuller defense will be provided in Chapter 5.

Upon examining these five criteria, one might wonder whether Kant has set himself an impossible task. For reflection on these five criteria might suggest that it is logically impossible for any principle to satisfy all five, which would entail, in Kant's terms, that there is no supreme principle of morality.

First, criterion [2], that the supreme principle be a categorical imperative, is the heart of Kant's conception of that principle. A categorical imperative is a rational command whose rational force – whose rational 'necessity'– would not rest on any of our particular ends or purposes. But recall Kant's means–ends conception of action. Acting in accordance with morality's supreme principle requires acting with some end in mind. If all action aims at an end, but the supreme principle of morality does not acquire its rational force from our having willed particular ends, then at what end do morally obligatory actions aim? Kant seems to be forced toward the conclusion that, despite our particular ends or purposes, there is some end or other we are obligated to take into account with our choices. There must, Kant believes, be a "universal" end (G 4:393) or an end "that is in itself a duty" (MM 6:383) But what is this end? It would have to be an end that, no matter what other ends we rationally will for ourselves, we must also value as an end. We might wonder whether there really is such an end, one that we *must* will and that therefore grounds duty.

Here, a second challenge emerges for Kant: Suppose there is an end that is also a duty, an end that it is rationally mandatory for us to value. Recall Kant's means–ends theory of action: Ends are valuable state of affairs, and our actions serve as means to bring about those ends. Yet criterion [4] states that the supreme principle must not be consequentialist. Kant's project thus requires identifying some end that we are required to value, but valuing that end appropriately does not amount to trying to *bring about* that end. This may seem puzzling: What else can it mean to value an end other than to try to bring it about? To value one's health is to try to make oneself healthy, to bring about health as an end. But as Kant sees it, the supreme principle of morality must not only rest on an end, it must rest on an end which, despite being valuable regardless of our other ends, is appropriately valued in some way besides being an end we seek to bring about. Skepticism that such an end exists seems reasonable.

Thus, Kant needs to identify a distinctive sort of end or value and a distinctive way in which, by doing what we are morally obligated to do, we value that end. Finally, one might worry that Kant appears committed to defending a theory of morality that is very remote from human concerns. In arguing that the supreme principle of morality must be a categorical imperative, Kant seems to claim that in fulfilling our moral obligations, we are not advancing our ends or purposes. Acting morally, on this picture, does not serve any of our particular ends or purposes. It does not seem to bear any obvious relation to making us *happier* or better off. We might worry that Kant divorces morality from human concerns – from our particular ends, we may say – that it may seem to have no point at all. Kant thus needs not only to show that there could be a moral principle that satisfies his five criteria – some of which are in apparent tension with each other – but that we have reason to *care* about whether our conduct, and the conduct of others, conforms to this principle. (We will return to some of these worries in Chapter 8.)

Hence, it is reasonable to be skeptical about Kant's search for a categorical imperative to serve as morality's supreme principle. Still, if he can identify a principle that does all this, that would be a first-rank philosophical achievement.

Further Reading

Samuel Kerstein's Kant's Search for the Supreme Principle of Morality (Cambridge, 2002) adopts an interpretive strategy for the Groundwork similar to mine, though we differ on what Kant's criteria for the supreme principle of morality are. Kerstein offers a condensed discussion of his strategy in "Deriving the supreme moral principles from common moral ideas," in T.E. Hill (ed.), Blackwell Guide to Kant's Ethics (Wiley-Blackwell, 2009). Christine Korsgaard's "Kant's analysis of obligation: The argument of Groundwork I," *The Monist* 72 (1989): 311–340, particularly section III, indicates how the early portions of that text use a "motivational analysis" of the good will to identify morality's supreme principle. Jonathan Dancy's Ethics Without Principles (Oxford, 2004) is the best-known articulation of particularism. W.D. Ross's classic The Right and the Good (Oxford, 2003) is the canonical source for modern-day ethical intuitionism.

2 The Categorical Imperative and the Kantian Theory of Value, Part I

In this chapter, we will introduce one of the formulations Kant provides of the Categorical Imperative, the supreme principle of morality. This formulation, the Formula of Humanity, has been widely influential in many areas of ethics. Our chief aim is to describe this formulation and indicate why it satisfies the five criteria for the supreme principle of morality that we arrived at in Chapter 1. If in fact the Formula of Humanity satisfies these criteria, and these criteria are the correct criteria for identifying the supreme principle of morality, then Kant will have succeeded in showing that the Categorical Imperative, or at least one expression of it, is actually morality's supreme principle.

In the course of our discussion of the Formula of Humanity, we will pursue two other tasks which must be tackled if we are to fully appreciate Kant's theory of morality. The first is to outline Kant's taxonomy of duties. Although Kant believed that our moral obligations are ultimately to be justified by reference to the Categorical Imperative, morality's supreme principle, he nevertheless believed that the Categorical Imperative generated a set of duties that could be broken down on the basis of two fundamental distinctions: the distinction between perfect and imperfect duties on the one hand, and the distinction between duties to others and duties to oneself on the other. In this chapter, we will elaborate these two distinctions and fill in the taxonomy of duties based on these distinctions, as well as showing how these various categories of duty reflect the moral demands imposed by the Formula of Humanity.

The second task is to use the Formula of Humanity to begin filling in Kant's theory of value. As I noted in the preface, Kant has a distinctive theory of value that is often underappreciated by philosophers who engage with his moral theory. The Formula of Humanity highlights important components of that theory of value.

2.1 Kantian Morality and Value

Morality exists because value exists. If there were nothing of value, morality would have no subject matter. So when we talk about morality, we are talking about values – what we do (or should) care about. Morally good people – the morally virtuous, we might say – are good because they respond to value in the right way. And the difference between right and wrong, between what is morally permissible and morally obligatory, is a difference relating to differences in value. We act rightly when we respond correctly to moral value, and we act wrongly when we either respond incorrectly to moral value or assign moral value to the wrong kinds of things.

These claims about morality and value may seem uncontroversial, even trivial. But they are not uncontroversial among philosophers, especially those sympathetic to Kantian ethics. In fact, philosophers have often interpreted Kant as rejecting such claims about morality and value. Instead of understanding Kantian ethics as grounded in a theory of moral value, these philosophers interpret Kantian ethics as concerned solely with moral rules and with the supreme principle of morality. On this understanding, value hardly enters into Kant's thinking about ethics at all.

In my estimation, by divorcing morality from value, this interpretation of Kant's ethics makes his views obscure and makes an already difficult theory even more elusive. A full defense of a value-based interpretation of Kant's ethics is beyond the scope of this book. Nevertheless, I offer in this book what I believe to a more credible interpretation of Kant's ethics, one that puts his account of moral value front and center.[1] As we will see, for Kant, *rational agency* is the central moral value. I will argue that this view is in fact plausible as an overall approach to Kant's ethics as well as being philosophically attractive. But it is a difficult view to appreciate in isolation from alternative or rival views. Hence, our investigation of Kant's theory of moral value begins not with Kant but with an investigation of another moral theory often compared to his: utilitarianism.

2.2 Utilitarianism, Value, and Valuing

Though utilitarian moral theory has deep roots in Western philosophy, it was first given systematic expression by three nineteenth-century British thinkers: Jeremy Bentham, John Stuart Mill, and Henry Sidgwick. Since then, utilitarianism has been developed and refined extensively, to the point where there are now literally dozens of permutations of utilitarianism discussed among philosophers. Nevertheless, the core idea behind utilitarianism can be expressed in this *utilitarian standard for right action:*

[1] Perhaps no Kantian has done more to suggest that Kant is misread if we assume that he lacks an account of value than Barbara Herman. See in particular her essay, "Leaving deontology behind," in her Practice of Moral Judgment (Harvard, 1993).

A person's act is right if and only if no other act the person could have performed would result in greater net welfare for all affected by the act.

Let's try to unpack the utilitarian standard a bit.

First, what do utilitarians have in mind by 'welfare'? The utilitarian standard is sometimes expressed in terms not of welfare, but in terms of 'happiness,' 'utility,' or 'well-being.' While there might be slight differences in meaning among these terms, the notion of welfare invoked by utilitarians is straightforward. Welfare is simply whatever contributes to making people's lives go well. Utilitarians have strenuous disagreements about the best *theory* of welfare. Some believe that welfare ultimately reduces to pleasure and pain. Others think that welfare is a function of having your desires satisfied rather than frustrated.[2] These theoretical disagreements aside, though, utilitarians generally agree about the sorts of things that contribute to welfare. Having enough to eat, being free of physical pain, and cultivating good friendships are examples of what makes one's life better. In contrast, loneliness, illness, and frustration are examples of what makes one's life worse.

The utilitarian standard requires that we perform an act if no other act would result in greater net welfare. 'Net welfare' refers to the difference between an act's positive contribution to welfare – how much it makes people's lives better – and how much it detracts from people's welfare – how much it makes people's lives worse. Many acts are such that they have both positive and negative consequences for people's welfare. Keeping a promise to one person may mean not attending to the needs or desires of another. Quarantining a person with a virulent infectious disease reduces her liberty, but protects others from developing that disease. Punishing a child causes him pain or distress, but may help him develop better judgment in the future. Utilitarianism recognizes this fact and proposes that we act rightly when we perform an act that has the best *overall* results for welfare. We act rightly, then, if there was no act that is better in terms of how much welfare it brings about. Utilitarianism is thus an outstanding example of what we called in Chapter 1 a consequentialist theory of morality. For on the utilitarian view, all that matters in determining the rightness or wrongness of an act is how good its consequences are, and, in particular, how much welfare results from an act's being performed (particularly in comparison with alternative courses of action).

Finally, utilitarians insist that the welfare of all those affected by an act must be taken into account. Utilitarians often present this point by saying that morality should aspire to *impartiality* among the welfare of individuals. From a moral perspective, no one's welfare should count for more than anyone else's.

[2] Mill is a complicated case: Though he seemed to believe that all value is ultimately grounded in happiness, he seemed to think of happiness as a composite of a variety of intrinsic values, such as virtue.

Utilitarianism thus requires us not simply to consider our own welfare or the welfare of people we know when we engage in moral decision making. We must also take into account those we do not know but whose welfare will be affected by our acts, those on the other side of the globe, and perhaps the welfare of non-human animals[3] and human beings who do not yet exist.

The utilitarian standard thus claims that any act that *maximizes* net welfare is right, and all right acts maximize net welfare. Now, utilitarianism is a theory that has been subject to many criticisms over the past two centuries, and the theory's defenders have proven very resourceful in answering these objections. In the end, by defending Kantianism, I am explicitly rejecting utilitarianism. Nevertheless, this book's purpose is not to critique utilitarianism, so we will largely set these debates aside in order to focus on how utilitarianism's theory of moral value differs from Kant's.

So what do utilitarians believe has moral value? Welfare – and *only* welfare. Anything else we might value ultimately derives its value from welfare, according to the utilitarian. Some things that we value, such as money or a reputation for being trustworthy, are valuable, utilitarians believe. But they are not intrinsically valuable or valuable in their own right, according to utilitarians. Rather, their value rests on their being *means* to welfare, the only thing that is intrinsically valuable or valuable in its own right. Money or a good reputation can help us acquire welfare. Other things that we value, such as friendship or good health, are not valuable because they are means to welfare. Their value instead rests on being *constituents*, or components, of welfare. A person who has rewarding friendships or is in good health has some of the things that make their life go well. Hence, like the means to welfare, the constituents of welfare derive their value from their relation to welfare.

The claim that all value ultimately reduces to the value of welfare is a bold one. Everything valuable, on this view, is valuable because of its relation to welfare, the only thing that is valuable for its own sake. But many philosophers, even some who are not utilitarians, have thought that it is very plausible that all value reduces to the value of welfare. Consider something that you value: your favorite pair of shoes, having lunch each day with your co-workers, a lovely spring blossom. For each of these things, it seems like a reasonable question to ask, 'why are these things valuable?' Moreover, the right answer seems clear: they are valuable because they ultimately contribute

[3] Some utilitarians, most notably Bentham, have held that the welfare of animals also contributes to net welfare and so needs to be taken into account in determining right and wrong. Whether this is so turns on whether or not welfare is understood in terms of attributes animals possess (for instance, the susceptibility to pleasure and pain). As the discussion in Section 7.3 will suggest, I agree that animals and their welfare matter morally, though not in the way consequentialists have maintained.

to happiness, or, to use the utilitarian language, because they contribute to welfare. But it does not look like a reasonable question to ask 'why is welfare valuable?' This seems like a misguided question because not only is welfare valuable, it is *not* valuable for the sake of, or as a means to, anything else. Hence, whereas the value of welfare appears to explain why everything besides welfare is valuable, nothing is needed to explain why welfare is valuable. Welfare looks like as good a candidate as any for what is intrinsically or fundamentally valuable.

Again, there is much, much more to be said about utilitarianism. But what we need to notice at this point is that utilitarianism has a *monistic* theory of moral value. A monistic theory is a theory that posits one and only one fundamental value. For the utilitarian, that value is welfare. Kant (as we will see) also has a monistic theory of moral value, but he posits that rational agency, not welfare, is the sole fundamental moral value.

Utilitarianism is monistic in a second way. 'Value' is a complicated idea. To this point, we have been talking about 'value' in terms of those things that have value. We have been treating 'value' as a noun. But 'value' is also a verb, something we *do*. And there are different ways of valuing things, or of responding to what is valuable about them. I value my anniversary by remembering and celebrating it. I value the World Cup by enjoying it every four years. I value mountains by visiting them, admiring them, and appreciating them. Valuing is therefore a diverse activity, and different sorts of values call for different sorts of valuing. As one non-utilitarian philosopher puts it, to 'be for' or to value something can take many diverse forms, including "loving it, liking it, respecting it, wanting it, wishing for it, appreciating it, thinking highly of it, speaking in favor of it and otherwise intentionally standing for it symbolically, acting to promote or protect it."[4]

An adequate theory of morality needs to tell us what has value. But it also needs to tell us *how* to value what is valuable. Utilitarians say that welfare alone has value. And how are we to value welfare, according to the utilitarian? The utilitarian standard says that an act is right just when it brings about as much welfare as possible. We are to maximize welfare. Or, put differently, the utilitarian attitude toward welfare is that we are to *promote* it to the greatest extent possible. Promoting welfare is the proper attitude to have toward the value of welfare, and welfare alone has intrinsic moral value. Note that the utilitarian not only holds that there is but one intrinsic value, but that there is only one correct way to value that value: by promoting it.

Utilitarianism thus offers a monistic theory of value in two different senses. It recognizes only one fundamental value and only one proper way to value what is valuable. I have already hinted that Kantian ethics is monistic in the first

[4] Robert Merrihew Adams, *A Theory of Virtue* (Oxford, 2006), p. 15.

sense, recognizing only one fundamental moral value, but disagreeing with utilitarianism about what the value in question is. For the utilitarian, it is welfare, and for the Kantian, rational agency. But as we will see later on, with respect to valu*ing*, Kantian ethics is not monistic, but pluralistic. For Kant thought that there is more than one way to properly value rational agency from a moral perspective.

2.3 Kant's Formula of Humanity

Let us return to the agenda set in Chapter 1 and resume our effort to grasp why, according to Kant, the Categorical Imperative is the supreme principle of morality. Unfortunately, Kant confuses matters by proposing that there are in fact several different versions of the Categorical Imperative that are nevertheless equivalent expressions of the same underlying principle. We will return later to the relationship among the different versions of the Categorical Imperative. For the moment, though, we turn to one version of this principle.

Kant's Formula of Humanity states:

> Always act so that you use humanity, whether in your own person or in the person of any other, always at the same time as an end, never merely as a means. (G 4:429)

As with the utilitarian standard, we should unpack the components of the Formula of Humanity.

This principle claims that we are to treat a person's "humanity" in a particular way. One common misunderstanding about this principle results from the unfortunate term 'humanity.' Kant does not have in mind here human beings or the human species. Rather, 'humanity' refers to our capacity to guide our choices and actions on rational terms. More specifically, humanity is our capacity to set ends and the means to those ends by using our rational abilities (MM 6:392). Recall from our earlier discussion of hypothetical imperatives Kant's means–ends view of action: When we act voluntarily, our acts are means to our ends and are rational insofar as they realize our ends. This is a view he shares with utilitarians. Kant recognizes that one way we use our rational capacities is in order to discern the best (or at least adequate) means to our ends. After all, sometimes people pursue their ends irrationally, by selecting means that are insufficient to their ends. A person might want to enjoy a lavish retirement but underestimate the amount of money he needs to save for it. An aspiring rock musician may not recognize how much touring and self-promotion is necessary for such a career. Or (and here I speak from firsthand experience) students may want 'A' grades in their courses but not have the study habits or skills to get high marks. One of the main challenges of human life is figuring out how to achieve our ends, and though we often succeed, we can also fail. Meeting this challenge is a matter of having true beliefs about the world: about whether particular actions will result in our ends being achieved. Philosophers have taken to calling the kind of rationality we exercise when we try to discern the best means to our ends *instrumental rationality*.

Kant sees instrumental rationality as one of our rational capacities. But the central rational capacity that defines humanity is the capacity to rationally appraise and select our ends. In each of the cases in Section 1.3, the individuals not only had the power to rationally ascertain the means to their ends; they also had the power to scrutinize these ends, determine if those ends are worth pursuing, and, if not, pursue other ends in their stead. The woman who opts for a Mexican vacation does so presumably because she believes there is something satisfying, desirable, or pleasant about it. But it is not inevitable that she opts for the Mexican vacation. She is able to reflect upon that end and consider whether it really is a worthwhile end to pursue. Her choosing that end is an exercise of her humanity because she chooses it as a result of rationally endorsing it or finding it good. As Kant might put it, her choosing that end is an example of exercising her capacity to set ends according to reason.

Thus, beings with humanity are not simply given their ends or purposes by nature or habit. Non-human animals have ends, at least inasmuch as they clearly engage in behavior that is means to their ends. The dog who fetches a thrown stick has as her end the return of the stick to her human companion. Her retrieval and return of the stick is her means to that end. But the dog does not rationally scrutinize or select her ends. While non-human animals exhibit a variety of forms of intelligence – and could thus be called 'rational' in one sense – non-human animals do not (as far as we can tell) have the capacity to question or appraise their ends. The woman planning her vacation can pose for herself the question, 'ought I vacation in Mexico?' The dog chasing the thrown stick does not, and presumably cannot, pose for herself the equivalent question (in mental 'dog-ese') 'ought I return the stick?' On the other hand, Kant's use of the term 'humanity' should not mislead us into thinking that only members of the human species could possibly possess humanity. Kant clearly thought of adult humans as the clearest examples of beings with humanity, but, as we hinted at in Chapter 1, he seemed open to the possibility of beings of other species having the rational capacities that constitute humanity. Perhaps someday we will discover that we had been wrong all along about some animal species and conclude that they can rationally evaluate their ends and thus have humanity. Or perhaps we will someday be visited by an intelligent alien species that has humanity. In any event, Kant's Formula of Humanity does not say that we are to treat *human beings* in a certain way. Rather, we are to treat what Kant takes as a defining attribute of human beings – our capacity to set ends and the means to those ends by using our rational abilities – in a certain way.

2.4 Treating Humanity Merely as a Means

To Kant's mind, our humanity, which includes our instrumental rationality, means that we are rational agents – or, as I will put it, that we enjoy *rational agency*. In saying that we are morally obligated to treat humanity as end in itself, Kant's Formula of Humanity thus directs us to value rational agency. So whereas happiness is the central moral value for utilitarians, rational agency is the central moral value for Kantians. (We will have more to say about the value Kant ascribes to happiness in Chapter 8.) Still, we have not yet said how the Formula of Humanity directs us to value rational agency. There are, in my estimation, two complications here.

The first is what Kant intends by treating someone's rational agency as an "end in itself." We have already been introduced to Kant's means–ends conception of action. If the Formula of Humanity requires us to treat rational agency as an end, then his means–ends conception of action might be taken to imply that the Formula of Humanity requires us to bring about rational agency or cause it to come into existence. After all, Kant standardly takes an 'end' to be the state of affairs at which a person's action aims. When we act, we engage the world around us to assist us in *realizing* our ends (in the way that if a person's end is to become a schoolteacher, she acts with the aim of making it the case that she becomes a schoolteacher). As we shall see, that is not the sense in which humanity is supposed to be treated as an end "in itself," according to Kant. The Formula of Humanity does not ask us to bring about rational agency (or rational agents) or cause them to exist. Hence, we will need to understand how treating something as an end differs from treating something ('humanity' in particular) as an end *in itself*.

The second complication is that Kant's Formula of Humanity seems to contain two clauses: that we are never to treat rational agency merely as a means, *and* always to treat it as an end in itself. Grasping this moral principle necessitates understanding each of these clauses. But it also necessitates understanding how the clauses are related. Does any act that treats rational agency merely as a means also fail to treat rational agency as an end in itself? Does any act that fails to treat rational agency as an end in itself also treat rational agency merely as a means? Here I will suggest that treating rational agency merely as a means and not treating it as an end in itself are not co-extensive: While every act that treats rational agency merely as a means fails to treat it as an end in itself, not every act that fails to treat rational agency as an end in itself also treats it merely as a means. Not treating rational agency as an end in itself turns out to be a broader notion than treating rational agency merely as a means. Let us address this second complication first before circling back to the first complication: how precisely to understand treating humanity as an end in itself.

In order to act effectively, we often have to make use of objects as means to our ends. We use vehicles to convey us to where we desire to be. We use cookware to prepare our food. And we use electronic gadgets to gather information to enable us to pursue a variety of different ends. Such choices and actions take advantage of the causal properties of those objects in order to advance my ends. Kant noticed something important about many of our actions: They take advantage of the causal properties of 'humanity,' or rational agency, in order to advance our ends. When I take out a loan, the loan officer who approves my application is a means to my securing the funds I desire. Without the officer's approval (an exercise of her rational agency), I could not secure the desired funds. When my physician gives me advice about my diet, he is a means to my acquiring knowledge needed to improve my health. Without his choosing to provide me that advice (and exercise of his rational agency), I would lack the knowledge I seek in order to improve my health. The students I teach are means to my earning a paycheck. Without students agreeing to enroll in my courses (an exercise of their rational agency), I would not have the students necessary to earn a living. And in many such cases, I (or, more accurately, my rational agency) functions as means *for* other people and *to* their ends. For the loan officer and the bank that employs her, I am a means to creating a debt which, if repaid, will increase the bank's profits and provide the loan officer her salary. For the physicians, patients are means to income. And for students, their instructors are means to the achievement, knowledge, or credentials they seek.

As Kant recognized, there is nothing necessarily morally objectionable about treating rational agency as a means. Each of us does so dozens of times each day, and it would be hard to imagine human life where we did not do so. Human beings are highly interdependent creatures, and we possess different skills or resources. Much of human activity, especially our economic activity, involves using skills or resources that we have in order to acquire or make use of the skills or resources of others. Through such exchanges, we exercise our rational agency and thereby expand our capacity to pursue our ends effectively.

In and of itself, treating rational agency as a means is therefore morally innocuous. However, the Formula of Humanity indicates that an important moral boundary is crossed when our actions treat humanity "merely as a means" – or, as Kant sometimes put it, when our actions treat humanity *only* as a means. Rational agents are distinct from other objects that we may use in the service of our ends. Unlike vehicles, cookware, and electronic gadgets, we rational agents have ends to which are committed, as well as the capacity to choose those ends and the best means through which to pursue them. Our having rational agency makes us more than just "things," according to Kant. We are, instead, "persons" (G 4:428). And while Kant allows that it is permissible for rational agents to be treated as thing-*like*, using their rational agency with the aim of realizing one's ends, he disallows treating rational agents only or *exclusively* as things. Some of our actions treat rational agency as if it were nothing more than a means to the achievement of our ends. When we do so, Kant believes, we fail to value rational agency properly.

Here is an example of what Kant has in mind (G 4:429–430). Suppose that Jan has as one of her ends acquiring money for some purpose or other, but she lacks any other means to acquire that money except through a personal loan that she is quite aware she will never be in a position to repay. Knowing that only an apparently sincere affirmation of her intent to repay the loan will enable to secure the loan, she decides to misrepresent to a sympathetic friend, Keith, her intention of paying back the money. She ends up borrowing the money from Keith under false pretenses.

So described, this '"false promisor"' acted wrongly in misrepresenting her intention (and ability) to repay the borrowed funds. But in what sense has Jan treated anyone's *rational agency* merely as a means? Jan's securing the loan serves to advance her rationally chosen ends. But Keith, the friend from whom she borrows the money, has 'humanity' as well. He is a rational agent with ends of his own. Keith presumably lends Jan the money to pursue his ends, among which (we may reasonably assume) is that he will be repaid. (Keith is genuinely making a loan, not engaging in an act of charity.) But Keith's ends, and the fact that Keith lends the money with those ends in mind, seem to play no role in Jan's decision to misrepresent her intention to repay. Kant's worry about such conduct is not that the loan will turn out to be adverse to Keith's interests. Rather, Kant would point out that Jan, having good reason to believe that *Keith's* ends will not be served by her "false promise," does not treat Keith's ends as the slightest obstacle to her action. Her lie, if efficacious, will result in Keith unknowingly exercising his rational agency so as to serve Jan's ends, but not his own. Jan's lie thus treats Keith's rational agency – his capacity to set ends and identify the means to those ends – as a causal capacity existing solely to serve her ends. Keith's "humanity" is thus not accorded the same respect or concern by Jan as she accords her own.

Again, Kant finds nothing inherently morally objectionable about enlisting others' rational agency in the service of our own ends. Indeed, doing so is the essence of cooperative behavior: In an honest lending transaction, Jan would advance her ends (securing the desired money) by convincing Keith to advance his ends (not ending up financially worse off due to the loan). As Kant puts it, it should be possible for our actions to "contain" the ends of those with whom we interact (G 4:430). Jan's lie to Keith makes it impossible for Keith to pursue his ends while Jan pursues hers.

Many commentators have interpreted Kant's Formula of Humanity as a principle requiring that we not treat others in ways to which they cannot, either in actuality or in principle, consent to being treated.[5] On this interpretation, Jan wrongs Keith because either (a) Keith would not have consented to the loan were he aware that Jan did not intend to repay, or (b) Keith could not have consented to the actual arrangement, since he was not aware that Jan was acting under false pretenses. These commentators are correct in that many acts that treat humanity merely as a means are neither consented to nor can be consented to. To fully consent to some way of being treated, in full knowledge of the nature of the arrangement, is to give one's rational endorsement to being treated in that way. The very fact of one's consent means that one's rational agency is treated as something more than a purely causal power to bring about someone's ends. Consent of this kind thus strongly suggests that a person's act is not wrong, according to the Formula of Humanity. However, I do not believe we can *equate* treating someone merely as a means with treating them in ways that to which they cannot or do not consent. Not actually consenting to being treated in a certain way usually entails that one *is* thereby treated merely as a means. Conversely, actually consenting to being treated in a certain way usually entails that one is thereby *not* treated merely as a means. But there are exceptions to these claims. As shall be discussed in Section 6.5, Kant argues that if lying is necessary in order to preserve one's life, then such a lie, an act to which one necessarily *cannot* consent, does not treat another merely as a means and is therefore morally permissible (LE 27:448). On the other hand, there are acts which, according to Kant, one might rationally consent to (suicide, selling oneself into slavery) that are nevertheless wrong because they treat one's own rational agency as a means. Nevertheless, analyzing treating humanity merely as a means in terms of consent helps to illuminate the core insight of the Formula of Humanity, particularly insofar as it functions as a principle of interpersonal morality. The interactions among rational agents, according to Kant, should, to the extent possible, be *transparent.* We cannot avoid trying to influence each other's choices or behavior. But those efforts at influencing one another must be compatible with respect for one another as rational agents, as beings entitled to set our own ends and to pursue those ends.

A common complaint among Kant's critics is that the Formula of Humanity, and especially the notion of treating someone's humanity merely as a means, is vague. Later (Section 2.9) I will propose that it is less vague than it seems – that in fact the notion of *respect* for rational agency lies at the heart of this principle. Still, these critics are correct inasmuch as there are a variety of types of acts that treat rational agency merely as a means, and these acts fail to respect rational agency through a variety of different mechanisms.

[5] Most prominently, Onora O'Neill. See "A simplified account of Kant's ethics," in T. Regan (ed.), *Matters of Life and Death* (McGraw-Hill, 1986).

Sometimes, we wrongfully *circumvent* rational agency: In getting Keith to loan her the money despite her having no intention or ability to repay, Jan hopes to get Keith to act in ways that serve her ends without his being fully aware of a fact (i.e., that she will not repay) that bears on his ends. She thereby tries to advance her ends by working around or circumventing Keith's rational agency so that Keith will exercise that agency on her (Jan's) behalf. Other instances of treating others' humanity merely as a means *co-opt* their rational agency. From the liar's standpoint, lying is effective at advancing his ends when it influences the beliefs of another rational agent so that she will choose or act in ways conducive to the liar's own ends. A liar hopes that his lie will lead another rational agent to have a false belief that she will in turn rely upon in deciding what to do. The liar hopes that, because of his lie, she will act in ways that advance his ends. The liar thus clandestinely puts others' rational agency to work in the service of his ends. In other cases, we treat humanity merely as a means by *disregarding* it altogether. A doctor who administers a medication without her patient's consent, or a person who sexually assaults another without the latter's consent, fails to engage with others' rational agency in situations where those others might well not perceive these forms of treatment as something that serves their ends.

Treating humanity merely as a means thus involves treating a person's capacity for choice, either of ends or of means, not as worthy of respect but simply as a tool or instrument. Again, we probably cannot enumerate all of the ways in which this can take place. Nevertheless, that we are not to treat rational agency merely as a means entails strong moral presumptions against the use of force or coercion; lying and willful deception; impairing or damaging someone's rational capacities so as to impair their ability to exercise that agency; killing rational agents, particularly those who do not wish to die; manipulating others' beliefs, attitudes, or choices; paternalistic actions, aimed at compelling or inducing people to choose as others wish them to; and, in general, to do only what others have agreed to or at least could agree to. What links all of these impermissible behaviors is that they betray that the moral agent in question views rational agency, whether found in herself or in others, purely as a set of cogs in a causal system, cogs to be influenced or navigated so as to advance one's ends but not to be taken into account or consulted prior to action. Kant's Formula of Humanity thus propounds a moral ideal wherein our interactions with rational agents should be governed by the aim of treating them transparently and as rational equals.

2.5 Humanity as an 'End in Itself'

What, then, of the other component of Kant's Formula of Humanity – that we are to treat rational agents as ends in themselves? This demand is, I propose, distinct from but related to the moral demand not to treat rational agency merely as a means.

This becomes clear when we consider another of the duties Kant outlines: the duty to promote the ends, or happiness, of others. Consider a figure we may call the *rugged individualist.* Kant describes him as someone

> for whom things are going well while he sees that others (whom he could very well help) have to contend with great hardships, [and] thinks: what is it to me? Let each be happy as heaven wills or as he can make himself; I shall take nothing from him nor even envy him; only I do not care to contribute anything to his welfare or to his assistance in need! (G 4:423)

This rugged individualist neither assists others to achieve their ends nor expects the assistance of others in achieving his ends. And yet, Kant says, the rugged individualist's unwillingness to aid others is contrary to the Formula of Humanity.

But why so? If all that the Formula of Humanity required is that we not treat rational agency merely as a means, the rugged individualist's indifference to the happiness or "welfare" of others would not violate that Formula. The rugged individualist preaches a 'live and let live' outlook, neither soliciting nor accepting others' aid or cooperation. Hence, he does not treat others *merely* as a means largely because he has adopted a policy of neither treating others as means to his ends nor of being himself treated as means to others' ends. Kant claims that the Formula of Humanity is not only a 'negative' principle, however. It does not simply identify *constraints* on how we treat rational agency. In order to treat rational agency as an end in itself, "it is not enough that the action does not conflict with humanity in our person as an end in itself; it must also *harmonize with it*." The human species might be able to survive if all adopted the rugged individualist's outlook on life. Nevertheless, Kant argues, such an outlook does not positively 'harmonize' with humanity. The ends of others must "as far as possible be also *my* ends," so that everyone endeavors "to further the ends of others" (G 4:430).

Despite its not treating humanity merely as means, indifference to others' happiness nonetheless does not treat their rational agency as an end in itself, according to Kant. Kant does not say quite enough here about why we must, in order to treat humanity as an end in itself, seek to promote others' chosen ends. So here is an attempt to fill in Kant's thinking on this matter: A community of rugged individualists would not treat each other merely as means, and, to that extent, they would respect each other's humanity. But their indifference to one another's happiness suggests that they would not really *value* each other's humanity fully. When we seek to advance another person's ends, we value those ends inasmuch as those ends express the rational commitments of that person; her ends are, after all, the ends she has rationally chosen as the objects of her pursuits. Hence, our advancing a person's ends amounts to valuing her as a person, and because those ends are the ends of a rational agent, promoting those ends recognizes the value of that person qua rational agent. Refraining from treating rational agents merely as means respects their integrity. But seeking to promote their ends fully *recognizes* their value as rational agents. Indifference to one another's ends will, to Kant's mind, preclude *discord* among rational agents. But actively seeking to advance one another's ends brings those ends into a state of harmony wherein the value of each rational agent is recognized through the promotion of her ends.[6]

The rugged individualist thus fails to treat humanity as an end in itself, despite not treating anyone's humanity merely as a means. This resolves our first complication regarding the Formula of Humanity: what Kant intends by treating humanity merely as a means and as an end in itself. But what of our second complication: that the Formula of Humanity thereby expresses two unrelated moral principles? Kant sometimes seems to admit that the Formula of Humanity expresses two distinct principles: "a human being is an end for himself as well as for others, and it is not enough that he is not authorized to use either himself or others merely as means (since he could then still be indifferent to them); it is in itself his duty to make the human being as such his end" (MM 6:395). Although the Formula of Humanity gives rise to two distinct sorts of duties, I do not think that it expresses two unrelated principles. To see why, we need to interrogate Kant's notion of an end in itself. As we noted in Section 2.4, Kant typically thinks of ends as the outcomes at which our actions aim. Such ends are the ends arising from 'inclination,' or desire. But that does not seem to capture how humanity is supposed to be any kind of end for Kant. In not treating humanity merely as a means, we are not aiming to bring about rational agency – to cause it to exist or for there to be more of it. In advancing others' ends and thereby promoting their happiness, we are aiming to bring about particular outcomes as a result of our actions – namely, that the ends of others are realized. But even here, the *ends* of other rational agents are our ends. Their rational agency is not our end in Kant's usual sense of that term.

It seems, then, that in dubbing humanity an end 'in itself,' Kant was striving to ascribe to our rational agency a distinctive kind of worth or value. Other ends, he says, are "relative" ends, "ends that a rational being proposes at his discretion as *effects* of his actions." These are not ends in themselves because their status as ends – i.e., as state of affairs to be pursued through action – are conferred upon them by our willing them as ends. Their value is thus contingent

[6] Here Kant seems to be gesturing at the social ideal he calls *the kingdom of ends*. See Section 8.7 for details.

upon our willing them. Humanity, in contrast, is an "objective" end, not an end whose value derives from its being a 'discretionary' effect of our actions (G 4:428). Humanity is not an end to be "effected," since that would render its value "relative." Rational agency is thus properly valued not by our "effecting" it or by our bringing into existence. As Kant glosses it, humanity's status as an end can also stated in terms of its being an "independently existing end" or "the subject of all possible ends" (MM 4:437).[7] My suggestion is that to say humanity is an end in itself is for Kant to declare that humanity alone is a final end or an end *in its own right*. All other ends acquire their significance by virtue of the fact that we rational agents exercise our humanity and choose those ends. Those ends' value depends upon rational agency, rather than vice versa. But the value of rational agency is "independent," not dependent upon anything else. Humanity justifies other things (our ends) having value, but nothing justifies its value. Humanity is an end in itself because it is the 'end of the line' from the standpoint of moral justification: Nothing explains *its* value, but it in turn explains all other value.

The notion of humanity as an end in its own right helps illuminate the underlying relationship between the two ideas incorporated in Kant's Formula of Humanity. We saw earlier, in connection with the rugged individualist and the duty to promote others' happiness, that not all instances of not treating humanity as an end in itself are instances of treating humanity merely as a means. The rugged individualist, in refusing to promote others' ends, does not take others' ends, which are expressions of others' humanity, as an end. But he does not thereby treat others' humanity as a mere means. Conversely, whenever a person's rational agency is treated merely as a means, it is *also* not treated as an end in itself. When Jan makes her false promise to Keith, she inverts the justificatory relationship between humanity and our ends, for she treats Keith's humanity or rational agency as a means subservient to her ends. Keith was not given the opportunity to authorize Jan pursuing her ends via the loan. His rational agency is thereby treated solely as a means to her ends rather than as an end in itself.

2.6 Kant's Taxonomy of Duties: Perfect and Imperfect Duties

Although treating humanity merely as a means and failing to treat it as an end in itself are clearly grounded in a common moral ideal, Kant's Formula of Humanity nevertheless highlights two distinct ways in which we fail to treat humanity as an end in itself: by treating rational agency merely as a means, and

[7] The term that is typically translated as 'end in itself,' – *Zweck an sich selbst* – might also be translated as 'self-sufficient' or 'self-standing' end, underscoring how humanity's value is independent of other ends we will.

by not promoting others' chosen ends. In fact, this distinction is the basis of a fundamental division in how Kant understands our duties.

Kant divided our duties into categories known as *perfect duties* and *imperfect duties*. What does Kant mean by saying that a duty is 'perfect'? A perfect duty requires the performance of particular actions. Duties not to lie, not to harm others, not to coerce others, and so on are duties we fulfill by doing (or perhaps more often, not doing) certain kinds of actions. We will see in Section 6.5 that whether Kantian ethics implies that *every* act of these kinds is wrong – every lie, for example – has been a matter of controversy. But what it is not controversial is that Kant believed that it belongs to the nature of such actions that they treat others merely as means. Our earlier example of Jan, the false promisor, exemplifies a violation of a Kantian perfect duty. Jan's own end of securing money for herself is not itself impermissible. However, the means she took to that end, the action itself, treated Keith's rational agency merely as a means. Kant's perfect duties thus require that we treat rational agents as ends by constraining or limiting the means by which we pursue our ends. Predominantly, then, Kant's perfect duties are 'negative,' or duties of *non-performance*. The perfect duties dictate which ways of treating humanity are *forbidden*.

Unfortunately, Kant is not only a verbose and turgid writer, he sometimes confuses readers by shifting his terminology. In the Metaphysics of Morals, where Kant offers his most thorough account of our various duties, he speaks not of perfect and imperfect duties to others, as he does in the Groundwork, but of "duties of respect" and "duties of love" toward others. However, we can surmise that duties of respect toward others, because they are "owed to others," require the performance of particular actions and hence correspond to perfect duties. Kant emphasizes that in fulfilling these duties we show respect to our fellow human beings by not treating their humanity merely as means. Furthermore, the demands placed upon us by our duties of respect require what Kant calls "modesty" on our part, a willingness to permit the ends of others to restrict how we pursue our ends (MM 6:462).

The counterpart of perfect duties, the imperfect duties or "duties of love," do not require the performance of particular actions, but instead require commitment to certain ends as a matter of personal policy. One such duty is the duty transgressed by our aforementioned rugged individualist: the duty to promote others' happiness by advancing their ends. The rugged individualist fails to fulfill this duty because he is utterly indifferent to the happiness of others. However, we should not infer from this conclusion that Kant thought that this duty requires altruistic zeal or that we do everything possible to promote others' happiness. For one, imperfect duties are duties of *wide latitude*. For example, the duty of promoting others' happiness – the duty of beneficence – does not require that we do everything within our power to promote others' happiness. This duty gives us some choice over the time or manner by which we fulfill it. For example, it would seem to require that we at least occasionally support charitable causes, but it does not tell us which charitable causes to support (whether to give to UNICEF or to Oxfam, for example). Moreover, it would seem to allow us not to give to charitable causes when we lack the resources to do so (when we are unemployed, say) so long as we are willing to support them in times when our resources are abundant.

Moreover, Kant held that perfect duties take precedence over imperfect duties. It would not be morally acceptable, for instance, to lie to your boss about a friend's qualifications for a job even if getting the job would promote your friend's happiness (or promote the most happiness overall). Our perfect duties constrain the morally acceptable *means* by which we pursue various ends, and Kant believed that good ends (including the happiness of others) cannot morally justify deploying means – that is, performing actions – that violate perfect duties. Perfect duties make the rational agency of others a "negative" end – that is, an end that limits our pursuit of other ends. The imperfect duties make the rational agency of others a "positive" end, an end that we seek to realize.

It is not entirely obvious why Kant thought that perfect duties take precedence, but here is a possible line of defense: When performing an act that violates a perfect duty, an agent is usually doing something more morally objectionable than when she fails to act so as to advance the ends prescribed by an imperfect duty. For perfect duties limit our moral *options* to a greater degree than do imperfect duties. In the course of pursuing one's ends, one must not, for example, tell a lie in order to advance one's financial interests. Imperfect duties, being duties of wide latitude, tell us not that there is some specific act we must (or must not) do. Rather, they propose to us a range of actions which, in varying degrees, further the end prescribed by the duty in question. An individual who, on one occasion, opts not to (for example) act so as to promote others' happiness thereby does nothing to help fulfill her imperfect duty of beneficence. But given that such duties are duties of wide latitude, she will have other opportunities to do so. Such is not the case when one violates a perfect duty. Thus, more forceful moral criticism seems appropriate when a person violates a perfect duty, for she will not have another opportunity to fulfill that duty. A person cannot 'make up' for violating a perfect duty such as keeping a promise by keeping another promise later on. Hence, while Kant would insist that failing to honor one's imperfect duties is no less wrong than failing to honor one's perfect duties, the latter is more objectionable from a moral perspective.

The fact that the conditions for fulfilling imperfect duties are more lenient than the conditions for fulfilling perfect duties, along with Kant's use of the term 'imperfect,' leads some readers to think that imperfect duties are not genuine duties or are somehow lesser than perfect duties. In one sense, that is correct. For, as we noted, perfect duties take precedence over imperfect duties, so that conflicts between the former and the latter must be resolved in favor of fulfilling the former. But the imperfect duties are still duties, Kant insists, and we deserve praise or blame for fulfilling them or not.

In some circumstances, it may appear that we do not have any latitude with respect to our imperfect duties. Consider, for instance, an example made famous by the utilitarian philosopher Peter Singer.[8] While walking by a shallow pond, you notice a young child struggling in the water. It becomes apparent that you are the only person who can help the child, who (it is obvious) may well drown and die. You are an excellent swimmer, and while rescuing the child might take a few minutes and you will end up spoiling your favorite pair of pants, these are not great costs or inconveniences. Undeniably then, you have a duty to rescue the drowning child. Singer, being a utilitarian, arrives at this conclusion by toting up the net welfare. You lose things of very modest value (your time, your pants) if you rescue the child, but these losses are more than offset by what would be lost if you did not rescue the child (the child's future and her future happiness, the happiness of her friends and loved ones, etc.). The moral mathematics, if you will, clearly favors rescuing the drowning child.

Kantians arrive at this conclusion by a different route. Each of us is subject to an imperfect duty to promote others' happiness. But this is a duty of wide latitude. So why think that you would be obligated *in this particular situation* to save the drowning child? Or to put it differently: The duty that would justify rescuing the drowning child is an imperfect duty, the duty to promote others' happiness. But intuitively in this case, we do not have the latitude *not* to rescue the drowning child. Rescuing the child looks like a perfect duty, not just one opportunity among many to fulfill an imperfect duty.

Here I think Kantians should reason[9] as follows: The imperfect duty is a duty to commit oneself to a particular end – namely, the happiness of others. This is the duty of *beneficence*. How do we know if a person is in fact committed to an end? Doubtless this is not an easy question to answer. But situations in which a person can *greatly* advance a particular end at very little *cost* to herself are likely to shed a great deal of light on how committed a person is to a given end. As Kant states elsewhere, "the greater the natural obstacles (of sensibility) and the less the moral obstacles (of duty), so much the more merit is to be accounted for a good deed, as when, for example, at considerable self-sacrifice I rescue a complete stranger from great distress" (MM 6:228). Here Kant seems to

[8] "Famine, affluence, and morality," *Philosophy and Public Affairs* 1 (1972): 229–243.

[9] My own thinking on this issue is inspired by Marcia Baron's treatment of a similar case in M. Baron, P. Pettit, and M. Slote, eds., *Three Methods of Ethics* (Wiley-Blackwell, 1997), pp. 17–18.

claim that if a person fulfills a momentous duty despite great "natural obstacles" – that is, despite the large self-sacrifice involved – then such an act is especially meritorious and thereby deserving of special moral praise. But it would follow that if a duty is similarly momentous but requires very *little* by way of personal sacrifice (dirtying your pants, in this case), then it would be especially blameworthy not to fulfill it. The ease with which the duty can be fulfilled suggests that a person who fails to fulfill it is not very deeply committed to the end prescribed by the duty – to promote the happiness of others. And in the case of a drowning child, the happiness of others can be dramatically meliorated with only a very modest sacrifice on your part. Matters are different when the risk or inconvenience to oneself is much greater (if, say, the child were struggling in strong surf during a tropical storm) or if the benefit to others is modest (the child is not drowning but has merely thrown his beach ball far into the pond). In those circumstances, we would not likely doubt your commitment to others' happiness if you failed to provide aid. But the low cost and high stakes of the drowning child example makes it a test case for ascertaining the depth of your commitment to others' happiness. By failing to help the drowning child, you have shown that your commitment to the end of advancing others' happiness is so weak that we may reasonably infer that you have not fulfilled your imperfect duty in that regard.

Thus, the Kantian can grant to the utilitarian that more happiness is often created when we promote others' happiness. Furthermore, the Kantian can agree with the utilitarian that, in particular cases, we violate our obligation to be beneficent toward others when we fail to aid them. But the Kantian arrives at this conclusion not by comparing the *amount* of happiness created by the act with the amount of unhappiness it creates. Rather, the Kantian sees this as an example where our commitment to others' happiness as an end, which is prescribed to us as an imperfect duty of wide latitude, is in effect a duty of strict or narrow requirement in these specific circumstances.

Still, this example highlights a distinctive feature of imperfect duties: We can only discern whether a person fulfills her imperfect duties by looking at the pattern of her conduct over time. While a single action (or inaction), such as whether you jump in the water to rescue the drowning child, can be powerful evidence about your commitment to the ends prescribed by your imperfect duties, no act taken in isolation can tell the whole tale. For although *not* saving the drowning child would be strong evidence of not being committed to the end of beneficence, saving the drowning child would not prove that a person who is never again beneficent toward others is committed to that end. Only the pattern of a person's behavior over time can tell us whether the commitment essential to an imperfect duty is in fact present – whether the person has genuinely *willed* the end in question.

Beyond beneficence, Kant recognized two other general kinds of imperfect duties to others, which he also calls "duties of love." These are duties of gratitude and of sympathy. The former asks us to honor and esteem those who benefit us. Again, the latter is not a duty that requires us to act in a certain way. Rather, the imperfect duty of sympathy asks us to cultivate our natural feelings of compassion toward others, to feel joy when others succeed or flourish, and to experience dismay when they fail or suffer (MM 6:457). (This duty will be discussed further in Chapter 8.)

2.7 Kant's Taxonomy of Duties: Duties to Oneself

Perfect duties, as we have seen, prescribe means, and are duties of strict performance. Imperfect duties prescribe ends, and are duties of wide latitude.

Kant's taxonomy of duties requires another crucial distinction. Recall that Kant's Formula of Humanity states that we are to treat humanity as an end and never only as a means, whether the humanity resides in others or *in ourselves*. In Kant's moral theory, we therefore have moral obligations not only to other people, but also obligations to ourselves.

The concept of "duties to self" may strike you as foreign or odd. Philosophers nowadays rarely talk about duties to self. However, philosophers in Kant's time would not have blinked twice at the notion that we have moral obligations to ourselves. And a moment's reflection suggests that contemporary philosophers dismiss the notion of duties to ourselves too quickly. We tend to think of moral goodness or moral virtue in other-directed terms, as utilitarians such as Mill seemed to. A morally good person is someone who is particularly attentive to the needs or wants of others. Being good thus requires sympathy, sensitivity, sacrifice, and so on. But we do sometimes think that how people treat themselves is morally significant too. A person who will not defend herself against vicious gossip seems to lack self-respect. A person who is unambitious, lacking goals or aspirations, is a sluggard. These judgments are moral judgments, moral appraisals of how people treat themselves. Granted, the attitudes that accompany judgments that individuals have failed to fulfill their duties to others tend to differ from the attitudes that accompany judgments that individuals have failed to fulfill their duties to themselves. When one person wrongs another, the person wronged (and perhaps those who know of the wrong) tends to feel resentment or blame. When a person wrongs herself, the appropriate attitudes are instead more colored with disappointment or regret. But even though the attitudes or responses seem to differ, both sets of attitudes or responses are moral in nature, thus suggesting that duties to self are genuine. More generally, skeptics about duties to oneself bear the burden of answering the following line of thought: Suppose that

Kant's Formula of Humanity is correct. It illustrates that the fact that others are rational agents is the source of the obligations we owe them. But we too are rational agents. This implies that our own rational agency is a source of obligations as well. Skeptics could claim that there is a morally relevant difference between ourselves and others so that while we have obligations to others we lack any obligations to ourselves. But the skeptic must indicate what this difference is – it is not enough simply to say that we differ from others in that their rational agency or humanity is *theirs*, while our own rational agency or humanity is *ours*.

More can be said to defend the plausibility of duties to ourselves, but they are undeniably central to Kant's division of duties. As with duties to others, Kant categorizes duties to self as perfect or imperfect. The former are "limiting" or "negative" duties forbidding us to act contrary to our "moral self-preservation" or "moral health." The latter are positive duties that enjoin us to make our own perfection one of our ends, and, in particular, to cultivate our capacity to realize our ends. "The first principle of duty to oneself," Kant states, "lies in the dictum 'live in conformity with nature,' . . . that is, to *preserve* yourself in the perfection of your nature; the second in the saying, '*make yourself more perfect* than mere nature has made you'" (MM 6:419).

Kant further divides the category of perfect duties to oneself into what he terms duties to ourselves as "animal beings" (MM 6:422) and duties to ourselves as "moral beings" (MM 6:429). The former set of duties are duties we owe ourselves that pertain to our physical bodies. The central such duty is the duty of self-preservation, which Kant takes to entail duties against suicide, physically disabling or handicapping ourselves, incapacitating ourselves with drugs, etc. The thought behind these perfect duties to ourselves as animal beings is that our bodies are the instruments by which we exercise our rational agency, and so we must not hamper our body's capacities to act on our rationally chosen ends. A rational agent, an agent with humanity, who incapacitates or kills herself makes it harder (or impossible!) to make rational decisions and implement them. Hence, killing oneself, etc., are actions that fail to treat our own rational agency as an end in itself. (We will consider whether Kant is right about this in Section 7.2) The other perfect duties to ourselves as animal beings are duties not to imbibe in food or drink in ways that interfere with our powers of "skill and deliberation" (MM 6:427) and not to engage our sexual capacities merely for the sake of "lustful" pleasures or "animal impulses" (MM 6:424–425). Section 7.1 offers a discussion of Kant's views on the ethics of sex, so we will leave consideration of the latter duty until then.

The other category of perfect duties to oneself are the duties concerning our "moral" nature. These include a duty to avoid "avarice," which Kant defines as "restricting one's own enjoyment of the means of living so narrowly as to leave one's own true needs unsatisfied" (MM 6:432); a duty not to make oneself servile to others; and a duty not to lie. Admittedly, it is hard to see a common thread in the perfect duties to ourselves as moral beings. Recall that perfect duties to ourselves aim to preserve our 'moral nature' or 'moral health.' Take, for instance, the duty concerning avarice. Kant distinguishes avarice from other vices relating to the acquisition or use of means to one's ends, vices that violate our duties to others. Greed, for example, in which one acquires and uses more than is necessary for one's needs, is at odds with our duty to love others, presumably because the excesses of greed preclude needy others using our means in the service of their ends. Avarice violates duties to oneself because it leaves one's own needs unmet, which (Kant thought) posed a threat to our moral nature or moral health because those with unmet needs are more tempted to act immorally to meet said needs. (See Section 8.6 for more on the "indirect duty" to meet one's needs and pursue one's own happiness.) The duty to avoid servility has a similar basis in maintaining our moral natures. We violate this duty when we fail to show respect or esteem for ourselves, particularly in comparison with other moral agents. Here Kant says that we are not to sell ourselves into slavery, acquire debts so great that others will have power over us, or fail to defend our rights. Such actions amount to "waiving any claim to moral worth in oneself" (MM 6:435). Servility thus represents a more direct assault on our moral natures than does avarice. Whereas avarice undermines our ability to act morally, servility in effect denies that ability.

The puzzle here is Kant's inclusion of lying as violating a perfect duty to oneself. Kant regarded lying as the "greatest violation of a human being's duty to himself" as a moral being (MM 6:429). Here Kant distinguishes between an "external lie" (a lie told to others) and an "internal" or "inner lie." Both are serious moral wrongs, in Kant's estimation, but not because of the harm, either to the liar herself or to others, that might be caused by a lie. Both forms of lying are instead wrong because they "annihilate" a person's "dignity as a human being." An internal lie is worse than an external lie, however, because such lies make a person "contemptible in his own eyes." Unfortunately Kant does not define "internal" or "inner lie" for his readers, and the examples he provides suggest that he may not have had *lying* in mind:

> Someone tells an inner lie . . . if he professes belief in a future judge of the world, although he finds no such belief within himself but persuades himself that it could do no harm and might even be useful to profess in his thoughts to one who scrutinizes hearts a belief in such a judge in order to win his favor in case he should exist. Someone also lies if, having no doubt about the existence of this future judge, he still flatters himself that he inwardly reveres his law, though the only incentive he feels is fear of punishment. (MM 6:430)

Kant's examples are both "inner lies" regarding a future judge – that is, God. The former "lie" involves a person who harbors doubts about God's existence but hopes that, if God exists, then if he professes "in his thoughts" that God exists, God will favor him. The latter "lie" involves a person who believes in this "future judge" but deceives himself about the motivation behind his abiding by God's word. Neither of these strike me as lies in the usual sense, for they lack the characteristic friction between the liar and the audience that defines lying. In neither case is the 'liar' attempting to influence anyone's beliefs regarding God's existence or her own motivation to abide by God's word. These "inner lies" do not involve a person believing some statement her belief in which she misrepresents to someone, herself included.[10]

As I see it, the mental acts to which Kant's examples refer are not best classified as lies, "inner" or otherwise. Rather, they are examples of *self-deception*, instances in which a person affirms a belief, despite not being fully persuaded to accept the belief on the basis of the evidence available to her, because she has ends that would be served by affirming the belief. In the former case, the reluctant theist desires to be in the good graces of God (if he exists). In the latter case, the believer desires to be seen, in her own eyes or perhaps in God's, as pious, abiding by God's word not from callous self-interest but from some 'higher,' more admirable motive. In each case, what the individual 'knows' about herself and her own attitudes is at odds with what she affirms in her own mind or in her own consciousness. She shows a form of insincerity or a lack of integrity. As Kant puts it, her "inner judge" condemns her for a lack of "conscientiousness" in her believing (MM 6:430).

Thus, while it seems a stretch to call these mental acts "lies" of any sort, they are instances of self-deception that Kant would have good reason to find morally objectionable. The kind of "insincerity" I have identified as self-deception is a "rotten spot" in human nature, according to Kant, because it threatens to spread into our relations with others (MM 6:430–431). Stephen Darwall attributes to Kant the thesis that this sort of self-deception threatens the integrity of our moral judgment inasmuch as it amounts to a failure to judge impartially.[11] In this respect, the duty not to engage in these "inner lies" is an adjunct of another duty advocated by Kant. Kant says that in addition to the various duties to oneself, there is a "first command" of duties to oneself, a duty of *self-knowledge*. "[K]now your heart – whether it is good or evil, whether the source of our actions is pure or impure" (MM 6:441). As Kant saw it, we often deceive ourselves about our own motives, depicting our reasons for action as more morally upright and admirable than they in fact are. We must therefore be

[10] Seana Shiffrin offers a useful account of lying along these lines in *Speech Matters: On Lying, Morality, and the Law* (Princeton, 2014), pp. 12–15.

[11] "Self-deception, autonomy, and moral constitution," in A.O. Rorty and B.P. McLaughlin (eds.), *Perspectives on Self-Deception* (University of California Press, 1988), pp. 424–425.

diligent and dogged in examining not only what we do, but also our motives for doing it.

Kant is correct, then, in arguing for a duty not to engage in these "inner lies" – though, as I have argued, they are best classified as instances of self-deception rather than lies in any ordinary sense. Put in positive terms, we have a duty to cultivate and exercise *integrity in our self-examination.*

This still leaves the matter of lies to others: "external" lies. Does Kant succeed in showing that such lies violate a duty to ourselves by threatening our moral self-perfection? Here Kant is much less convincing. First, note that Kant does not need to show that lies to others violate duties to ourselves in order to have a substantive basis for morally condemning lying. As we noted earlier in Section 2.6, lying wrongs other rational agents because it treats their rational agency merely as a means to the liar's ends, in violation of the Formula of Humanity. But Kant's own explanation of why lying violates perfect duties to ourselves rests on undefended claims regarding the purpose of human communication:

> communication of one's thoughts to someone through words that yet (intentionally) contain the contrary of what the speaker thinks on the subject is an end that is directly opposed to the natural purposiveness of the speaker's capacity to communicate his thoughts, and is thus a renunciation by the speaker of his personality, and such a speaker is a mere deceptive appearance of a human being, not a human being himself. (MM 6:429)

In truth, Kant's rhetoric here is overheated and the required argumentation absent: He gives us no reason to think that communicating our thoughts is the natural purpose of communication (and, as we shall see in Section 7.1, we have good reason to be skeptical, even on Kantian grounds, of grounding Kantian ethical arguments in claims regarding the "natural purpose" of our bodies and their capacities). So while Kant is on solid ground in arguing that self-deception violates duties to oneself, his argument that lying violates such duties is less compelling.[12] (We will have occasion to revisit Kant's views on lying to others in Section 6.2.)

Underlying all the perfect duties to ourselves as moral beings is a capacity Kant calls *conscience.* In each human psyche, Kant argues, there exists an "inner court" or ideal judge with which we morally evaluate our choices and actions. This inner court can also warn us before we act wrongly. And though Kant does not say so explicitly, he would certainly agree that developing

[12] For a discussion of Kant's views on the wrongfulness of lying, see my "The murderer at the door: What Kant should have said," *Philosophy and Phenomenological Research* 79 (2009): 17–46. For a somewhat more sympathetic account, see Stefano Bacin, "The perfect duty to oneself as a moral being," in A. Trampota, O. Sensen, and J. Timmerman, *Kant's Tugendlehre: A Comprehensive Commentary* (de Gruyter, 2013), pp. 247–255.

conscience and heeding its verdicts is itself a duty inasmuch as conscience is a necessary element of moral decision making (MM 6:400).

The imperfect duties to oneself all fall under the heading of what Kant calls the duty of "natural perfection": "A human being has a duty to himself to cultivate his natural powers (powers of spirit, mind, and body), as means to all sorts of possible ends. He owes it to himself (as a rational being) not to leave idle and, as it were, rusting away the natural predispositions and capacities that his reason can some day use" (MM 6:444). This duty thus requires that we not allow our natural capacities and talents to wither away. Rather, we must cultivate the mental capacities for reasoning, imagination, etc., as well as bodily capacities, such as our physical strength or natural talents and skills. In cultivating these various capacities, we make it more likely that we will be able to effectively pursue and realize our chosen ends. A person with humanity – the capacity to choose her ends and the means to those ends – will nevertheless not exhibit successful rational agency if she lacks the capacities to pursue and realize these ends.

Thus, fulfilling this duty is a way to value our own rational agency by making that agency more fruitful or efficacious. Again, because this duty is an imperfect duty, it does not require that we cultivate all our capacities to the greatest degree. This duty gives us the freedom to decide which of our capacities to develop according to our preferences or goals. One person might meet this duty by becoming skilled at accounting and sailing, while another might meet this duty by becoming skilled at knitting and marksmanship.

In satisfying our moral duties to ourselves, we are, according to Kant, enhancing our own moral self-perfection and clearing a path toward moral virtue, the state in which we subject our wills and our choices to the requirements of morality. Moral virtue is nothing more than "the moral strength of a human being's will in fulfilling his duty." (MM 6:405) A morally virtuous person does what she morally ought to do because she morally ought to do it and does not waver in doing it even when tempted to do otherwise.

A final note regarding duties to self: We noted in connection with duties to others that Kant associates perfect duties with "duties of respect" and imperfect duties with "duties of love." Kant's distinction between duties of respect and duties of love does not carry over to duties to oneself, however. Indeed, Kant denies that we have any *direct* duty to love ourselves, where that duty is understood as a duty to promote our own happiness (G 4:430–431, MM 6:388). (We will clarify precisely in what sense Kant thought we have a duty to promote our own happiness in Section 8.6.) We cannot have a duty to promote our own happiness because, according to Kant, we cannot be under an obligation to do what we will inevitably do anyway. As embodied beings, we humans will invariably be concerned to promote our own happiness, Kant argues. But then the promotion of one's own happiness is not any sort of "constraint" on our choices and actions and hence makes no demands on our choices and actions. All duties to self, whether perfect or imperfect, are thus concerned with preserving or perfecting one's rational agency, not with the immediate promotion of one's ends.

We can now represent Kant's taxonomy of duties fully (I have placed lying in *italics* to highlight my earlier claim that it does not seem to fit well into Kant's taxonomy).

DUTIES	TO SELF	TO OTHERS
PERFECT (prescribe specific means or actions)	As animal beings: • Self-preservation • Maintaining physical body (no incapacitation, disabling, succumbing to sexual lust) As moral beings: • Ensuring fit between one's means and one's needs/ends (avarice, etc.) • Exact respect from others (not being servile) • Integrity in self-examination • *Not lying*	Treat others' humanity as an end in itself, not merely as means. Do not (for example): • Deceive • Break promises • Pursue one's ends through coercion • Engage others in courses of action to which they cannot consent • Cause injury
IMPERFECT (prescribe ends or purposes)	Natural perfection: cultivation and development of physical and rational powers	• Beneficence • Gratitude • Sympathy

FUNDAMENTAL OR OVERARCHING DUTIES

- Self-knowledge
- Conscience

2.8 Duties of Right, Duties of Virtue

A final distinction that bears on Kant's taxonomy of duties is that between *duties of right* with *duties of virtue*. The former are duties for which "external lawgiving" is possible, the latter duties for which external lawgiving is not possible (MM 6:239). Some duties are such that compliance with them can be compelled by "external lawgiving" – that is, it is possible that a person can be coerced into acting in accordance with them. The duty not to steal other's property, for example, is a duty that a person could be coerced into fulfilling by the threat of being apprehended and punished. Such a duty is a duty of right, according to Kant, because such "external constraint" is possible. Indeed, others have the right to use coercion to compel us to fulfill these duties (MM 6:239, 6:383).

Duties of virtue, on the other hand, are duties to adopt a particular end. And while others can coerce us into acting in a particular way, they cannot coerce us into adopting a particular end. "Setting an end," Kant says, cannot be compelled by external lawgiving or coercion because setting an end "is an internal act of the mind" (MM 6:239). Therefore, while others can coerce us to do things that do not reflect our ends, they cannot coerce us to *will* some end (MM 6:381). Consider again, our duty of beneficence, our duty to promote others' happiness. Laws could be passed that penalize those who do not act altruistically ('mandatory charity' is not incoherent). But no law could be passed that penalizes those who lack charity as an end. The law might compel us to act charitably, but it cannot compel us to act charitably for the sake of the end of being charitable. In that case, the law would "prescribe external actions that lead to an end without the subject making it his end" (MM 6:239). Duties of virtue, then, because they require us to adopt ends, are not enforceable through coercion, threats, or other social sanctions. They are, Kant says, duties rooted in "free self-constraint" rather than constraint by the causal power of others (MM 6:379, 6:382).

Duties of right are central to Kant's political philosophy. As Kant saw it, governments exist so as to make "external freedom" or independence possible for all, and they do so by exercising their power to threaten or coerce those who would limit others' freedom. Governments thus play the central role in enforcing duties of right, but cannot enforce duties of virtue (MM 6:231–232, 6: 327–338).[13]

On its face, this distinction seems to closely track Kant's distinction between perfect and imperfect duties. Duties of right seem to correspond to perfect duties in that both categories of duty relate to the performance (or nonperformance) of particular acts. It thus seems possible to compel or coerce a person into fulfilling her perfect duties. Similarly, duties of virtue seem to correspond to imperfect duties in that both categories of duty relate to the adopting of ends rather than the performance of particular acts. Moreover, it might seem that all duties to others are duties of right, since we can typically be compelled or coerced to act in particular ways toward others, whereas we cannot typically be so compelled or coerced regarding how we treat ourselves. However, these correspondences are not exact. For one, the central *imperfect*

[13] Those seeking an understanding of Kant's political philosophy can do no better than Arthur Ripstein, *Force and Freedom: Kant's Legal and Political Philosophy* (Harvard, 2009).

duty toward others – the duty to promote others' happiness – is a duty of virtue because (again) we can be compelled to act in ways that promote others' happiness even when our end in doing so is not their happiness (we want to enhance our reputation for charity, for example). Conversely, a central perfect duty toward ourselves, self-preservation, is one whose fulfillment can be compelled or coerced. (Consider that in medieval Europe, authorities attempted to discourage suicide by disinheriting the suicidal person's descendants or denying that person Christian burial.) But even this duty is such that we cannot be compelled or coerced to preserve ourselves for that very end. I may be threatened with eternal damnation if I commit suicide, but that threat cannot make me will self-preservation (as opposed to the avoidance of pain or torture) as my end.

These observations underscore that this distinction is just what Kant says it is: a distinction between duties for which external incentives can compel or coerce their fulfillment and duties for which that is not the case (because the duty requires willing an end, not the performance of an act as a means to a presumed end). This distinction shows that Kant was concerned to remind us of a fact that it is easy to overlook: Only some of our duties are, or even should be, enforceable through incentives provided by coercion, disapproval, or other external incentives.

2.9 Valuing Rational Agency

Let us recap Chapter 2 to this point. We have been trying to understand the moral significance of Kant's Formula of Humanity, including:

- what it is to treat humanity or rational agency as an end in itself rather than as a means only.
- how the Formula of Humanity gives convincing explanations of what is wrong with behaviors such as false promising, deception, indifference to others' happiness, etc.
- how Kant uses the Formula of Humanity to create his taxonomy of duties, rooted in the distinctions between (a) perfect and imperfect duties, and (b) duties to others and duties to oneself.

Furthermore, we began by noting that utilitarianism, a chief theoretical rival to Kantianism, is a monistic theory of morality in two different ways: first, it recognizes only one fundamental moral value (well-being); and, second, it understands right and wrong in terms of a single way to value well-being (promoting it). Kantian ethics, I have suggested, is monistic on the first score, but disagrees with utilitarianism about the nature of what is morally valuable. For Kantians, rational agency, rather than happiness, is fundamentally valuable. This in turn provides Kantianism with a different account of impartiality. Recall that utilitarianism places great weight on its notion of impartiality, that all individuals are to be treated equally by taking their well-being into account equally. On this view, we are not entitled to give our own well-being, or the well-being of those we know or care about, greater weight than anyone else's. Does impartiality have a role in Kantian ethics? Yes, but it functions differently in Kantian ethics. First, whereas utilitarians understand impartiality in terms of taking each individual's *well-being* as having equal moral significance, Kantians understand impartiality in terms of each individual's *rational agency* as having equal moral significance. The rational agency of any one individual, on the Kantian view, should not be seen as more morally significant than the rational agency of another.

However, I also hinted that Kantianism is pluralistic on the second score, holding that there is more than one morally justifiable way to properly value rational agency. With the Formula of Humanity, Kant is gesturing at one of the ways that rational agency is supposed to be valued. In honoring the Formula of Humanity, how exactly are we valuing rational agency?

Like many Kantians, I believe that *respect* toward rational agency is the attitude that underlies Kant's Formula of Humanity. But respect is itself a multifaceted concept, and in order to tease out the kind of respect for rational agency that I believe Kant has in mind, we will need to disentangle the various ways in which we use the concept of respect, as well as how Kant uses it.

One initial problem here is that Kant often does not use the language of respect (in German, *Achtung*) in connection with the Formula of Humanity. Rather, Kant often describes respect not as an attitude we show toward humanity or toward rational agency, but as an attitude we show toward morality or toward the moral law (G 4:400–404, C2 5:74–76). Indeed, Kant states that any "respect for a person is properly respect for the [moral] law" (G 4:402n). Some philosophers have therefore concluded that a properly Kantian view of respect sees it as directed at morality, not at rational agency.

However, Kant does not seem to limit respect to respect for morality, and, on a number of occasions, he describes respect as a feeling or attitude directed toward individual rational agents. "Respect," he claims, "is always directed only to persons, never to things" (C2 5:76). We have a duty to show respect for our own selves (MM 6:403) and to show our neighbors "the respect necessary for every human being" (MM 6:448). Indeed, Kant comes very close to saying that in showing respect for others, we obey the Formula of Humanity's demand that we treat others' rational agency always as an end and never merely as a means. Respect, Kant says, is to be understood as responding to the "dignity of humanity" in others, and the "duty of respect" for others is expressed in a principle "not to degrade any other to a mere means to my ends" (MM 6:450).

The evidence suggests, to me at least, that Kant thought of respect as directed both at individuals and their rational agency *and* at morality or the moral law. To insist that Kant thought respect was directed exclusively at one or at the other is unreasonable. In fact, I believe we can go a step further and argue that respect for morality and respect for rational agency turn out, in the end, to merely be slightly different names for the same thing. For, as I have argued, respecting rational agency is the most fundamental moral attitude, the attitude that morally decent people take toward themselves and others. As Kant says, "respect for a person is properly respect for the [moral] law," so to show respect for rational agency *just is* to show respect for morality understood as an abstract ideal. For Kant, there is no clear sense to be made of respect for morality and the moral law aside from respect for rational agency. Respect for rational agency simply gives content to what it is to respect morality or the moral law.

This still leaves the question of precisely what respect for rational agency, or, as many philosophers would say nowadays, 'respect for persons,' amounts to. We use the word 'respect' in many ways.[14] An expert mountain climber might admonish a novice to "respect the mountain." Here 'respect' means something like *fear* or *hold in awe.* Two athletic rivals might say that they "respect each others' ability," meaning that they *recognize or esteem* each others' ability (C2 5:76). We sometimes speak of respect for another person's property, denoting that another person's property *should not be intruded upon*. Kant references this sense of respect when he remarks that the duty to respect someone is analogous to the duty "not to encroach upon what belongs to anyone" (MM 6:449).

Given this diversity of meanings, it might appear that respect is too amorphous a notion to be useful in moral philosophy. However, I believe that woven through these various meanings of respect is a concept that is philosophically useful and seems to capture what Kant has in mind with his Formula of Humanity.

First, respect is a relation. Respect is always respect *for* something or someone. In terms of the Formula of Humanity, it directs us to relate both to ourselves and one another as rational agents. On Kant's picture, we live in a world populated with rational agents who have the capacity to choose their ends and the means to those ends. In performing only those acts that treat that capacity as an end and not merely as a means, we satisfy two ideals: one concerning relations among rational agents, and a second concerning how we rational agents treat our own rational agency.

Second, respect is an attitude that acknowledges *boundaries* between things. The mountaineer who respects the peak is implicitly reminding herself that the peak is distinct from her and does not conform to her wishes to climb it. So too for assertions to respect another's property: To respect someone's property is to

[14] See the seminal discussion of respect by Stephen Darwall, "Two kinds of respect," *Ethics* 88 (1977): 36–49, as well as Carl Cranor, "Toward a theory of respect for persons," *American Philosophical Quarterly* 12 (1975): 309–319.

see it as in some important sense off limits for one's own use or enjoyment. Respect is an attitude that marks moral distance or distinctness (MM 6:449).

At the same time, though, Kantian respect is an attitude that can sometimes be reciprocal. Mountains and personal property cannot respect us back. But rational agents can exhibit respect for one another as rational agents: They can see another person's rational agency as distinct from their own and available for their use only with the rational authorization of that person. Others respect your property only by making use of it with your consent. As noted above, others are permitted to benefit from making use of your rational agency, thus making use of your humanity as a means to their ends. However, they show respect for your rational agency by enlisting your agency in the service of their ends only with your rational authorization. Carrying the analogy one step further, when your actions treat others merely as means, you are in a sense trespassing upon others' rational agency, making use of that agency for your purposes with insufficient regard for the purposes of the person whose agency you use. But if others' rational agency establishes a boundary that we may not trespass in the service of our own ends, then so too does our rational agency establish a boundary that we may not trespass even in the service of our own ends.

Finally, respect is strongly associated with *deference*. A judge may issue a ruling that I disagree with, but I may nevertheless respect the verdict – that is, I agree to abide by the ruling despite my disagreement with it. In doing so, I treat the judge as a kind of authority to whom I defer. Kant's Formula of Humanity likewise directs us to treat rational agents as authorities over their own choices and affairs. We may not necessarily agree with the choices other agents make. We may believe the ends they are pursuing are frivolous or ill-advised, or we may believe the means by which they are pursuing their ends is imprudent or irrational. Kant is happy to permit us to rationally *persuade* others that their ends or the means by which they pursue them are wrong-headed. But when we violate or treat others merely as means, we sometimes use non-rational means (deception, for example) in an effort to lead others to act in ways conducive to ends of *our* choosing. We in effect wrongfully exert authority over another rational agent who, concerning her own choices at least, has a form of authority to which we are morally obligated to defer. The value of rational agency thus constrains how we ought to treat other rational agents. And in the case of our imperfect duties, such as the duty of beneficence, our duty is to promote others' happiness by helping them secure *their* chosen ends, regardless of whether those are ends we ourselves endorse. As Tennyson wrote, when it comes to the ends that others see as central to their happiness, ours is not to reason why.

Respect, then, is an attitude of deference wherein we acknowledge the boundaries between rational agents. The Formula of Humanity asks us to see rational agency as generating a limitation on how we use our rational agency.

In the case of others, we must see their rational agency as a limit on how we pursue our own ends. In the case of ourselves, we must treat our own rational agency, as well as the mental and bodily resources needed for its effective exercise, as a limit on how we pursue our own ends.

2.10 The Five Criteria Revisited

In Chapter 1, we traced how Kant settles upon five criteria that the supreme principle of morality must satisfy. With an understanding of one formulation of the Categorical Imperative, the Formula of Humanity, we are in a position to determine whether that principle in fact satisfies Kant's criteria. I conclude this chapter by trying to make the case that the Formula of Humanity appears to satisfy these criteria. This will not be our last discussion of these matters, since some of the objections to Kant's ethics that we will address in Part II of this book pertain to whether Kant satisfies his own criteria.

Let us begin with the criteria that, in my estimation at least, we can be most confident that the Formula of Humanity satisfies: criteria [1], [3], and [4].

Criterion [1] was that the supreme principle of morality *provides plausible explanations of moral obligations we already recognize.* As we will see in Chapter 6, there are some hard cases for Kant's ethics, situations where it may not be clear what the Formula of Humanity implies we ought to do or where what it seems to imply is controversial or counterintuitive. Nevertheless, our discussion of the Formula of Humanity in this chapter has illustrated that it can provide a credible account of our moral obligations. Indeed, I hope to have shown that it provides satisfactory explanations of various obligations we recognize, including obligations not to deceive or coerce, to further others' happiness, and, to the extent possible, to secure others' rational authorization to treat them as we do. Kant also argues for duties of gratitude, as well as duties to cultivate sympathy, to subject our moral choices to the demands of conscience, and to pursue knowledge of our own motives and character. All of this, to my eyes, accords well with what we would have thought our moral obligations consist in before laying eyes on Kant's ethical writings. And while Kant's inclusion of duties to self in his taxonomy of obligations may strike us as surprising, the notion that we stand in a distinct moral relation to ourselves is not totally foreign to our moral thinking; and, in any case, duties to self are sensibly grounded in Kantian morality. For just as other agents have the capacity to set ends according to reason, we have that capacity as well, and it is no less deserving of respect in our own case than in that of others.

These facts in turn show that the Formula of Humanity satisfies criterion [3]: that the supreme principle *be whatever principle governs the choices of the morally good will.* A morally good will is one motivated by a sense of duty, rather than by inclination or desire. How, then, does a person of morally good will perceive others? For the morally good will, others are not merely resources or tools with which to advance her own ends. If that were the case, the morally good will's treatment of others *would* be motivated by inclination or desire. She must then perceive others not only as means to her ends, but as ends in their own right, ends that constrain how they may be treated. Their humanity thus operates for her as an end in itself. Likewise, a morally good will understands her own humanity as placing limits on how she may pursue her ends.

That the Formula of Humanity asks us to respond to value by respecting it helps us see how it satisfies criterion [4]: that it *be a non-consequentialist principle*. David Cummiskey has argued that Kantians should be consequentialists.[15] So whereas utilitarians are consequentialists who seek to promote welfare, Kantians should be consequentialists who seek to promote rational agency. On Cummiskey's view, Kantians should be willing to treat someone's humanity merely as a means if the consequences are good enough – in particular, if by treating humanity merely as a means we enable more people's humanity to be treated as an end in itself. This view therefore licenses trade-offs between the humanity of some and the humanity of others. On Cummiskey's view, a politician might well be justified in lying to the public if doing so would promote valuable ends. For example, suppose that if the public knew about a particular threat to public health, they might panic and engage in counterproductive behaviors, such as looting, staying home from work or school, etc. But such a politician, even though he has admirable aims in lying to the public, would not be providing the facts on the basis of which members of the public could decide for themselves how to respond to this public health threat. Of course, the politician could nevertheless try to assure the public that the threat is minimal and could take measures to minimize the negative consequences of the public's reaction (by increasing the number of police on the streets, say). His lie could promote ends the public cares about, but he does so by failing to respect members of the public as rational agents.

To understand the Formula of Humanity in consequentialist terms is to overlook the role of respect in treating humanity as an end in itself. As we discussed earlier, to respect something is to treat it as a boundary, as something with an authority to which one must show deference. Respect is therefore the sort of attitude that blocks trade-offs of the sort that Cummiskey's "Kantian consequentialism" allows. For to respect a person's humanity is to see it as imposing an inviolable limit on how she may be treated as a rational agent. The logic of respect, I argue, has a non-consequentialist character, and so because the Formula of Humanity enjoins us to respect rational agency, it too has a non-consequentialist character.

15 *Kantian Consequentialism* (Oxford, 1996).

That said, it is important to note that the consequences of an action can play a *subsidiary* role in Kantian ethics. It might appear that Kant's ethics provides us a criterion for moral wrongness, captured in the Categorical Imperative, that fails to recognize the heterogeneity of moral wrongs. Actions that fail the Categorical Imperative all do so in the same way and for the same reason – they treat rational agency merely as a means instead of as an end in itself. This is a binary attribute, rather than a matter of degree: An action either does or does not treat rational agency as an end in itself. That Kant's ethics adopts this binary picture of moral right and wrong seems at odds with our sense that even among morally impermissible acts, some are morally worse than others. Murdering someone is *more* wrong, it seems, than telling a modest lie in order to advance one's interests. Kant's ethics thus seems to level down these moral differences, incorrectly treating all wrong actions as equally morally objectionable.

In one respect, this line of thinking is on target: A properly Kantian view of morality could not claim that different acts are *more or less* wrong. Again, either an act treats rational agency as an end in itself or it does not. There is, however, space for a properly Kantian view of morality to take into account the consequences of morally wrong actions so as to accommodate the thought that morally impermissible actions can vary in morally discernible ways.

Suppose that two different acts are each wrong they fail to show respect for rational agency. Note that how, and how much, such acts materially affect rational agency can vary, and often we will have stronger moral reasons to object to having our rational agency disrespected based on how it is disrespected, and, in particular, based on how different forms of treatment undercut or thwart our rational agency. A lie that convinces me to buy a product advertised on a television infomercial does not undercut or thwart my agency to the extent that a lie convincing me to marry a potential suitor does. If effective, the former lie will result in inconvenience, lost funds and time, etc., but my overall capacity to choose my ends and act in pursuit of those ends will only be slightly affected (and hardly at all over the long term). In contrast, the second lie will influence my agency in more far-reaching ways. By marrying a would-be suitor, I undertake marital obligations that determine how I am morally permitted to exercise my rational agency subsequently. Moreover, such a marriage can influence the means available in the pursuit of my ends (for example, my income, my level of education, where I domicile), as well as which ends I recognize as available to me (marriage may make me more likely to consider having children, etc.). By being enticed into the marriage on the basis of a lie, the history of my life as a rational agent is profoundly and irreversibly altered, whether for good or ill. The trajectory of possible avenues through which I can exercise my rational agency is far more substantively altered by this lie (if it is effective in persuading me to marry) than it is substantively altered by the lie which may lead me to buy the product advertised on the infomercial.

This example illustrates how actions which are wrong according to Kant's Formula of Humanity can nevertheless vary in how morally objectionable they are for reasons that Kantianism can readily acknowledge – namely, that such acts vary in how much they impact our capacities for rational agency. This is not to say that such acts vary in their wrongness. Rather, they vary in their *badness*. Hence, Kantians need not jettison their binary view of right and wrong – that all actions are right (or wrong) for the same reasons and to the same measure – to acknowledge that actions can vary in their moral objectionability.

It may seem odd to propose that Kantian ethics can recognize two moral yardsticks: rightness and wrongness, on the one hand, and degrees of badness on the other. But this is not problematic. For rightness and wrongness remain the more fundamental notions. An action or maxim that is not wrong cannot be made wrong, on the Kantian view I am proposing, by having bad enough results regarding our rational agency. Conversely, no suggestion is made that an otherwise wrongful action or maxim is made right by having good enough results regarding our rational agency. That the results of violating our obligations can matter to how *bad* those violations are does not undermine the overall Kantian account of moral *obligation* outlined in this book. Hence, acknowledging that consequences count morally need not push Kantian ethics in a consequentialist direction: The consequences of an action for our rational agency do not determine its rightness. Right and wrong remain independent of the value of an action's consequences. A consequentialist account of the badness of morally impermissible actions or maxims is compatible with a Kantian – and non-consequentialist – account of moral permissibility.

Let me now address the two criteria, [2] and [5], where it may seem less obvious that the Formula of Humanity is up to par.

Criterion [2] stated that morality's supreme principle must *be an imperative that it is rationally necessary for us to adopt* – that is, *a categorical imperative*. To say that the Formula of Humanity is an imperative that it is rationally necessary for us to adopt is to say that failure to adopt it would amount to a form of irrationality. To say that the Formula of Humanity is a categorical imperative is to say that its rational force does not depend on our particular ends or purposes – that it applies to us simply insofar as we are rational beings. As we noted at the end of Chapter 1, there is something puzzling about the possibility of a principle satisfying these criteria. In the case of a hypothetical imperative, its rational force is clear: If I have willed a particular end, then it is surely irrational not to perform those actions which (best) realize that end. But the Formula of Humanity tells us to 'will' an end too. It directs us to have, in addition to our particular ends, another end in mind when we act: rational agency, whether in ourselves or others. Notice that humanity is not a freestanding end – that is, it is not an end we value or 'will' apart from the actions we perform in pursuit of other ends. When, for instance, we deal honestly and truthfully with others, there are in effect two ends associated with that act: the humanity of those others, as well as whatever particular ends we are pursuing with our acts and utterances. If I sell an item to a would-be buyer and am truthful about its features, defects, and history, then I treat the buyer's humanity as an end in itself while also pursuing my end of acquiring money by selling the item. To treat others humanity as an end in itself is thus a kind of adverbial end – not an end pursued in isolation, but a property or aspect of how we pursue other ends.

However, that humanity is an end we pursue in conjunction with other ends does not make the rational force of the Formula of Humanity *dependent* on those other particular ends. Rather, the Formula of Humanity directs us to value a specific end: rational agency in ourselves and in others, *irrespective of what our other ends are*. This is the sense in which it has the force of a Categorical Imperative: Whatever one's particular ends are, they are to be pursued subject to the constraint of treating humanity as an end.

This suffices to explain how the Formula of Humanity satisfies criterion [2]. But it may seem murky why we *must* value humanity – why failure to do so evinces any kind of irrationality. In what respect is it irrational to pursue one's ends without bothering to treat others and their ends with respect? Why couldn't someone go through life being unconcerned for her own humanity, or that of others, without being justly accused of irrationality?

To make sense of the rational inescapability of respecting humanity, let us imagine engaging someone skeptical of the Formula of Humanity who asserts, "I choose not to respect rational agency, not to treat humanity as an end in itself." We then ask our skeptic, "Do you choose your ends and the means to them?" Assuming the skeptic answers yes, the skeptic thus acknowledges that she possesses the property Kant calls humanity. Suppose we then challenge our skeptic as follows:

> You said earlier that you, an agent who chooses her ends and the means to them, nevertheless choose not to value humanity, the capacity to choose one's ends and the means to them. Why should we treat your choice not to respect humanity as worthy of respect?

The skeptic cannot give a coherent reply to this challenge, for, in claiming that we should treat his choice not to respect humanity as worthy of respect, *the skeptic is appealing to the claim that his own humanity is worthy of respect.* The legitimacy of the skeptic's rejection of the value of humanity – its worthiness to be respected – presupposes that humanity is to be respected. And if the skeptic's own humanity is to be respected, then the skeptic must, if she believes she is not similarly obliged to respect the humanity of others, likewise respect the humanity of others. The rejection of humanity as an end in itself presupposes the very sort of valuing of humanity that the Formula of Humanity requires. Skepticism about the respect for humanity thus seems incoherent, for the cogency of the *denial* that humanity is a distinctive source of moral reasons for action implies that humanity *is* a distinctive source of moral reasons for action. As the prominent Kantian philosopher Christine Korsgaard puts it:

> Kant saw that we take things to be important because they are important to us – and he concluded that we must therefore take ourselves to be important. In this way, the value of humanity itself is implicit in every human choice. If complete normative scepticism is to be avoided – if there is such a thing as a reason for action – then humanity, as the source of all reasons and values, must be valued for its own sake.[16]

Much more can be said to defend (and criticize) this line of argument. But it provides a powerful expression of what philosophers would call a *transcendental argument*: an argument wherein a skeptic about some claim – call it claim C – must presuppose the truth of C in order to intelligibly raise the skeptical worry in the first place. The Formula of Humanity thus appears to represent a rationally inescapable categorical imperative. For even in questioning it, we affirm its rational authority.

Finally, let us consider criterion [5]: that the supreme principle must *be a principle conformity to which requires only that we are practically rational beings*. As I mentioned in Section 1.8, this criterion raises troubling metaphysical difficulties that require a separate discussion (Chapter 5). Hence, I can only offer a tentative defense here of the Formula of Humanity in connection with [5]: In order to treat humanity always as an end and never as a means, what must we be able to do? We must only be able to see the capacity for rational agency as a consideration that must shape our choices. In the case of perfect duties, rational agency serves as a constraint on the performance of particular actions. In the case of imperfect duties, rational agency is supposed to function as one of our ends – or, to put it differently, the rational agency of ourselves and of others is supposed to serve as a standing ideal. Shaping our choices in accordance with the Formula of Humanity is not a matter of possessing a certain body of theoretical knowledge or technical skill. Hence, we do not have to be blessed with special abilities or insight in order to abide by it. Rather, all that the Formula of Humanity demands is that the reasons for which we act be responsive to the humanity of ourselves and others. Note that this does not mean that conforming to the Formula of Humanity is *equally* easy for all

[16] *The Sources of Normativity* (Cambridge, 1996), p. 122. Kant seems to hint at a similar reply to the skeptic at G 4:429.

individuals. For example, those blessed with greater capacity for sympathy, for instance, will be more likely to be beneficent toward others. Those with greater powers of introspection will be better equipped to achieve moral self-knowledge. Nor will our efforts at treating humanity as an end in itself always succeed. Our efforts at furthering others' happiness may be frustrated, for instance. But merely treating humanity as an end in itself is something that virtually any agent can do. For all it demands is that our rational will be oriented toward a particular good.

2.11 Conclusion

This chapter has shown how the Formula of Humanity satisfies the five criteria Kant offers for the supreme principle of morality. Kant's Formula of Humanity illustrates how Kant believed rational agency is worthy of respect, and in this regard, he placed rational agency, rather than well-being, at the center of his moral thinking.

We see in Kant's taxonomy of duties what respecting rational agency implies with regard to our moral conduct. In the next chapter, we will consider a second formulation Kant gives of the Categorical Imperative. We will analyze this formulation to determine if it too satisfies Kant's criteria, and, in so doing, we will discover a second way in which, according to Kant, we are to value rational agency: by manifesting or embodying it in our choices.

Further Reading

Some influential discussions of the Formula of Humanity include Thomas Hill, "Humanity as an end in itself," *Ethics* 91 (1980): 429–450, and Christine Korsgaard, "Kant's Formula of Humanity," *Kant-Studien* 77 (1986): 183–202. Richard Dean offers a thorough examination of the place of humanity in Kant's ethics in *The Value of Humanity in Kant's Moral Theory* (Oxford, 2006). Joshua Glasgow contests Dean's interpretations in "Kant's conception of humanity," *Journal of the History of Philosophy* 45 (2007): 291–308. For contrasting defenses of the claim that rational agency is the sole source of unconditioned value, see Christine Korsgaard, *The Sources of Normativity* (Cambridge, 1996) and David Sussman, "The authority of humanity," *Ethics* 113 (2003): 350–366. Marcia Baron provides an excellent account of Kant's taxonomy of duties in the contribution on Kantian ethics to *Three Methods of Ethics: A Debate* (Blackwell, 1997). Robert Johnson takes a Kantian approach to duties to self in *Self-Improvement: An Essay in Kantian Ethics* (Oxford, 2011). Some of the more useful discussion of Kant on lying include James Mahon, "The truth about Kant on lies," and David Sussman, "On the supposed duty of truthfulness: Kant on lying in self-defense," both in C. Martin (ed.),

The Philosophy of Deception (Oxford, 2009). Those seeking a deeper understanding of utilitarianism should consult J.S. Mill's classic and widely reprinted essay "Utilitarianism," as well as J.J.C. Smart and Bernard Williams' Utilitarianism: For and Against (Cambridge, 1973) and William Shaw's Contemporary Ethics: Taking Account of Utilitarianism (Wiley-Blackwell, 1999).

3 The Categorical Imperative and the Kantian Theory of Value, Part II

The previous chapter focused on the Formula of Humanity. But, as we know, Kant offers a number of versions of his supreme moral principle, the Categorical Imperative. The best known, and most heavily scrutinized, is the *Formula of Universal Law:*

> Act only on those maxims that can be willed as universal laws.

Kant seemed to view this version of the Categorical Imperative as the 'official' version of morality's supreme principle. Indeed, he sometimes states that this Formula *is* the Categorical Imperative (G 4:421, MM 6:225–226).[1] Other times, Kant states that the different versions of the Categorical Imperative are different representations of the moral law, varying only in how easily they are grasped by our "intuition" (G 4:436). Yet despite the apparent primacy Kant attributed to this Formula, it does not play as prominent a role in some of his ethical writings as we might expect it to play. For instance, the Metaphysics of Morals offers many discussions of our particular ethical duties, but in virtually none of these does Kant argue for these duties by appeal to the Formula of the Universal Law and its procedures.

In any case, the purpose of this chapter is to unpack the meaning of the Formula of Universal Law, with special attention to how it directs us to value rational agency in a different way than the Formula of Humanity directs us to respect rational agency. As we will see, the Formula of Universal Law imposes a kind of consistency test on our choices, a test that reflects the idea that when our choices are rationally consistent, we are valuing rational

[1] Careful readers will note that Kant often presents the Formula of Universal Law alongside the very similar Formula of the Universal Law of Nature: "*act as if the maxim of your action were to become by your will a* **universal law of nature**" (G 4:421. See also G 4:424; C2 5:44, 5:69). Disagreement exists over whether this Formula differs substantively from the principle that we must be able to will our maxims as universal laws, which Kant calls the "canon of moral appraisal of action in general" (G 4:424). In any event, Kant seemed to have held that thinking of our maxims as potential "laws of nature" helps us to deliberate about the morality of our maxims and so serves as a model or "typic" for moral deliberation, irrespective of whether it is a distinct formulation of the Categorical Imperative (C2 5:67–71).

agency by manifesting or exhibiting it. We will also investigate how Kant uses the Formula of Universal Law to generate the taxonomy of duties described in Chapter 2. Our maxims, I will propose, can be inconsistent in two different ways, corresponding to Kant's contrast between perfect and imperfect duties. Finally, we will consider whether the Formula of Universal Law satisfies the five criteria Kant identifies for the supreme principle of morality.

3.1 Maxims: Subjective Principles Expressing Reasons for Action

The Formula of Universal Law tests the morality of our actions *indirectly*. That is, it directs us to *act* only on "maxims" that can be willed as universal laws. The moral permissibility of our actions, according to this Formula, thus depends on their maxims, whose moral permissibility this Formula tests *directly*. The first step in understanding the Formula of Universal Law is therefore to understand Kant's concept of a *maxim*. Kant makes several direct statements concerning the nature of maxims, from which their defining characteristics can be teased out.

First and foremost, maxims are practical principles, or principles on the basis of which a person chooses and acts. A maxim, Kant says, is a "principle of volition" (G 4:401), a "principle on which a person acts" (G 4:420), a "principle of acting," or "the principle in accordance with which the subject acts" (G 4:421).

Second, Kant repeatedly calls maxims "subjective" principles (G 4:401, 4:421; C2 4:19; MM 6:225, 6:389). As we shall see momentarily, Kant seemed to intend that maxims have some degree of generality. Nevertheless, what renders maxims "subjective" is that they are "principles that one makes for oneself" (C2 5:20) or principles by "which the subject himself makes his rule (how he wills to act)" (MM 6:225). A maxim is thus a principle on the basis of which a particular individual chooses and acts, and so are to be "regarded by the subject as holding only for his will" (C2 5:19). Kant repeatedly contrasts the 'subjectivity' of maxims with the 'objectivity' of practical *laws*. Laws are 'objective' practical principles because they hold not merely for one individual but for "all rational beings" (G 4:401) or are "valid for every rational being" (G 4:421. See also C2 5:19). While maxims do not hold for all rational beings, Kant did seem to have in mind that a maxim is not simply a 'one-off' principle, a principle that can only apply to a single act taken in isolation. A maxim, according to Kant, is a "rule" (MM 6:225) for the "*general* determination of the will" (C2 5:19, emphasis added).

Taken altogether, Kant's remarks suggest that a maxim is a principle that applies only to a single rational individual rather than to all of them, but nevertheless functions as a kind of general rule or *policy* for that individual.[2] This suggestion is reinforced when we consider the concrete examples Kant gives of maxims:

- "from self-love I make it my principle to shorten my life when its longer duration threatens more troubles than it promises agreeableness" (G 4:422)
- "when I believe myself to be in need of money I shall borrow money and promise to repay it, even though I know that this will never happen" (G 4:422)
- I will "let [my] talents rust and be concerned with devoting [my] life merely to idleness, amusement, and procreation – in a word, enjoyment" (G 4:423)
- "I do not "care to contribute anything to" the "welfare" of others" or provide them "assistance in need" (G 4:423)
- "let no insult pass unavenged" (C2 5:19)
- "everyone may deny a deposit which no one can prove has been made" (C2 5:27)

Each of these maxims is a general rule or policy an individual chooses for herself.

Though Kant does not say so explicitly, he seemed to hold that maxims can be part of the psychological explanation of a person's behavior: If someone is observed avenging some past insult, then the maxim "let no insult pass unavenged" could be part of what explains her observed behavior. But Kant clearly believed that maxims do not merely *explain* action. For note that when Kant speaks of maxims, he deploys language connoting activity or purpose on our part. Maxims are "principles of volition" – that is, of choice or of will; we "make" maxims for ourselves and "subject" ourselves to them, so that maxims come to be "regarded" as holding for us, etc. Running throughout Kant's philosophy is a fundamental contrast between nature and reason. The natural world is essentially passive, a domain in which things are changed but do not change via their own activity. Reason, in both its theoretical operations (whereby it seeks to acquire belief and knowledge) and its practical operations (whereby it engages in choice and action), is an essentially *active* capacity. In depicting reason as an active capacity, Kant was explicitly rejecting the picture of reason propounded by the Scottish philosopher David Hume, who remarked that "reason is wholly inactive, and can never be the source of so active a principle as conscience, or a sense of morals."[3] Kant's use of active language in describing maxims suggests that the choice of maxims is an

[2] Barbara Herman, "Moral deliberation and the derivation of duties," in *The Practice of Moral Judgment* (Harvard, 1993), chapter 7.

[3] *A Treatise of Human Nature*, book III, part 1, section 1.

activity of reason – that maxims serve as expressions of what an individual understands herself to have reason to do. As we noted in Chapter 2, Kant saw human beings as rational agents. They are agents because they have agency, the capacity to choose and act. And they are rational because their choices reflect what they suppose they have reason to do. As Kant puts it, we have rational wills, capacities to choose and act on the basis of reasons. "The will," Kant famously said, "is a kind of causality of living beings insofar as they are rational" (G 4:446).

So, in choosing and acting on the basis of reasons, there is a statement of a rule or principle that captures why we hold it is rational to act in that way. This statement expresses a person's maxim. Recall our woman who buys a plane ticket for a vacation in Mexico. One way to home in on her maxim is to ask 'why did she do that?' or 'what are her reasons for doing that?' Obviously, we would have to know a good deal about her to answer that question adequately. But we might well guess that she acts as she does for the same sorts of reasons many people do: They enjoy breaks from work, find sunny climates relaxing, want to visit such a climate, need a way to travel there, etc. So we might surmise that her maxim is something like

> When I have time and sufficient funds, I will buy a plane ticket to travel to a relaxing vacation destination.

Notice that this statement could well be her response to our question, 'why did you do that?' And that is the defining mark of a maxim: A maxim expresses a person's reasons for acting in a particular way in light of certain other facts.

Before turning to how maxims are structured, let us first address two common, but misguided, objections to Kant's account of maxims. The first objection is that there are many actions that do not seem to have maxims associated with them. For example, there does not seem to be any statement that captures my reasons for sneezing. This simply illustrates that Kant did not think that maxims underpin all of our behavior. Rather, maxims underpin all of our *voluntary* behavior. Hence, Kant would agree that there are not maxims that purport to justify involuntary behaviors such as sneezing. But this is not a very substantial concession on his part, for I doubt anyone thinks that sneezing is morally permissible or impermissible. That we cannot use the Formula of Universal Law to morally assess involuntary behavior thus raises no worries, because involuntary behaviors are not the kinds of behaviors subject to moral assessment anyway.

Another common objection to Kant's account of maxims is that very often we are not aware of our behavior being justified or motivated by a maxim. In our day to day lives, we often act, not exactly impulsively, but without much reflection on our reasons for so acting. We wash our hands, go to work, greet our friends, prepare for sleep, read books, and so on without having any justifying rule or maxim in mind. In these cases, we do not act mindlessly, but we do act more or less automatically. This objection is misplaced, however, because it is not a requirement on acting on a maxim that a person necessarily be aware of or attend to the maxim underwriting a particular action when she performs it. A person who picks up an apple is not usually consciously thinking 'I'll pick up an apple as a snack when I'm hungry.' But if we could interrogate her for her reasons for picking up an apple, the answer that would emerge from such questioning is her maxim. So Kant's claim that all our voluntary behavior is justified (or unjustified) on the basis of our maxims does not require that we be aware of these maxims when we act on them.

3.2 The Structure of Maxims

Let us now turn to the common structure shared by all maxims. Recall from Section 1.3 the idea of action having a means–ends structure. An action is the means by which a certain end, or state of affairs, is brought about. Hence, a maxim, because it is the rule an individual takes to justify her action, will refer to the action (or means) as well as the end sought by the action.

Notice that several of Kant's examples include 'when' clauses: The individual will perform a certain action for the purpose of realizing some end she wills *when* a particular set of circumstances obtains. Kant thus recognized that, when we act, we often think that our action is rational only under some conditions or circumstances. The rule 'I will visit the dentist whenever I have a toothache in order to relieve my discomfort' is a rule the rationality of which depends on a certain condition or circumstance being met: having a toothache. The same holds true for most of our actions: We take them to be rationally justified in some circumstances, but not in others. Kant thus understands maxims as having three elements: an act, an end, and a set of relevant circumstances. The general form of a maxim is therefore[4]

I will do act **A** in circumstances **C** to achieve end **E**.

This general form provides a handy acronym for determining if a principle is in fact a maxim: ACE.

Every maxim will therefore satisfy the ACE form and include these three components.

[4] John Rawls, "Themes in Kant's moral philosophy," in E. Forster (ed.), *Kant's Transcendental Deductions* (Stanford, 1989), p. 83.

Maxim	Act	Circumstances	End
When I have time and sufficient funds, I will buy a plane ticket to travel to a relaxing vacation destination.	Buy a plane ticket	When I have time and sufficient funds	To travel to a relaxing vacation destination
In order to acquire needed money, I will borrow from others even knowing that I cannot repay.	Borrow from others	Knowing I cannot repay	To acquire needed money
"[F]rom self-love I make it my principle to shorten my life when its longer duration threatens more troubles than it promises agreeableness" (G 4:422).	Shorten my life (suicide)	Whenever the future is on balance bad ("threatens more troubles than it promises agreeableness")	"Self-love," i.e., in order to maximize pleasure and/or minimize pain for myself

With some maxims, it may not be apparent what some of the elements are. When we reflect on our maxims, we sometimes omit one of more of the three elements. Consider the rule:

Whenever my phone rings, I will answer it.

Here the rule refers to an action (answering the phone) and a set of circumstances (whenever it rings). But it appears to omit the end served by answering the phone. Perhaps the maxim would be something like

Whenever my phone rings, I will answer it in order to communicate with whomever is seeking to communicate with me.

where:

A = answering the phone
C = whenever the phone rings
E = in order to communicate with whomever is seeking to communicate with me.

In other cases, we may not be explicitly aware of either a maxim's relevant circumstances or its end. An extremely aquaphobic individual might guide her behavior according to the rule:

I will never be in the ocean.

Here both the circumstances and the end are left out. A fuller description of her maxim would be

I will never be in the ocean under *any* circumstances for *any* reason.

In effect, then, the aquaphobic's maxim strikes her as rational regardless of the circumstances or the end.

A = not being in the ocean
C = any set of circumstances
E = any end or purpose

3.3 Universalization

The Formula of Universal Law tests for the moral permissibility of a person's actions by testing the moral permissibility of the maxim she takes to justify her action. The Formula of Universal Law is a principle-testing principle – a 'law,' as Kant would put it, that tests the rules, or maxims, implicit in our actions for their moral permissibility. And the moral permissibility of acting on a maxim, according to Kant, turns on whether it can be willed as a universal law. So what does it mean to will one's maxim as a universal law?

The first step in determining if a maxim can be willed as a universal law is to *imagine* or *conceive* it as a universal law – that is, not simply as a principle that justifies one person's action on a particular occasion, but as a principle that everyone acts on in all the same relevant conditions, i.e., when they have the relevant end and act in the same circumstances. When we identity a maxim's *universalized counterpart*, we are imagining or conceiving a person's maxim as if it were a universal principle for all rational agents, or, as Kant sometimes put it, as if the maxim were a "universal law of nature" (G 4:421).[5] So for any particular maxim, there exists its universalized counterpart that does not refer to a particular individual:

Individual's maxim	Universalized counterpart
In order to acquire needed money, I will borrow from others even knowing that I cannot repay.	Whenever anyone needs money, he or she will borrow from others despite knowing that he or she cannot repay.
When I have time and sufficient funds, I will buy a plane ticket to travel to a relaxing vacation destination.	Whenever a person has time and sufficient funds, he or she will buy a plane ticket to travel to a relaxing vacation destination.

[5] For the logically inclined: As I understand universalization, all three variables within a maxim fall within the scope of its universalization. The universalized counterpart of a maxim is thus expressible as "For all individuals x, x does A in circumstances C to achieve end E." Universalization is *not* such that one of the variables falls outside its scope (as would be the case if, say, the end were embedded as the antecedent of a conditional whose consequent was a maxim's universalized counterpart. E.g.: "For all individuals x that seek to achieve end E, x does A in circumstances C.") This bears on how I understand the contradictions generated by the universalization of morally impermissible maxims.

As we shall see, exactly what Kant had in mind when he stated acting on a maxim is morally permissible only if it can be willed as a universal law is a source of almost endless controversy. But before inserting ourselves into that controversy, we must address a prior worry.

As we saw earlier, Kant thought of maxims as principles that justify actions in light of our chosen ends and in particular circumstances. Maxims are "rules" for the "general determination" of our wills. This conception of maxims reflects the thought that when a person acts on a reason, she understands that reason not merely as justifying her acting in that way on that particular occasion. Rather, she understands that reason as justifying her acting in that way on other occasions that share all the same relevant features as the present one. The individual who acts on the maxim "I will visit the dentist whenever I have a toothache in order to relieve my discomfort" does not suppose that this maxim justifies her visiting the dentist *only* when she has a toothache on July 26, 2012. Unless she changes her mind about the rationality of this maxim, she must also suppose that this maxim justified her visiting her dentist when she had a toothache on April 6, 1997 and would justify her visiting her dentist when she has a toothache on November 23, 2017. Again, she might not have always endorsed this maxim, and she may not endorse it in the future. (Perhaps she will end up converting to a religion that believes toothaches are punishments God inflicts on sinners.) But the point is that *so long as* she endorses this maxim, she takes herself to have a sufficient reason to act on the maxim whenever the circumstances included in the maxim are satisfied. If she did not take herself as having a sufficient reason to act on the maxim whenever the circumstances included in the maxim are satisfied, her choices would be rationally inconsistent and inexplicable. This illustrates that reasons *generalize* across time: All other things being equal, what is sufficient reason for performing a given action at one time in a particular set of circumstances is also a sufficient reason for performing that same action at another time in a set of circumstances that share all the same features that made it a sufficient reason to act in the first instance. And since maxims are statements of a person's reason for acting, maxims generalize across time as well.

But with his Formula of Universal Law, Kant is proposing that maxims are morally permissible only if they generalize in a different way: If an action is morally permissible only if its maxim can be willed as a universal law, then Kant is hinging this Formula on the thesis that morality rests on universalization across *persons* or agents. We will turn to different interpretations of what this universalization amounts to in subsequent sections of this chapter. But why should that be – why should whether my action is morally permissible depend on whether its maxim can be universalized across persons? Why is it impermissible to act on a maxim that holds only for the person whose maxim it is?

This is a question that Kant (and Kantians[6]) struggle with. Maxims, Kant says, are not objective practical laws, "laws to which one is unavoidably subject" (C2 5:20). They "merely *qualify* for a giving of universal law" (MM 6:389). But Kant insists that there must be an objective or universal law that governs the choice of maxims by rational beings. Indeed, the existence of such a law is implicitly assumed by rational agents when they engage in practical deliberation about what to do. Pauline Kleingeld offers this description of Kant's argument for the existence and nature of such a law:

> Agents who regard themselves as facing a decision and as deliberating about possible maxims of actions ascribe to themselves (implicitly or explicitly) the capacity to guide their actions on the basis of reasons. They ask themselves how to act and why. Their questions do not confine themselves to questions of expediency and prudence, because if and when they seriously ask themselves *why* they would act in a certain way, their reflection naturally leads to questions regarding ends and general principles of acting. Such agents ask themselves not merely whether certain actions are instrumental in achieving a given end, but also whether the end itself is worth pursuing (and why).[7]

I take Kleingeld (and Kant) to be arguing as follows: In choosing what to do, rational agents are choosing among possible maxims to act upon. As we saw in our discussion of hypothetical imperatives in Section 1.3, whether, in acting on a given maxim, we will in fact achieve that maxim's end determines whether that maxim is instrumentally rational. But deciding among maxims is not guided solely by how instrumentally rational different maxims are. Given (say) two maxims, each of which an individual concludes is equally instrumentally rational, there remains the further question of which maxim to adopt: Answering the question 'will doing A achieve my end E in circumstances C?' does not answer the question 'ought I pursue E in C?' Indeed, that latter question can only be settled by reference to a more general principle – a 'law,' in Kant's terms – that does not already assume that some end ought to be pursued. Unless the law dictating how to choose among possible ends or maxims does not refer to ends, we would confront an endless regress. For if the 'law' dictating how to choose among possible ends or maxims referred to an end – along the lines of 'choose one's maxims on the basis of whether they advance end E' – that would simply beg the question: Why ought one choose maxims that advance end E? The procedure by which we rationally decide among possible maxims, Kant thought, must break out of the loop of principles referring to possible ends. We cannot decide to adopt maxim M on the

[6] See, for example, Christine Korsgaard's "publicity argument" in *The Sources of Normativity* (Cambridge, 1996), as well as my critique of it ("Egoism and the publicity of reason: A reply to Korsgaard," *Social Theory and Practice* 25:3 (1999): 491–517).

[7] "Moral consciousness and the 'fact of reason,'" in A. Reath and J. Timmermann (eds.), *Kant's Critique of Practical Reason: A Critical Guide* (Cambridge, 2010), p. 68.

basis of a law that is itself maxim-like. The law in question must instead, as Kant says, be "formal" rather than "material" – a law requiring that our maxims be universal or 'objective' (C2 5:27, 5:31). Thus, the very act of practical deliberation – the act of deliberating about which maxims to adopt – presupposes the existence of an objective law that "holds without the contingent, subjective conditions that distinguish one rational being from another" (C2 5:21). Our reasoning about what to do thus implies that our maxims are subject to a requirement that they be universalizable. Absent such a law to serve as the fundamental law for practical reasoning, our maxims are rationally groundless or "arbitrary" recommendations, according to Kant (MM 6:389).

Again, we have not yet elaborated precisely what Kant's requirement of universalizability amounts to. But we have some insight into why Kant imposes this requirement on our maxims: For Kant, that we are rational agents is the most central moral fact. Our rationality not only determines how we are to be treated (as the Formula of Humanity states, as ends in themselves). Our rationality also imposes requirements on how we choose and act. That our maxims be universalizable is arguably the most basic of these requirements.

3.4 Interpreting Kant's Formula of Universal Law: Three Observations

We turn in the next section to competing interpretations of the Formula of Universal Law and its universalization requirement. Before doing so, some observations regarding this version of Kant's Categorical Imperative are in order, observations we will draw upon in evaluating the competing interpretations.

The Formula of Universal Law is intended be a test for the moral permissibility of maxims – that we are to act only on those maxims that can be willed as universal laws. We are to identify the universalized counterpart and suppose that it serves not only as our own maxim, but as a maxim that others adopt and act upon. We thus will the maxim 'as a universal law.' It is crucial to emphasize that the Formula of Universal Law tests whether maxims can be *willed* as universal laws. The trouble with morally impermissible maxims, Kant seems to say, is not that the maxims *themselves* cannot be universalized or cannot serve as universal laws. Rather, what makes these maxims morally impermissible – their 'wrongmaking' property, we might say – emerges when we envision them being endorsed by the rational will. This suggests that, ultimately, the Formula of Universal Law hinges moral right and wrong not on maxims per se, but in the *attitudes* (the beliefs, aims, etc.) of the agent who wills the maxim.

Second, in saying that morally impermissible maxims cannot be willed as universal laws, Kant argues that morally impermissible maxims generate a *contradiction.* As the next two sections will indicate, rival interpretations of the Formula of Universal Law diverge primarily in how they understand this contradiction. However, this observation, in conjunction with the observation in the previous paragraph, indicates that the Formula of Universal Law condemns maxims toward which those agents who will those maxims have contradictory attitudes. In other words, when an agent wills a morally impermissible maxim, there is something contradictory or inconsistent about the attitudes that constitute the act of willing that maxim.

Finally, recall the first criterion Kant identifies for the supreme principle of morality: that it provide plausible explanations of moral obligations we already recognize. Note that this criterion requires something stronger than that supreme principle logically *entail* the moral obligations we already recognize. It requires that the principle explain *why* we have the moral obligations we already recognize ourselves as having. Put more precisely, criterion [1] will not be satisfied if the best interpretation of the Formula of Universal Law implies merely that

(a) An act is wrong if and only if its maxim cannot be willed as a universal law.

Rather, criterion [1] requires for its satisfaction that

(b) An act is wrong if and only if *and because* its maxim cannot be willed as a universal law.

Put differently, the supreme principle of morality should not function merely as a *decision procedure* for figuring out which maxims (or which actions) are right and which right. It should also home in on what makes maxims morally permissible and so function as a *criterion of right action.*[8]

3.5 Contradiction: The False Promisor Case (and Two Mistaken Interpretations)

Let us finally attempt to hash out the disagreements among rival interpretations of the Formula of Universal Law. As we shall see, some common interpretations of the Formula of Universal Law are inadequate because they do not make the moral impermissibility of maxims depend on the consistency of the agent's

[8] For discussion of this important distinction, particularly as it applies to Kant, see Cynthia Stark, "Decision procedures, standards of rightness, and impartiality," *Nous* 31 (1997): 478–495, and Mark Timmons, "Decision procedures, moral criteria, and the problem of relevant descriptions in Kant's ethics," *Jahrbuch fur Recht und Ethik* (Annual for Law and Ethics), v.5 (Duncker & Humblot, 1998), pp. 389–417.

attitudes or they fail to provide a plausible explanation of the obligations we already recognize.

Kant says that acting on a given maxim is permissible if it can be willed as a universal law – i.e., if it is possible for its universalized counterpart to be willed. The trickiest part of the Formula of Universal Law stems from that little word 'can.' Let us use Kant's false promisor example as a way of developing the different interpretations of that 'can.'

The false promisor is someone who makes a promise he does not intend to keep, and, in fact, lacks the resources or ability to fulfill the promise. He

> finds himself urged by need to borrow money. He well knows that he will not be able to repay it but sees also that nothing will be lent him unless he promises firmly to repay it within a determinate time. He would like to make such a promise, but he still has enough conscience to ask himself: is it not forbidden and contrary to duty to help oneself out of need in such a way? (G 4:422)

As we might expect, the answer to this question turns on the false promisor's maxim: "when I believe myself to be in need of money I shall borrow money and promise to repay it, even though I know that this will never happen" (G 4:422).

Kant observes that acting on such a maxim might well be desirable from the false promisor's point of view. If the false promisor could secure the money he desires by acting under these false pretenses, his 'future welfare' might be served, but it is a further question 'whether it is right.' To determine if it is right, we must convert this maxim into a 'universal law.'

> I then see at once that it could never hold as a universal law of nature and be consistent with itself, but must necessarily contradict itself. For, the universality of a law that everyone, when he believes himself to be in need, could promise whatever he pleases with the intention of not keeping it would make the promise and the end one might have in it itself impossible, since no one would believe what was promised him but would laugh at all such expressions as vain pretenses. (G 4:422)

Once universalized, the false promisor's maxim, Kant argues, ends up being inconsistent. Indeed, the maxim "must necessarily contradict *itself*," according to Kant. How are we to understand what makes this universalized maxim self-contradictory?

One popular answer is known as the *logical possibility* interpretation. This interpretation draws attention to Kant's remark that willing the universalized version of the false promisor's maxim would make *the promise* impossible. On this interpretation, the contradiction in question is that, in acting on this maxim, the false promisor would be attempting to make a false promise in a hypothetical world where, because the false promising maxim is universalized, promises could not be made. Why not? Presumably, a world in which this maxim was universalized would be one where the practice of promising could not exist. Everyone else in this hypothetical world, including potential lenders, operates according to the false promisor's maxim and so would have no reason to expect that the loan will be repaid (or at least no reason to expect it to be repaid simply *because* the false promisor made a promise to do so). In this hypothetical world, uttering the words "I promise to pay back the money I borrowed" would do nothing to help the false promisor secure the money she seeks. Lenders would therefore laugh at promises as "vain pretense," as Kant observes. In effect, the false promisor must will a contradiction: that promising must be possible in a world where it is in fact impossible.

Suppose that Kant is right in concluding that the universalization of the false promisor's maxim would make promising (and therefore acting on the maxim of false promising) logically impossible. Is this a plausible way of understanding the contradictions that make acting on a maxim morally impermissible? More precisely, does the logical impossibility interpretation help to explain, in a recognizable and intuitively plausible way, what is morally objectionable about acting on such maxims?

First, we must not misunderstand what the logical impossibility interpretation alleges. We might suppose that Kant is arguing that maxims of false promising are wrong because acting on them would *destroy* a socially useful practice. So much of human life is interdependent, predicated upon expectations we form of one another's conduct. Promising is one very powerful way of creating such expectations and holding others accountable for meeting them. A world without promises would be a world without marriage, legal contracts, and other formal mechanisms of promising. A world absent such "covenants," as the English philosopher Thomas Hobbes famously pointed out, would be profoundly insecure, a world in which life is "solitary, poor, nasty, brutish, and short."

But if this were Kant's account of the moral impermissibility of false promising, he seems perilously close to being something we know he is not: a utilitarian, albeit of a sophisticated sort. I do not doubt that Kant thought that a world without the trust engendered by promises, in which promises are mere utterances taken seriously neither by those who make them nor by those to whom they are made, would be a very dismal world from the standpoint of well-being. Yet this sort of reasoning is, at root, utilitarian. Making false promises – and all the more, a universal practice of making false promises – is bad for human well-being. Kant would agree, but we should not expect him to ground his argument for the wrongfulness of false promising in such utilitarian considerations.

So the fact that most of all of us would be *worse off* in a world where a particular maxim is universalized is not a likely interpretation of what Kant means in saying that a morally impermissible maxim "must necessarily contradict itself' when universalized. The trouble, however, is that there does not seem to be any better explanation for what makes it wrong to act on a maxim it would be literally impossible to act on if everyone else adopted it. The logical possibility interpretation places great moral weight on the fact that some moral wrongs occur against the backdrop of social *conventions*. In the case of promising, most every society develops a set of rules and expectations that make promising possible – certain utterances and so on that count as making a promise, etc. The false promisor would, in the hypothetical world where her maxim has been universalized, be trying to act on (and benefit from) a non-existent convention. Imagine travelling to a community that has no conventions for promise making and trying to make a promise to someone in that community. You would fail to make a promise, as Kant predicts.

Yet hinging the moral permissibility of our maxims on conventions in this way causes several problems for the logical impossibility interpretation of the Formula of Universal Law. First, a large portion of morality does *not* seem to depend on conventions. Most every society has 'conventions' against people killing one another in that people ordinarily expect that they can go about their daily lives without being killed. But it seems strange to think that what would be wrong with a maxim involving killing (say, 'I will kill other human beings when doing so is conducive to my own interests') is that in a hypothetical world where such a maxim were universalized, one could not act on it. For one, as the many examples of lawless societies on the verge of political breakdown illustrate, it is not true that one could not act on such a maxim if it were universalized. A world in which everyone embraced the maxim

> I will kill other human beings when doing so is conducive to my own interests

is one in which murder would be unfortunately common. But it is surely not a world in which it would be logically impossible to kill others. The logical impossibility interpretation seems not even to imply that such a maxim is morally impermissible, much the less why it is so.

Second, even if universalizing such a maxim were logically impossible, the logical impossibility interpretation reverses the relationship between a maxim's wrongfulness and the conventions that enable acting on a maxim. Killing, for instance, is not wrong because it is contrary to a convention against killing. Rather, conventions against killing arise because it is wrong for some other reason – that is, moral communities discourage killing and establish 'conventions' against killing because they recognize powerful moral reasons against killing. Yet the logical impossibility interpretation is ill positioned to identify what these other reasons are.

These two considerations indicate that the logical impossibility interpretation fares badly with respect to criterion [1], as it seems straightforwardly unable to explain some of our actual moral obligations and provides an implausible explanation (appealing to conventions) of others.

Finally, the logical impossibility interpretation does succeed in highlighting something irrational about the attitudes of those who will morally impermissible maxims. According to this interpretation, acting on a maxim's universalized counterpart is impossible: The false promisor could not make promises in a world where his maxim is universalized. Acting on such maxim would be inconsistent, even irrational. No one can do the impossible, so it is irrational to will the impossible. Nevertheless, I do not see that this inconsistency succeeds in illustrating what is morally objectionable about willing morally impermissible maxims. If Kant is correct about universalizing a maxim being a rational requirement built into practical deliberation, then willing a maxim of the form 'I will do act A in circumstances C to achieve end E' when one could not do A (once the maxim is universalized) is certainly ill-advised. Yet I do not perceive anything morally objectionable about this volition, i.e., about willing to do what one cannot do. To say to the false promisor, "you could not make promises in a world where your maxim holds as a universal law" is to implicitly assert that it is wrong for him to perform this act because he cannot perform it. But it is hard to see how that amounts to recognizably *moral* criticism, any more than pointing out to an engineer that she cannot build a perpetual motion machine is to issue a recognizably moral criticism of her plans to build such a machine. Thus, the logical impossibility interpretation also does not provide a satisfactory account of the contradictory nature of morally wrongful maxims, in particular, how they are morally objectionable once willed.

A second common interpretation focuses on Kant's statement that a morally impermissible maxim is one whose universalization makes "the end one might have in it itself impossible." Return to the false promisor's maxim:

> When I believe myself to be in need of money I shall borrow money and promise to repay it, even though I know that this will never happen.

Its universalized counterpart is

> Anyone who believes himself/herself to be in need of money shall borrow money and promise to repay it, even though the borrower knows that this will never happen.

In a world governed by this universalized maxim, all parties would adopt and act upon this maxim and assume others do the same. Again, Kant predicts that if this maxim were a universal law, the practice of making and honoring promises would break down as a result. Those with money that they would otherwise be willing to lend out would no longer do so, reasoning that borrowers are unlikely to repay. In such a world, perhaps promises could be made in the minimal sense, but one could not achieve one's ends by promising. For funds would not be lent, and in general, promises would not be honored or even taken very seriously. Since the false promisor's end is to secure funds via a false promise, his end would not be one *he* could achieve in a world where his maxim is universalized. His maxim thus turns out to be self-defeating.

This *self-defeat* interpretation is also mistaken, though. Again, even if this interpretation of the Formula of Universal Law would entail many of the moral obligations we recognize, it does not provide a satisfactory explanation, in terms of the attitudes of the person willing the maxim, for why morally impermissible maxims are such. On this interpretation, the false promisor can act on this maxim but not successfully: She can make promises – and others can recognize them as promises – but she cannot achieve her intended ends by making promises. Yet the fact that a maxim would be self-defeating does not seem to correspond to any 'wrongmaking' features of that maxim. The false promisor is certainly being *imprudent* if he acts on this maxim in a world in which this maxim is universalized. After all, he will certainly fail to secure the funds he is seeking. But it is hard to see why being foolish in this way makes his acting on this maxim immoral. Someone intending to cheat at cards is acting foolishly in a game where every other player also intends to cheat. After all, any given player will fail to gain much of an advantage in the game if everyone else intends to cheat as well. But *that fact* does not make his intention to cheat immoral. And again, to say to the false promisor, "you could not achieve your end in a world where your maxim holds as a universal law" is not to subject him to recognizably *moral* criticism.

3.6 Rational Contradiction

In the end, then, we should reject both the logical impossibility interpretation and the self-defeat interpretation of Kant's Formula of Universal Law. Neither succeeds in explaining how there is something inconsistent and morally objectionable about willing an impermissible maxim as a universal law. To see how we might arrive at an interpretation that succeeds on this score, we need to confront some of Kant's odd locutions regarding maxims and their contradictoriness.

Often, Kant presents the moral impermissibility of maxims as a matter of such maxims being somehow at odds with themselves. A morally impermissible maxim "necessarily contradicts itself." A morally impermissible maxim, "as soon as it were made a universal law, would have to destroy itself" (G 4:403); could not "harmonize with itself" once universalized; and results (once universalized) in the "complete annihilation of the maxim itself and its purpose" (C2 5:28). This is strange talk on Kant's part. Unless a maxim literally was 'do A, and refrain from A, to achieve end E' or 'do A both to achieve and prevent the achievement of E,' a maxim cannot contradict itself. Nor can maxims – these abstract principles on the basis of which a person rationally justifies her action – destroy, annihilate, or fail to harmonize with themselves. Maxims don't act – agents act on them. Tempting though it is to dismiss this language as Kant indulging in metaphor, I will suggest that this language reveals a key feature of morally impermissible maxims.

Given that Kant could not have literally meant that maxims are contradictory or destroy themselves, etc., he must have meant that the act of *willing* these maxims is contradictory or disharmonious – that the attitudes of the individual willing the maxim are contradictory or irrational. A maxim, remember, is a statement expressing a person's reason for acting on a given occasion. In saying that a maxim "contradicts itself," etc., Kant appears to be claiming that what makes acting on a maxim morally impermissible relates to the consistency of a person's reasons – that, in some way or other, a person acting on an impermissible maxim is rationally contradicting *himself*. In other words, the 'can' in Kant's Formula is a *rational* 'can': that an impermissible maxim is one that cannot be rationally endorsed in a consistent or non-self-contradictory way.

Suppose we ask: Under what conditions is it rational to act upon a particular maxim? No doubt one condition is that it *must be possible to achieve the maxim's end by acting on that very maxim*. Kant seems to gesture at this idea when he points out that universalizing the false promisor's maxim makes both "the promise" *and* "the end one might have in it" impossible. Recall that the logical impossibility interpretation rested on the promise being impossible, the self-defeat interpretation on the end being impossible. My suggestion is that the relevant impossibility is 'compound': whether a person can achieve her end *by* performing the act prescribed by her maxim in the maxim's prescribed circumstances. As Kant argued elsewhere, "ought" implies "can" (MM 6:224). This means that one *ought* to act on a maxim only if by acting on that maxim one *can* achieve the end contained in the maxim. Or, to put it differently, acting on a maxim is *rational* only if, by acting upon it, one can achieve the end contained in the maxim.[9] In the case of the false promisor's maxim, what conditions must be met in order for his acting on this maxim to be rational? His maxim – "when I believe myself to be in need of money I shall borrow money and promise to repay it, even though I know that this will never happen" – is rational only if by acting on this maxim he can secure the money he seeks. But if his maxim is universalized – if anyone who believes himself/herself to be in need of money shall borrow money and promise to repay it, etc. – then he cannot successfully act on such a maxim. Hence, from the false promisor's

[9] John Rawls, *Lectures on the History of Moral Philosophy* (Harvard, 2000), pp. 170–171.

point of view, the ideally rational situation – the situation in which it is possible for him to achieve the end he seeks by acting on his maxim – entails that he wills his maxim

(a) When I believe myself to be in need of money I **shall** borrow money and promise to repay it, even though I know this will never happen

but also wills the *negation of its universalization*

(b) Anyone who believes himself/herself to be in need of money **shall not** borrow money and promise to repay it when he or she knows this will never happen.

In other words, the false promisor's willing (b) is a necessary condition of its being rational to act on (a). But note that (b) entails that the false promisor must also will

(c) When I believe myself to be in need of money I **shall not** borrow money and promise to repay it, even though I know this will never happen.

However, (c) and (a) contradict one another. The false promisor is both subject to a fundamental requirement of instrumental rationality – that acting on a maxim is rational only if it is possible to achieve that maxim's end by so acting – and to the Kantian requirement that his maxim be rationally consistently universalizable. But, I have argued, when his maxim is subject to these requirements, his will generates inconsistent commitments: Willing, and so acting upon, the maxim to which he was already antecedently rationally committed is rational only if he wills the universalization of his maxim's negation, which in turn implies willing the negation of the maxim itself. The agent is compelled to will both his maxim and that maxim's negation.

Let us call this interpretation of Kant's Formula of Universal Law the *rational contradiction* interpretation. On this interpretation, a maxim is self-contradictory (and hence, acting on it is morally impermissible) when, in order for an agent to achieve the end contained in her maxim, she must both will her maxim and will its negation. The rational contradiction interpretation thus understands the question

Can this maxim be consistently universalized?

as equivalent to

Does the rationality of the agent acting on this maxim, and more specifically, the rationality of her pursuing the end contained in the maxim, require both her willing the maxim and willing its negation?

It suggests the following procedure for evaluating whether a person's acting on a given maxim is permissible:

> Identify the maxim that person P is considering acting upon: "I will do act A in circumstances C to achieve end E."

Because maxims universalize across agents, P also wills the maxim's universalized counterpart:

> Identify the universalized counterpart of P's maxim: "Anyone in circumstances C will do act A to achieve end E."

A condition of its being rational for P to act on his maxim is that he is able to achieve his end. So ask:

> Is P's acting on this maxim rational (= P can achieve his end by acting on the maxim) only on the condition that others do not share the maxim with him, i.e., on the condition that the maxim **not** be universalized?

There are of course two possible answers here:

> IF 'YES':
>
> Then P wills both the maxim and it negation. The rationality of acting on his maxim requires that he be rationally inconsistent. Acting on this maxim is therefore morally *impermissible* or wrong.

> IF 'NO':
>
> The rationality of P's acting on his maxim does not require that P will both the maxim and its negation. The rationality of acting on his maxim does not require that he be rationally inconsistent. Acting on this maxim is therefore morally *permissible* or right.

The rational contradiction interpretation does not inherit the problems that the logical impossibility and self-defeat interpretations faced. While it agrees with both interpretations in holding that the false promisor would be unable to achieve his end in a world where all shared this maxim, it does not locate what is morally wrong with this maxim in the mere fact that the false promisor will be thwarted in his aims. Rather, it locates the wrongfulness of the maxim in the fact that the rationality of acting on this maxim requires the false promisor to have a contradictory set of attitudes toward the maxim (or its universalization). Note that this is a fact about the false promisor's maxim and the coherence of his rational attitudes. It is not a fact about the consequences of acting on the maxim or its universal adoption. Hence, it does not make Kant out to be a utilitarian.

Admittedly, Kant does not anywhere explicitly expound the rational contradiction interpretation. Nevertheless, we find hints of it when Kant makes statements that make the moral impermissibility of maxims depend on whether its end can be achieved by the person whose maxim it is. A morally impermissible maxim leads to the "complete annihilation of the maxim itself *and its purpose*" (C2 5:28, emphasis added). We are to appraise our actions, according to Kant, by ascertaining "whether, if the action you propose were to take place by a law of the nature of which you were yourself a part, you could indeed regard it as *possible through your will*" (C2 5:69, emphasis added). In any event, the rational contradiction interpretation best makes sense of Kant's insight that those who act wrongly have entangled *themselves* in contradiction. The false promisor, on this interpretation, must embrace contradictory attitudes toward his in order for his maxim to be rational.

3.7 What's Wrong with Morally Impermissible Maxims

Before considering how the Formula of Universal Law can be used to establish Kant's taxonomy of duties, we should take notice of how the rational contradiction interpretation provides a plausible account of our moral obligations, particularly in the terms established by criterion [1] for the supreme principle of morality. I complained earlier that neither the logical impossibility interpretation nor the self-defeat interpretation point to morally objectionable features of willing a morally impermissible maxim. How does my proposed rational contradiction interpretation fare on that count? I suggest that this interpretation links Kant's Formula of Universal Law to two insights already found in our pre-theoretical understanding of morality.

First, when we reflect on right and wrong, one natural conclusion is that morality is bound up with the notion of *fair play*. When people engage in moral wrongdoing, they are in some way not playing fair or not abiding by 'the rules of the game.' At the same time, these rule breakers expect others to abide by these same rules. But a situation in which some observe a rule while others disregard it is essentially unfair in that those who disregard the rule are making an arbitrary or groundless exception for themselves. They display a kind of arrogance, thinking that these rules do not apply them, prompting others to ask, "just who do you think you are?" Kant's Formula of Universal Law captures the intuitive force of this question and of the idea of morality as bound up with fair play. The Formula of Universal Law – based on the rational contradiction interpretation – prohibits individuals from acting on maxims the rationality of which depends upon others not sharing their maxims with them. The false promisor, for instance, desires there to be a rule in place (that promises not be made unless the promisor has reason to think she can fulfill them) that he can then exploit by acting on a conflicting rule. The Formula of Universal Law provides a sophisticated way to cash out the notion that the heart of immorality is wanting to make an exception of oneself, even to rules that one otherwise has reason to accept. Moral wrongdoers in effect assert that their aims in acting require one principle for themselves and another for the rest of us. Such assertions are rightly subject to *moral* criticism.

Secondly, we noted in Chapter 2 that Kant's Formula of Humanity serves to limit how individuals pursue their ends. The Formula of Humanity thus expresses the insight that a central facet of morality is that it functions to constrain our pursuit of our concerns. When we reflect on morality's role in human life, one uncontroversial conclusion is that by conforming to morality's demands, we must sometimes limit our pursuit of the ends we care about. The Formula of Universal Law expresses the same insight in different terms. Notice that maxims express what individuals take themselves to have reasons to do in particular circumstances. Hence, the rationality of acting on a maxim is captured by Kant's hypothetical imperative. Indeed, maxims can be seen as expressions of hypothetical imperatives, since their force as rational commands depends on the ends contained in them.[10] In "I will do act A in circumstances C to achieve end E" the rationality of acting to achieve E depends on the individual whose maxim it is having willed E as among her ends. As we have seen, the Formula of Universal Law tests these maxims for their moral permissibility. Hence, this formula, by determining which hypothetical imperatives morality permits us to act upon, also places limits on how we pursue our ends. The Categorical Imperative therefore functions as a test for the moral permissibility of our hypothetical imperatives, and, in so doing, captures the intuitive and familiar insight that moral wrongdoing occurs when we overstep moral requirements in the pursuit of our ends.

3.8 The Formula of Universal Law and Kant's Taxonomy of Duties

In Chapter 2, we were introduced to the two central distinctions in Kant's taxonomy of duties: duties to self versus duties to others, and perfect versus imperfect duties. There we articulated these duties in terms of the Formula of Humanity, indicating how the demands set out by these duties are rooted in the demand that we treat rational agency always as an end in itself and never merely as a means. Kant puts his Formula of Universal Law to parallel purposes, using it to articulate the four aforementioned categories of duty (perfect duties to self, perfect duties to others, imperfect duties to self,

[10] Of course, Kant is right to say that maxims, being "subjective," are not "imperatives," since imperatives, whether hypothetical *or* categorical, command objectively (C2 5:20).

imperfect duties to others). Of special significance is how Kant grounds the contrast between perfect and imperfect duties in a contrast in the kinds of rational contradiction generated by different kinds of maxims.

Not long after introducing the Formula of Universal Law, Kant indicates that maxims that fail that Formula's universalization test can fail it in two different ways:

> We must *be able to will* that a maxim of our action become a universal law: this is the canon of moral appraisal of action in general. Some actions are so constituted that their maxim cannot even be *thought* without contradiction as a universal law of nature, far less could one *will* that it *should* become such. In the case of others that inner impossibility is indeed not to be found, but it is still impossible to *will* that their maxim be raised to the universality of a law of nature because such a will would contradict itself. It is easy to see that the first is opposed to strict or narrower . . . duty, the second only to wide . . . duty. (G 4:424)

Here Kant suggests that the first way in which a maxim can be contradictory, that it "cannot be thought" without contradiction once universalized, corresponds to strict or narrower duty. In other words, those maxims which are contradictory in this first way violate perfect duties, duties that require the performance of particular actions on particular occasions. On the other hand, maxims that violate our wide duties – that is, our imperfect duties to adopt certain ends – are not contradictory once universalized because they cannot be "thought." Rather, Kant says, it is impossible to will these maxims, even if they can be thought.

The maxims that violate perfect duties and that violate imperfect duties are both contradictory once universalized. However, the contradictions generated by each differ. Our challenge, then, is to explain the different kinds of contradictions generated by impermissible maxims, and, in particular, to explain how the two kinds of contradictions embody the rational contradiction that (I have argued) characterizes morally impermissible maxims. Rather than addressing these tasks abstractly, I propose we look at the clearest examples Kant provides of these two kinds of contradictions.

The first is an example we have already addressed, the maxim of 'false promising.' As we noted above, it is rational for the false promisor to act on his maxim only if, by acting on it, he can achieve the end he seeks by so acting, namely, to secure money under false pretenses. But a condition of his being able to achieve that end is that others not share his maxim with him. That is, he wills as his maxim

> When I believe myself to be in need of money I **shall** borrow money and promise to repay it, even though I know this will never happen

while also willing that others adopt a contrary maxim

> When I believe myself to be in need of money I **shall not** borrow money and promise to repay it, even though I know this will never happen

It is thus a condition of its being rational to act on his maxim that he wills contradictory maxims. Kant says of such a maxim that it "cannot even be thought without contradiction as a law of nature" (G 4:424). As I interpret Kant's remarks, the contradiction that arises from trying to think of this maxim as a universal law is not literal. Rather, recall Kant's remark that we "must be able to *will* that a maxim of our action become a universal law" (my emphasis). Hence, what is incoherent is rationally willing a world governed by this maxim while also seeking the end incorporated in that maxim. The irrationality of the false promisor is a kind of "inner impossibility," Kant says. It is 'inner' because it is *internal* to the maxim: One cannot rationally act *on this very maxim* while also willing its universalization.

The other kind of contradiction, usually called a *contradiction in the will*, is best illustrated by Kant's fourth example of a morally impermissible maxim: a maxim of *non-beneficence*. Recall again Kant's rugged individualist, who is content both not to provide aid to others but also not to receive such aid (G 4:423). As we saw in Section 2.6, Kant held that we have an imperfect duty of beneficence, a duty to promote the happiness of others. We saw there how not having the happiness of others among one's ends fails to treat their rational agency as an end in itself. Here Kant offers a different avenue to the conclusion that utter indifference to others' well-being is wrong. Recall the ACE structure of maxims. Here Kant gives us two of the three essential elements in describing the non-beneficent person's maxim. The maxim 'I will neither contribute anything to others' welfare nor assist them when they are in need' provides us an action (or perhaps an inaction: refraining from aiding others) and a set of circumstances (whenever others are in need or one can contribute to their welfare). But it lacks an end. To what end might someone will a maxim of non-beneficence? Let us assume that the non-beneficent person's end in not aiding others is to enjoy "things . . . going well" for him without having to relinquish the time or resources needed to aid others or contribute to their welfare. The maxim 'I will neither contribute anything to others' welfare nor assist them when they are in need so as to enjoy my own welfare without having to relinquish any time or resources' cannot be consistently willed as a universal law:

> But although it is possible that a universal law of nature could very well subsist in accordance with such a maxim, it is still impossible to **will** that such a principle hold everywhere as a law of nature. For, a will that decided this would conflict with itself, since many cases could occur in which one would need the love and sympathy of others and in which, by such a law of nature arisen from his own will, he would rob himself of all hope of the assistance he wishes for himself. (G 4:423)

The person who adopts a maxim of non-beneficence is irrational from a practical point of view, Kant argues. How so? Here Kant says that willing such a maxim would put the will at "conflict with itself," because though there will inevitably be instances in which a non-beneficent person will need others' beneficence (their "love and sympathy"), by willing this maxim, the non-beneficent person thereby denies himself "any hope of the assistance he wishes for himself (G 4:423).

The contradiction in question is made clearer when we remind ourselves of the hypothetical imperative: that if we will some end, we are necessarily committed to securing the means to that end. The non-beneficent person wills that he not provide others with the means they might need in order to realize their ends, and so when this maxim is universalized, he wills that others not provide *him* with the means by which he might realize his ends. But in being rationally committed to his ends, he is thereby rationally committed to making use of the best means to those ends, even if those means are provided by others. In effect then, the non-beneficent person rationally wills that he be unable to realize the ends to which he is otherwise rationally committed. He wills his ends, but not all the possible means to his ends. His will is thus rationally at odds with itself.

But he is not at odds with himself in exactly the way the false promisor is. The false promisor's rational contradiction stems from the irrationality of acting on the false promising maxim while seeking to achieve the end incorporated into that very maxim. In contrast, the non-beneficent person's rational contradiction stems from the irrationality of acting on the maxim not to aid others in need while seeking to achieve other ends not specific to the maxim itself. That is, the false promisor can only achieve the *specific* end found in his maxim if he rationally wills that maxim for himself while rationally willing the contrary maxim for others. The non-beneficent person may well be able to achieve his end of enjoying his own welfare without cost to himself while willing that others adopt his maxim of non-beneficence. Nevertheless, given his commitment to achieving his ends in general, it would be irrational for him to will a maxim that will deny himself means he may need in order to achieve *other* ends he may have.

We see a similar sort of irrationality at work in Kant's other illustration of the Formula of Universal Law that generates an imperfect duty. We noted in Section 2.7 that Kant believed we have a duty to develop our talents. He arrives at the same conclusion by appeal to the Formula of Universal Law. He asks us to consider a person in "comfortable circumstances" who "prefers to give himself up to pleasure" instead of "enlarging and improving his fortunate natural predispositions" (G 4:423). Is this consistent with duty? Kant grants that it would be possible for everyone to adopt this maxim of letting our talents rust while devoting our lives to "idleness, amusement, [and] procreation." But such a maxim could not be willed as a universal law, for as a "rational being he necessarily wills that all the capacities in him be developed, since they serve him and are given to him for all sorts of possible purposes." Just as with the maxim of non-beneficence, a rational being committed to his ends cannot will that he be obstructed or frustrated in the pursuit of those ends. To will a life of indolence in which one's talents remain dormant and uncultivated is to will that the means that one may find useful in pursuing ends be made unavailable for subsequent use.

In both of these arguments regarding imperfect duties, Kant implicitly appeals to the notion that we are not fully self-sufficient beings – that whatever ends we may have, we will invariably find ourselves without the means sufficient to realize our ends. We depend both on others' beneficence and our own self-cultivation to provide ourselves the means to our ends. But by "natural necessity," we will our own happiness as an end (G 4:415), and since we achieve happiness by fulfilling our ends, we must necessarily will the means to the various ends that constitute our happiness. Hence, non-beneficence and failure to cultivate one's natural abilities are irrational and exhibit rational contradiction. For to both will one's ends and to will the non-satisfaction of those ends is to exemplify contradictory rational commitments. And in the case of the imperfect duties, the contradiction is *external* to the end sought in the maxim.

The perfect duties thus correspond to maxims that it is irrational to act upon while also willing the universalization of *that very maxim*. The imperfect duties thus correspond to maxims that it is irrational to act upon while also willing the ends found in *other* maxims.

3.9 The Formula of Universal Law and Rational Agency

Let us return, at long last, to Kant's theory of value, and what the Formula of Universal Law tells us about that theory.

We established in Chapter 2 that Kantian morality, like utilitarianism, is monistic inasmuch as it recognizes only one fundamental moral value. But whereas the utilitarian recognizes well-being as the sole intrinsic value, Kant recognizes rational agency as the sole intrinsic value. Kant's Formula of Humanity directs us to value rational agency by respecting it in ourselves and others, and, in particular, to treat rational agency as an end in itself instead of merely as a means.

In what sense do maxims that conform to the Formula of Universal Law value rational agency? We saw in the last section how, in striving to have beliefs that are rationally consistent, an individual is exhibiting a kind of rationality. Similarly with one's maxims: When an individual acts on a maxim whose universalized counterpart cannot be consistently universalized, she *manifests* or *exhibits* rational agency in choosing to act on that maxim. To manifest or exhibit value is a way of valuing something. Kant clearly thinks that when we act on universalizable maxims, we are manifesting or exhibiting rational agency in a direct way. We have made ourselves an instance of rational agency. It is important not to become confused here. 'Rational' is one of the trickiest of philosophical concepts. On the one hand, 'rational' means *capable* of rational thought or choice. We saw in Chapter 2 that, for Kant, we are rational agents in that we have humanity, the capacity to set our ends (and the means to those ends) according to reason. Our maxims are such that the rationality of *our* acting upon them must be compatible with others sharing them with us. When we act morally on Kant's view, we beings who are capable of rational choice actually manifest that rationality in our choices. And when we act immorally, we rational beings fail to live up to the standards of rationality because our attitudes are rationally inconsistent. We act *for* reasons (recall that a maxim is simply an expression of a reason for action), but our reasons fail to justify our action because they turn out to be inconsistent insofar as the rationality of our action depends on others not sharing our maxims with us.

Now, one might ask, 'What difference does it make if we are rational? What does Kant gain by claiming that immoral conduct is irrational, or that immoral conduct involves using our constitutive rational powers in irrational ways?' These are perfectly legitimate questions. They are descendants of an old philosophical chestnut: Why be moral? Kant's answer, as we have seen and will continue to investigate in the next section, is not that by behaving morally we necessarily benefit ourselves. Rather, Kant's answer seems to be that by behaving morally we are being what we in fact are: rational agents.

3.10 Universalization and Kant's Five Criteria

In Section 2.10, I attempted to show that we have good reason to think that Kant's Formula of Humanity satisfies the five criteria for the supreme principle of morality that we attributed to Kant in Chapter 1. Can the same be said about the formulation of the Categorical Imperative we have been considering in this chapter, the Formula of Universal Law?

Recall our five criteria. The supreme principle of morality must

[1] provide plausible explanations of moral obligations we already recognize,

[2] be an imperative that it is rationally necessary for us to adopt, that is, a categorical imperative,

[3] be whatever principle governs the choices of the morally good will,

[4] be a non-consequentialist principle, i.e., it must not make the rightness or wrongness of actions depend on the value of actions' consequences, and

[5] be a principle conformity to which requires only that we are practically rational beings.

Let us proceed in numerical order.

We will have occasion later to investigate some challenges to what the Formula of Universal Law actually implies about our moral obligations. As we will see, critics of Kant's ethics sometimes argue that the Formula of Universal Law implies that actions that are clearly wrong are *not* wrong and actions that are not wrong are *in fact* wrong. In a similar vein, other critics allege that the Formula of Universal Law is too malleable, so that a clever individual could justify most any action under its auspices. More sympathetic critics doubt that the Formula of Universal Law so roundly condemns actions such as lying and suicide, as Kant evidently believed.

We will give these criticisms a fair hearing in Chapters 5 and 6. But at first glance, it does seem that the Formula of Universal Law suffices to [1] *provide plausible explanations of our moral obligations* in a wide range of cases where we have fairly firm judgments. The Formula of Universal Law explains what is wrong with false promising (and with promise breaking), deception, and indifference to others' well-being. And it does so by rendering more exact some powerful intuitive ideas we have about the moral sphere: for example, that immorality consists in making exceptions for oneself to rules one wills for others and hence violates a sense of fair play.

The Formula of Universal Law also seems to satisfy criterion [2]. This principle directs us to adopt only maxims that can be consistently willed as universal laws, regardless of whether those maxims are such that by acting on them we promote our own ends. Hence, the Formula of Universal Law is not a hypothetical command, rooted in the rationality of pursuing our own ends, but *a categorical imperative* whose rational authority does not rest on how it advances our own personal ends. And, as we have seen, with the Formula of Universal Law, Kant has identified a second way in which the supreme principle of morality is *rationally necessary for us to adopt.* In willing maxims that cannot be universalized, we embrace inconsistency, the hallmark of irrational thought and belief.

Kant was thus a proponent of the thesis often called *moral rationalism.* Moral rationalism holds that the requirements of morality are requirements of rationality – or, put differently, that acting immorally amounts to acting irrationally. Kant is far from the only prominent rationalist among moral philosophers. Plato, Aristotle, and Hobbes all affirmed rationalism in some form or another. So too do Kant's rivals, the utilitarians. As utilitarians see it, the rational response to that which has intrinsic value (i.e., well-being) is to promote it. How, utilitarians ask, could it be rational to seek to bring about less intrinsic value instead of more? We see in Kant's Formula of Universal

Law a very different understanding of what rationality requires, and, as a result, a different version of moral rationalism. To be inconsistent in what one wills is to exhibit a form of irrationality. Consider the rationality of believing. One mark of a defective set of beliefs is that the belief set is inconsistent. A person who both believes that Saturn is the largest planet and believes that Saturn is not the largest planet is clearly defective insofar as she believes contradictory claims. (Of course, some philosophers would go so far as to say that holding inconsistent beliefs is impossible. I take no stand on that question. The example is only meant to illustrate a broader point about rationality – namely, the centrality of consistency among the demands of rationality.) Kant's Formula of Universal Law implicates individuals such as the false promisor in a similar sort of irrational contradiction. The false promisor both wills his maxim while also willing its negation. He is at rational cross purposes with himself, and, as such, he exhibits irrationality. Notice, as Kant does, that the false promisor is rational in one respect: If he can manage to secure the money he seeks by making a false promise, he will have secured his end. His maxim may well prove *instrumentally* rational or prudent. For, as Kant put it, his maxim is wholly consistent with his "future welfare." Yet his success will require that he will one maxim for himself and a contrary maxim for others.

What then of the morally good will? Do we have reason to think that its choices would be governed by the Formula of Universal Law? Someone who governs her choices by this principle would, I contend, come very close to our model of moral virtue. In choosing to act only on maxims that can be consistently universalized, an individual would embody not only a kind of practical rationality, but also a recognition of others as her moral equals. Her own rationally chosen ends, according to the Formula of Universal Law, can only confer instrumental rationality on her actions. In order for her actions to be fully rational, those ends must be ends that she wills others to share with her – or, as we put it earlier, she must not act on her maxim believing that it is rational to do so only because others do not share that maxim with her. The rational agency of others thus has equal standing to her own. For in abiding by the Formula of Universal Law, an individual implicitly understands herself as committed to a social ideal wherein her actions must be justifiable not merely in terms of her own ends, but in terms of the ends of others. The Formula of Universal Law would thus be a principle that *governs the choices of the morally good will* [3].

It should also be apparent why the Formula of Universal Law is a *non-consequentialist principle* [4]. It does not hinge the rightness of a person's action on its consequences, but on the action's maxim, and, more specifically, on whether that maxim can be universalized without requiring that person to will contradictory principles in order for it to be rational for her to act on that maxim. In a famous passage, Kant argues that since the supreme principle of morality cannot be based on the good 'effects' or consequences of acting on it, the only possible candidate for the supreme principle is the Formula of Universal Law.

> But what kind of law can that be, the representation of which must determine the will, even without regard for the effect expected from it, in order for the will to be called good absolutely and without limitation? Since I have deprived the will of every impulse that could arise for it from obeying some law, nothing is left but the conformity of actions as such with universal law, which alone is to serve the will as its principle, that is *I ought never to act except in such a way that I could also will that my maxim should become a universal law.* (G 4:402)

Hence, right and wrong are properties of maxims, not the effects of acting on those maxims.

In addition, some acts that would be permissible or obligatory according to a consequentialist standard (such as the utilitarian standard of right action) would be impermissible or wrong according to Kant's Formula of Universal Law. For example, sometimes making a false promise can end up having better consequences than not making it. Consider a person who takes out a small personal loan from a large corporate bank without intending to repay even though stating her intention to repay was a condition of her being lent the funds in the first place. She may well reason in utilitarian terms and conclude that she did no wrong in securing the loan by deceptive means. For her, the borrowed funds may help her fulfill very important ends and the burdens of repayment may be very great, whereas for a large corporate bank, a single unpaid loan will have little impact on its profitability, its employees, or its owners. On balance, then, it might appear that more overall happiness will result if she takes out the loan under false pretenses. From a utilitarian perspective, not only did she not act wrongly, she would have acted wrongly had she *not* misrepresented her intention to repay! Of course, utilitarians will remind us that we must keep in mind *all* the consequences of her actions, both short-term and longer-term. For example, not paying the loan will inhibit her future ability to borrow. But it seems at least conceivable that, on a utilitarian view, some agreements resting on false pretenses ought to be made because entering into them has the best overall consequences. In contrast, when considering the Formula of Universal Law, the goodness or value of an action's consequences do not determine whether an action is right, and, in this case, the Formula of Universal Law can supply a justification for the intuition that making a lying promise is wrong *despite* the overall weight of the consequences favoring doing so. As we have seen, in this case, the maxim

> When I believe myself to be in need of money I shall borrow money and promise to repay it, even though I know that this will never happen

is one that it is rational for the borrower to act upon only on the condition that others do not share it with her. Indeed, securing the borrowed funds – the end she has set in acting upon this maxim – is possible only when others do not adopt this same maxim. This holds true even if the overall consequences of her acting on this maxim are better than her not acting on it (or better than her acting on some alternative maxim).

This is of course only one example. Yet it illustrates that the Formula of Universal Law is non-consequentialist both in its own right and in terms of its practical implications.

Finally, let us turn to criterion [5], that the supreme principle of morality *be a principle conformity to which requires only that we are practically rational beings*. Again, a full treatment of the issues that [5] raises for the Categorical Imperative must wait for Chapter 5. Yet at the very least, conforming to the demands of the Formula of Universal Law does not appear to require extraordinary powers. It does not require that we be possessed of unusual powers of logical reasoning or an exceptional ability to modify the world so as to realize our ends. The Formula of Universal Law imposes requirements on our maxims – or, if you will, on the kinds of reasons that motivate our actions. Whether a consideration strikes us as a reason for doing something (whether, for instance, an animal's suffering resonates with us such that we see it as a reason to relieve that suffering) does not seem to be a capacity over which we exercise immediate or direct control. However, whether to act on a particular reason that we recognize is a power that rational beings typically have. Individuals with mental disorders that inhibit their ability to control their impulses lack this power. But, for the most part, competent moral agents can recognize reasons for action and decide whether those reasons are sufficient reasons to act. Hence, they are able to determine whether the principles that they take to justify their actions – their maxims – can be consistently universalized or whether, on the contrary, the rationality of pursuing that maxim depends on their willing that maxim for themselves but a different maxim for others. Doing so does not require any great feat of moral imagination or inquiry. It is only a matter of asking oneself if one would find it rational to act on a maxim if others did so as well.

Kant himself thought that conforming to morality's demands is made more difficult by our all-too-human tendency to be biased in morally evaluating our own choices. We are strongly prone to deceiving ourselves about our maxims and motives, Kant thought, often depicting our reasons for acting as we do in a false but flattering light. Note that Kant is not saying that we cannot categorize our actions into morally important kinds – as if it is a mystery to us whether we are deceiving someone, assisting someone in advancing her ends, etc. Rather, for Kant, what determines if our actions are praiseworthy and so have "moral worth" is the reasons for which they are done – that is, their maxims. After all, a person can fulfill her obligation in the sense of performing the act that conforms to what morality requires (refraining from lying, say). But it is a further question whether the action is done, as Kant says, "from duty" – that is, because the individual is *motivated* by a recognition that this action is what duty demands. Whether an obligatory action is done from duty and has moral worth requires us to look past the "actions one sees" to "their inner principles which one does not see" (G 4:407). But even here, the difficulty is not in ascertaining whether acting on a maxim is morally permissible. The difficulty is in ascertaining what maxim we in fact are acting upon on a given occasion (an issue engaged in Chapter 6). That may well be a barrier to moral righteousness, but it is not a barrier to knowing what is morally right. Hence, we may provisionally conclude that the Formula of Universal Law satisfies criterion [5].

3.11 Conclusion

The first three chapters of this book have sought to make a compelling case that Kant succeeded in what many philosophers believe was the central task of his ethical theory – namely, to defend the Categorical Imperative as morality's supreme principle. In particular, we

(a) outlined the five criteria Kant believed the supreme principle must satisfy,
(b) defended these as the proper criteria for the supreme principle,
(c) showed how one version of the Categorical Imperative, Kant's Formula of Humanity, satisfies these criteria, and
(d) showed how a second version of the Categorical Imperative, Kant's Formula of Universal Law, satisfies these criteria.

Along the way, we were introduced to Kant's classification of duties (perfect versus imperfect duties, duties to self and to others) and how these duties relate to the two different versions of the Categorical Imperative we considered. We also saw how Kant, though a monist about value in believing that rational agency is the sole fundamental moral value, was a pluralist about valu*ing* inasmuch as the Formula of Humanity asks us to respect rational agency whereas the Formula of Universal Law asks us to embody or exhibit rational agency.

One result of our inquiry may seem troubling: How can there be *two* supreme principles of morality? After all, the notion of a supreme principle implies that there is no rival principle that is as fundamental or basic to morality. We will have occasion later on, when considering an important objection to Kant's Formula of Universal Law, to analyze further the relationships among the formulas of the Categorical Imperative. Kant clearly thought that these two Formulas are intertwined:

to say that in the use of means to any end I am to limit my maxim to the condition of its universal validity as a law for every subject is tantamount to saying that the subject of ends, that is, the rational being itself, must be made the basis of all maxims of actions, never merely as a means but as the supreme limiting condition in the use of all means, that is, always at the same time as an end. (G 4:438)

Kant was not obviously wrong to think that the different "representations" of the Categorical Imperative are different expressions of the same underlying principle (G 4:436). For one, the two versions of the Categorical Imperative we have considered are oriented toward the same underlying value. I have argued that one feature uniting the Formula of Humanity and the Formula of Universal Law is that they direct us to value rational agency, albeit in different ways: the Formula of Humanity asks us to respect rational agency, whereas the Formula of Universal Law asks us to manifest rational agency. Furthermore, we have seen how these formulas imply similar moral verdicts about various actions. And each formula can be used as the basis for deriving Kant's taxonomy of duties (perfect vs. imperfect, duties to oneself vs. duties to others, etc.). Hence, it seems at least plausible that the Formula of Humanity and the Formula of Universal Law are *practically equivalent*, i.e., that they generate the same conclusions concerning the moral permissibility and impermissibility of our actions.

Finally, these two formulas are linked insofar as they rest on a similar picture of how we morally justify our actions. As noted in Section 3.8, Kant held that moral requirements are rational requirements – that, in acting immorally, we violate a standard of rationality. More specifically, an immoral act rests on a maxim that an agent wills while willing that maxim's negation for others. The agent is therefore choosing irrationally because she is choosing inconsistently. But equally central to Kant's understanding of morality is that our actions must be justifiable *to rational agents*. Take a maxim that violates the Formula of Universal Law – Kant's 'false promising' maxim, say. In acting on this maxim, an individual is exempting herself from a principle she rationally wills for everyone else. The rationality of pursuing the end contained in the false promising maxim thus requires that her maxim be shielded from others' rational scrutiny – that their interaction not take place on rationally transparent terms, that is, that the rationale for her actions must be concealed from potential lenders in order for those actions to be rational from her point of view. The false promisor is therefore unconcerned with whether her choice can be justified *to* other rational agents. Moreover, the false promisor acts without fully engaging other agents' rationality. In Kant's terms, she does not engage with their humanity and does not represent it as a check or a constraint on her choices. Instead, their rational agency is either exploited or circumvented in the service of her own ends. That her maxim cannot be universalized and her false promise treats humanity merely as a means have a common source: her failure to take seriously the moral (and rational) demand to justify her choices to other rational agents.

Further Reading

Perhaps no topic within Kant's ethics has received more attention from philosophers than the Formula of Universal Law. Onora O'Neil's work has been very influential in guiding scholarly discussion of the universalization test. See Acting on Principle: An Essay on Kantian Ethics (Columbia, 1975; published under the name Onora Nell) and Constructions of Reason: Explorations of Kant's Practical Philosophy (Cambridge, 1989), especially the essay "Consistency in action." An equally influential discussion is Christine Korsgaard's "Kant's formula of universal law," *Pacific Philosophical Quarterly* 66 (1985): 24–47. There Korsgaard proposes three interpretations of the Formula of Universal Law: the Logical Contradiction Interpretation, the Teleological Contradiction Interpretation, and the Practical Contradiction Interpretation. The 'rational contradiction' interpretation I defended in this chapter is not identical to any of these, but most closely resembles the Practical Contradiction Interpretation. Richard Galvin provides an excellent overview of the debates surrounding these rival interpretations in "The universal law formulas," in T. Hill (ed.), Blackwell Guide to Kant's Ethics (Wiley-Blackwell, 2009). The ACE structure of maxims is well explained by Josh Glasgow, "Kant's principle of universal law," in M. Timmons (ed.), Conduct and Character, 5th edn. (Thomson Wadsworth, 2006). For a similar account of the structure of maxims, as well as some strategies for dealing with false negatives and various complicated maxims, see Richard McCarty, "False negatives of the Categorical Imperative," *Mind* 124 (2015): 177–200. Hill's "The hypothetical imperative," *Philosophical Review* 82 (1973): 429–450, is a good starting place for understanding the rational force of the hypothetical imperative and why Kant denied that the supreme principle of morality can be an instance of it. O'Neill's "Universal laws and ends in themselves," *The Monist* 72 (1989): 341–361, is a valuable discussion of the relationships between the Humanity and Universal Law Formulas.

4 Dignity

Chapters 2 and 3 addressed two of the ideas for which Kant's ethics is well known: that our actions must be based on consistently universalizable principles (the Formula of Universal Law) and that morality requires us to treat rational agency as an end in itself, not simply as a means (the Formula of Humanity). This chapter addresses a third notion that Kant's ethics has helped to make popular: dignity. Over the past century or so, talk of 'dignity' has become ubiquitous within academic and popular circles. Recently, however, a backlash has arisen against dignity as an ethical concept. The bioethicist Ruth Macklin has gone so far as to declare dignity a "useless" concept in ethics.[1] Because this is a book on Kant's ethics, I will not attempt to consider all the various ways in which 'dignity' is used in different ethical discourses. Indeed, I very much doubt that there is a single 'right way' to understand this notion and its implications. Our goals will be more modest: to understand what differentiates the notion of dignity Kant invokes, and, in particular, to determine how central dignity is to Kant's ethics. Do Kant's claims about dignity add anything significant to Kant's ethical theory, or could he have said everything significant about ethics he wanted to say without invoking dignity at all? In pursuing these questions, we set aside for the moment the immediate project of the Groundwork: identifying and establishing the Categorical Imperative as the supreme principle of morality in light of the five criteria put forth in Chapter 1. We return to that task in the next chapter.

4.1 Some Non-Kantian Conceptions of Dignity

'Dignity' is both extremely popular and extremely contested. Virtually everyone agrees that dignity is important and that a person's dignity should be respected. But there is hardly any consensus on what dignity is or what respect for dignity entails. Dignity is sometimes seen as a foundational – and perhaps *the* foundational – concept underlying human rights. The United Nations Universal Declaration on Human Rights, adopted in 1948, declared in its first

[1] "Dignity is a useless concept," *British Medical Journal* 327 (2003): 1419–1420.

sentence that "all human beings are born free and equal in dignity and rights." "Bioconservatives" opposed to the use of technology to enhance human nature often rest their opposition on the belief that enhancements pose a threat to human dignity. Dignity is frequently invoked by Christian thinkers in works opposing abortion and contraception. But the dignity of women is also invoked by those supporting access to abortion and contraception. The Catholic Church claims that its stance that homosexuality is aberrant respects human dignity, while gay rights groups (including one called Dignity USA) proclaim that such a stance denies the dignity of non-heterosexuals. The chief organization that advocates for assisted suicide in the United States calls itself Death with Dignity. Unsurprisingly, those opposed to assisted suicide believe that allowing the practice denies individuals their dignity. As a moral ideal, then, dignity has proven to be highly appealing, but also highly elastic. One might conclude from this state of affairs that dignity is a suspect moral concept. Nick Bostrom concludes that "the idea of dignity has hit upon a winning formula by combining into one package gravitas, a general feel-good quality, and a profound vagueness that enables all constituencies to declare their allegiance without thereby endorsing any particular course of action."[2]

Though Kant is perhaps the most important historical contributor to the notion of dignity, other non-Kantian conceptions of dignity co-exist with the Kantian notion. We can thus make headway on understanding Kantian dignity by distinguishing it from some rival conceptions. Sadly, the number of such conceptions is too large for us to address all of them. Thankfully, we can distill from these conceptions some main strands.

For the ancient Romans, dignity (*dignitas*) was an attribute that only certain persons, mostly highborn, could have. Dignity belonged only to those with a particular status, such as nobles, and in this respect dignity was an essentially social concept. Those with dignity were owed a particular deference by virtue of their high rank. The Roman conception of dignity reverberates in the ways in which we deem the conduct of important or noteworthy persons (sometimes called 'dignitaries'!) unbefitting or unbecoming. For a justice of the Supreme Court, to appear on the bench with a torn and dirty robe would be "undignified" – that is, unsuited for a person of her office or stature. Similarly, this is the sense of dignity Shakespeare invokes in the prologue to *Romeo and Juliet,* when he states that the Montagues and Capulets were "both alike in dignity."

For the Romans, though dignity was a property only of persons, it was not a universal property of persons. Later, in Roman Catholic thinking, dignity was made universal but *plural*. On this understanding of dignity, all humans possess

[2] "Dignity and enhancement," in Adam Schulman (ed.), *Human Dignity and Bioethics: Essays Commissioned by the President's Council on Bioethics* (President's Council on Bioethics, 2008), p. 2.

it, but not in the same manner or to the same degree. Michael Rosen summarizes the views of nineteenth-century Pope Leo XIII as follows:

> all members of society have dignity, but their dignity consists in the role that is appropriate to their station within a hierarchical social order, one in which some are "nobler than others." Instead of sharing in equal dignity, the orders of society should differ in "dignity, rights, and power."[3]

This Catholic conception of dignity ascribes dignity to all human beings, but not the same dignity to all such beings. The dignity of priests differs from the dignity of laypersons, the dignity of women differs from that of men, and so on. Dignity relates to one's value within a larger social order.

Catholicism thus ascribed dignity to all, while the Romans attributed it to only a few. Yet both the Roman and the Catholic understandings of dignity rest it on a person's place within a social order. We may therefore call these conceptions of dignity *status* conceptions.

A second line of thought construes dignity as a moral quality manifest in some individuals. On this conception, dignity is a kind of moral benchmark or ideal achieved only by some. One of Kant's most pointed critics, Friedrich Schiller, saw dignity as an exemplification of a "noble disposition of mind," a "mastery of instinct by moral force." For Schiller, the dignified person is able to do what is morally right despite having powerful natural desires to the contrary. Thus, dignity is most apparent, according to Schiller, when a person does her duty despite hardships that might tempt her to violate that duty. Schiller thus saw dignity as a form of heroic self-control in the service of morality.[4] Sydney Carton, in Dickens' *A Tale of Two Cities*, is an example of Schillerian dignity. Carton knows that the revolutionary Darnay has been wrongly condemned to die. Realizing his physical resemblance to Darnay, Carton tricks his way into the prison, drugs Darnay, and has him removed from the prison. Carton then goes to his death, under the ruse that he is Darnay.

Clearly, this sort of dignity will not be universal. Rather, only those with an especially noble character can be dignified in this way. In light of its link with morally admirable acts, we can call this conception the *virtue* conception of dignity.

A final strand of thought about dignity associates it with a person's bearing or demeanor. Someone with dignity, on this conception, radiates a kind of tranquility, incorruptibility, and independence. Dignity marks out those who show composure, even majesty, under strain or stress. Those who advocate for a right to assisted suicide or euthanasia often claim that these modes of dying enable us to die "with dignity," and it is this sense of dignity that they have in mind. Those

[3] *Dignity: Its History and Meaning* (Harvard, 2012), p. 49.

[4] *On Grace and Dignity* (1793), G. Gregory, trans. (Schiller Institute, 1992).

who, for example, suffer from a profoundly painful disease may lack dignity of this kind, as their bodies are tormented and they cry out in pain. When such pain dominates one's experience, we lose our ability to attend to anything else and so lose the composure or serenity that characterizes dignity.[5] Advocates of death with dignity also contend that it is undignified to live in a condition where one is overly dependent on others or lacking in control of one's own situation or person. To be reliant upon others for meeting one's basic needs is to suffer a fate that many people find degrading or insulting to their dignity. The fact that we do not generally worry that children, who are often dependent or lacking in control in just these ways, are undignified is an indication that independence, placidity, and control reside near the heart of dignity.[6] Because this final strand of dignity thus focuses on features of a person's demeanor or outward appearance, I propose to call this *aesthetic* dignity.

4.2 Kant's Account of Dignity

Kant's understanding of dignity (*Würde*) bears some relation to dignity as status, dignity as virtue, and aesthetic dignity. However, it diverges from these conceptions of dignity in fundamental ways. Regrettably, to fully grasp Kant's understanding of dignity, we will need to disentangle the claims he makes about dignity, which seem obscure and even contradictory.

There are two questions we must address here: The first is, what (according to Kant) has dignity, or, better yet, what things are the *bearers* of dignity? I will try to show that the best answer to this question is that *rational agency* or *rational nature* has dignity. The second is, what is dignity? Here the best answer is that dignity is a distinctive measure of value.[7]

Recall that for Kant, "humanity" designates our rational capacity to set ends and the means to those ends. On three occasions, Kant indicates that we human beings have dignity because of our humanity. He speaks of "the dignity of a rational being, who obeys no law other than that which he himself at the same time gives" (G 4:434). As we know, Kant understands action in terms of maxims, principles expressing a person's reasons for action, referring to both the chosen end and the action that serves as the chosen means to that end. In this regard, we obey principles that we give ourselves, and it is only because we are rational agents, agents with "humanity," that we can give ourselves principles

[5] David Velleman, "A right of self-termination?," *Ethics* 109 (1999): 617–619, defends this view about how pain can undermine dignity.

[6] See Jyl Gentzler, "What is a death with dignity?," *Journal of Medicine and Philosophy* 28 (2003): 466–469.

[7] Failure to distinguish between what the bearers of dignity are and what dignity is (or what moral imperatives dignity generates) complicates discussions of Kant's view of dignity. See, for instance, Oliver Sensen, "Kant's conception of human dignity," *Kant-Studien* 100 (2009): 309–331.

for action. It is our capacity for "lawgiving itself" that "must for that very reason have a dignity" (G 4:436. See also G 4:439). We thus have dignity because we are rational agents or because of our practically rational natures. "Autonomy," or our capacity to rationally choose, and act on the basis of, principles, "is therefore the ground of the dignity of human nature and of every rational nature" (G 4:436).

This interpretation appears to conflict with other statements Kant makes about the bearers of dignity. For he sometimes suggests that morality, or our fulfillment of our moral duties, has dignity. He speaks of the "sublimity and inner dignity" of moral commands (G 4:425) or of the "certain sublimity and *dignity* in the person who fulfills all his duties" (G 4:440). To confuse matters further, he also states that "morality, and humanity insofar as it is capable of morality, is that which alone has dignity" (G 4:435), suggesting that both morality *and* humanity (or rational agency) have dignity. Yet a careful reading of these passages shows that Kant did not think of dignity as a property of morally dutiful actions or of morality itself. Rather, he seems to have had in mind that dignity is most evident or on display when we act in accordance with our duty from morally admirable motives. When we think of duty, Kant says, we think of being subject to morality's requirements, but we also "represent a certain sublimity and *dignity* in the person who fulfills all his duties." Note that Kant does not say that morality or the fulfillment of our moral duties *has* dignity. Rather, in fulfilling one's duties, one's dignity is clearly represented. Again, for Kant, fulfilling our moral duties is a matter of acting on maxims, or rationally chosen principles, that satisfy the Categorical Imperative. In order for us to act on morally permissible maxims, we must have 'humanity' or rational agency. To act on a morally permissible maxim is to exercise one's humanity in morally permissible ways. So, in fulfilling our moral duties, we therefore manifest our humanity, which (I argued earlier) is what has dignity. This is especially true when a person has few inclinations or "subjective causes" that speak in favor of doing her moral duty while there are many such inclinations or "subjective causes" against it (G 4:425). Our humanity, and hence our dignity, are most in evidence when a person faces inclinations or desires that are contrary to moral duty and yet overcomes these inclinations and does her duty anyway. An excellent runner's fitness is not most in evidence at the beginning of a race, when running on flat terrain. Rather, her fitness becomes most apparent when she has strong temptations to quit – near the race's end, as she ascends a steep hill, etc. Similarly, if virtue is, as Kant claimed, "the moral strength of a *human being's* will in fulfilling his duty" (MM 6:405), then it will be most fully on display when a person's inclinations or desires tempt her to act contrary to duty. This observation underscores that we must not assimilate states of the person that provide *evidence* of her dignity with dignity itself. Other aspects of a person – her choices, actions, psychological states, and the like – can remind us of her dignity. But only her rational agency, strictly speaking, possesses dignity, and, to the extent it is correct to speak of a person's choices, etc., as 'dignified' or as 'having dignity,' this is only because rational agency is the *source* of these other manifestations of dignity.

On my view, Kant was thus somewhat careless when he remarked that "morality, and humanity insofar as it is capable of morality, is that which alone has dignity" (G 4: 435). At its root, humanity or rational agency alone has dignity. But read in light of the other passages where Kant connects dignity to morality or moral virtue, Kant's error here is understandable: humanity alone has dignity, but dignity is most prominently displayed in acts of moral virtue.

The bearer of Kantian dignity is our rational agency or our rational nature. That still leaves a key question unanswered: What is dignity? Kant indicates that dignity is a kind of value or worth, or a measure thereof:

> everything has either a *price* or a *dignity*. What has a price can be replaced by something as its *equivalent*; what on the other hand is raised above all price and therefore admits of no equivalent has dignity. . . . that which constitutes the condition under which alone something can be an end in itself has not merely a relative worth, that is, a price, but an inner worth, that is, *dignity*. (G 4:434–435)

Those things whose value is measured by their price are *fungible:* It is morally permissible to exchange or replace these entities, either for other entities of the same kind or for entities of a different type. Kant says that all those things that satisfy human needs or provide us pleasure belong in this category. This presumably includes all material goods and wealth, as well as skills and labor. We are morally permitted to trade these things for one another, as we do when we barter or sell our goods or labor for money. In contrast, because it has dignity, our rational agency is "raised above all price" and has "no equivalent." Kant seems to have in mind that rational agency is a unique good in that we are not morally permitted to attach a price to it and to trade it for things to which prices may be appropriately attached. Consider selling someone into slavery: Kant believed that selling someone into slavery violates our moral obligations. Why? By indefinitely limiting a person's freedom and their control over their lives, slavery severely restricts the scope of their rational agency. The slave merchant treats a rational agent, who because of her dignity is beyond price, as if she had a price. In appealing to this notion of dignity, Kant in effect argues that, in order to satisfy our needs or wants, we can exchange what has price for something else which has price, but we may not exchange what has price for what has dignity. As Kant puts it, what has dignity has an "unconditional" and "incomparable" worth (G 4:436), a worth not commensurate with the "relative worth" of all that has price.

Unsurprisingly, Kant's notion of dignity carries echoes of his Formula of Humanity: "that which constitutes the condition under which alone something can be an end in itself has not merely a relative worth, that is, a price, but an inner worth, that is, *dignity*." As we know from Chapter 2, the only thing Kant counts as an end in itself is our 'humanity' or rational agency. Again, humanity is the sole bearer of dignity. And by virtue of bearing dignity, it enjoys special status. That which has price are means to our ends, and means can be exchanged for other means. Markets work efficiently when people can trade the means at their disposal for the means at other people's disposal in transactions that are mutually beneficial, i.e., that result in people having means that better enable them to pursue their ends. But that which is an end in itself is not simply a means to be used to realize our ends. It belongs to another category or metric of value altogether, and is therefore morally ineligible for exchange.

In the next section, we will outline more precisely how this conception of dignity differs from those described in Section 4.1. Before doing so, one last observation: For Kant, dignity stands in a dynamic relationship to moral *humility*. When we compare ourselves to the "moral law" – that is, when we evaluate our maxims against the demands of the Categorical Imperative – we experience what Kant calls "true humility" (MM 6:436). To experience true humility is to experience a kind of pain. For the moral law "strikes down self-conceit" – that is, it shows us the error of being too satisfied with our own moral character, alerting us to the ways in which we are tempted to make exceptions to morality's demands for the sake of our own interests and inclinations. (We explained in Section 3.8 how Kant thought of exempting ourselves from moral demands whose authority we recognize is the chief source of immorality.) Morality thus 'humbles' us, less in the sense of shaming or degrading us, but more in the sense of reminding us of our moral fallibility and our all-too-human tendency to find ways to circumvent the categorical demands morality presents to us (C2 5:73–75, 5:78). But at the same time that our awareness of the moral law humbles us, it reminds us of our capacity to act as the moral law bids us. That reminder induces self-esteem, and an awareness of our own dignity: "from our capacity for internal lawgiving and from the (natural) human being's feeling himself compelled to revere the (moral) human being within his own person, at the same time there comes an *exaltation* of the highest self-esteem, the feeling of his own inner worth, in terms of which he is above any price and possesses an inalienable dignity" (MM 6:436). Dignity (or, more accurately, the *feeling* of dignity) and humility thus serve as psychological counterparts, disclosing to us our potential, both positive and negative, as moral agents.[8]

[8] Jeanine Grenberg, *Kant and the Ethics of Humility* (Cambridge, 2005), offers a reconstruction of Kant's ethics focused around humility.

4.3 Kantian Dignity Versus Its Rivals

How, then, does the Kantian conception of dignity distinguish itself from its rivals? On what we called the status conception of dignity, dignity rests it on a person's place within a social order. Kantian dignity differs from the status conception in two ways. First, Kant asserts that all persons have dignity simply because they are rational agents. Kantian dignity is thus *universal*, as much a property of the poor, lowborn, or marginalized as of powerful elites. Secondly, Kantian dignity is *unitary*. There is only one kind of dignity: the kind that confers a distinctive value on all and only agents who choose their ends and the principles on which they act. There is not masculine dignity or feminine dignity, according to Kant's conception. Nor do generals have one kind of dignity, grunts another. For Kant, whatever distinctions there are within social hierarchy, these distinctions are not distinctions that track variations in individuals' dignity.

In a sense, Kant thought that dignity is a status. But it is a status that topples, rather than reinforces, social hierarchies. Kant's usage of dignity underscores a feature of his ethics that is often neglected: its deeply egalitarian character. In the Kantian mind, there are no inherent differences among human beings as far as moral status goes. It is sometime said that dignity carries a connotation of elevation or majesty – that we are to "look up to" what has dignity. Kant agrees – but we are to look up to all rational beings, treating them as ends in themselves.

On the virtue conception of dignity, dignity is a kind of moral merit or esteem based on a person's character and actions. As we saw in Section 4.2, Kant agrees with Schiller (and other advocates of this conception) that our dignity is most apparent to us, and to others, through our morally virtuous actions. For when we act in morally virtuous ways, we are reminded of the freedom afforded by our humanity, a freedom to embrace or to spurn morality's demands. But Kantian dignity does not confer upon us a value that turns on our moral choices. The morally virtuous person has dignity, but so too, according to Kant, do the worst of criminals. Again, because dignity is unitary, individuals do not have more or less of it. For dignity is an attribute we have just insofar as we are rational agents who choose our ends and maxims. We do not acquire dignity through our praiseworthy acts, nor do we suffer a loss of dignity through our blameworthy acts. Our dignity, Kant says, is "inalienable" (MM 6:436). Dignity is thus not a potential realized through our choices or our environment. Dignity is an unwavering moral constant, a status we need not seek out nor one we can renounce or fritter away.

Lastly, the aesthetic conception of dignity associates it with observable features of a person's demeanor, a serene self-control or self-mastery. Kant would likely agree that in manifesting such characteristics, a person gives evidence of her dignity. Indeed, when he enumerates the duties we owe to ourselves by virtue of having dignity, he remarks that "complaining and whining, even crying out in bodily pain, is unworthy of you" (MM 6:436). However, Kant would clearly reject the aesthetic conception of dignity too. Again, the aesthetic conception makes dignity a quantitative matter, possessed to a greater or lesser degree by different individuals. But for Kant, all rational agents possess dignity to the same degree. Furthermore, for Kant, *only* rational agents possess the special value associated with dignity, whereas the aesthetic conception seems to allow that non-rational entities, such as objects in nature, could have it. Finally, Kant would reject this conception of dignity for making it a phenomenal or observable fact about individuals. As Kant puts it several times, because dignity is borne by our rational natures, it is an "inner" property of us, a property that cannot be located in or on our bodies.

4.4 Dignity and the Duty of Respect

As we noted in Section 2.7, Kant believed that the proper attitude toward humanity is that of respect. Given that humanity is also the basis of dignity, it is unsurprising that for Kant respect is also the attitude that dignity should elicit from us:

> Every human being has a legitimate claim to respect from his fellow human beings and is *in turn* bound to respect every other. Humanity itself is a dignity; for a human being cannot be used merely as a means by any human being (either by others or even by himself) but must always be used as the same time as an end. It is just in this that his dignity (personality) consists, by which he raises himself above all other beings in the world that are not human beings and yet can be used, and so overall *things*. (MM 6:462)

By associating dignity with respect, Kant thus clarifies what respecting humanity amounts to.

First, in rejecting the virtue conception of dignity, Kant indicates that the sort of respect humanity demands from us is what Stephen Darwall has called "recognition respect."[9] To give something or someone recognition respect is to give some fact about it consideration in our choices or actions. Recognition respect is not earned, nor does it vary in degree among those things entitled to it. More specifically, those things entitled to recognition respect constrain how we may treat them. Darwall identifies several possible candidates for those things entitled to recognition respect, including the law, institutions, and nature. However, Kant held that only one thing is entitled to recognition respect – namely, humanity or rational agency. His Formula of Humanity is a principle

[9] Darwall, "Two kinds of respect."

requiring us to respect rational agency and to honor a fundamental constraint in how we treat it: to always treat rational agency as an end in itself and never merely as a means. Our humanity, and hence our dignity, 'raises' us 'above' mere things whose value consists in their price. Kant makes this link between respect, dignity, and recognition explicit: "The *respect* that I have for others or that another can require from me . . . is therefore recognition of a *dignity* in other human beings, that is, of a worth that has no price, no equivalent for which the object evaluated could be exchanged" (MM 6:462).

The respect that we owe to those beings with dignity thus differs from what Darwall calls "appraisal respect." Appraisal respect is given to someone or something on the basis of their earned merits or excellences. Two rivals might respect one another in this regard. But this notion of respect is the kind of respect that we would owe according to the virtue conception of dignity. For that conception of dignity makes it dependent on a person's actions, achievements, or merits, whereas Kantian dignity does not depend on any of these.

That Kantian dignity rests on our rational agency sometimes leads to confusion about what would be required by the Kantian demand that we respect dignity. Consider this example, offered by Michael Rosen:

> One way of dealing with people that indisputably treats them merely as a means is treating them purely as physical objects. Suppose that it is a cold and windy day and a group of people are standing together in a line, waiting for a bus. You go and stand behind them so that they act as a windbreak for you. Clearly you are using them as a means and nothing else – they are advancing your interests and you are not acknowledging them as persons . . . Nevertheless, although your using the bus queue as a windbreak is to use the people in it as a means only, it does not seem that you are doing anything morally objectionable.[10]

Rosen believes this example is problematic for the Kantian claim that to treat someone with dignity is to treat them as ends, not merely as means: You would be treating your fellow bus riders merely as means, but this does not seem at odds with their dignity, nor does it seem morally objectionable.

What Rosen overlooks is that the Formula of Humanity requires that we not treat rational agency merely as a means, not that we not treat *persons* merely as means. While it is true that you would be treating the other bus riders as means (or, perhaps more accurately, using their bodies as means), you do not thereby treat their rational agency merely as means. Indeed, in standing behind them, you do not 'use' their rational agency at all. It is not morally imperative in this case to (for example) seek out their consent or cooperation. Note that this might not be the case under slightly modified circumstances. If your fellow bus riders are huddled together because they are co-religionists engaged in a prayer ritual, your standing directly behind them might interfere

[10] Rosen, *Dignity: Its History and Meaning*, p. 82.

with their shared ends (you may be a distraction or your presence may detract from the desired solemnity of their ritual). Again, the Formula of Humanity dictates how we are to interact with others insofar as we are rational agents, and what it requires (or forbids) cannot be ascertained merely by considering one's own behavior. What matters is how that behavior engages with other rational agents and their ends. This illustrates that an important aspect of abiding by the Formula of Humanity is understanding when our behavior does or does not impinge on others' rational agency and hence when we must consciously engage with them as rational agents in order to treat them as ends in themselves. (That part of being a conscientious moral agent is being aware of when our behavior impinges on others' rational agency is a claim we will return to when we address the 'false negatives' objection to Kant's Formula of Universal Law in Section 6.3.)

That Kant rejects aesthetic dignity also sheds light on another example discussed by Rosen.[11] In 1987, a German satirical magazine was convicted of defaming a prominent German politician with an illustration of him as a copulating pig. The courts ruled that the illustration 'devalued' the politician and deprived him of his human dignity. Here we might worry that being depicted in an unflattering, even insulting, light is part of the price political leaders pay for having power in a democratic society. Should we prohibit satirical political expression because it 'deprives' people of their dignity? Kant would say no, precisely because it is not possible for us to be deprived of our dignity through others' representations of us. Arguably, the German politician is treated merely as a means: He is depicted as a pig in order to advance the artist's ends. These may be admirable (promoting worthwhile political reform) or contemptible (getting a cheap laugh). But this depiction, if it is interpreted in a literal way as suggesting that he is not a rational agent but an animal unable to control his carnal impulses, cannot be at odds with his having humanity or dignity. The satirical depiction could be seen as a kind of defamation at odds with Kant's Formula of Humanity. We could be deprived of our dignity only if we could be deprived of the rational agency on which our dignity depends, and, short of death,[12] there appears to be no way to rob us of our capacity to set our own ends and identify the best means for the realization of those ends. The only way the German politician could be deprived of his dignity by the insulting caricature is if dignity meant something other than what Kant meant: aesthetic dignity, the kind of dignity associated with being represented as composed and noble.

[11] Rosen, Dignity: Its History and Meaning, pp. 75–76.

[12] Though I argue elsewhere that some suicidal persons have degraded or compromised capacities for practical reason. See "Suicide intervention and non-ideal Kantian theory," *Journal of Applied Philosophy* 19 (2002): 245–259, and "A Kantian defense of prudential suicide," *Journal of Moral Philosophy* 7 (2010): 489–515.

These conclusions underscore that, in a strict Kantian sense, it is impossible for someone to behave in a way that is "undignified." For if by "undignified," one means literally *without dignity*, Kant would deny that one can lose one's dignity through one's conduct. Dignity is, after all, "inalienable." Similarly, it is not possible, in a strict Kantian sense, for us to fail to treat someone "with dignity." For if treating "with dignity" amounts to *conferring* dignity on a person, then this is confused from a Kantian perspective. Dignity is not something we give to others. Even more fundamentally, dignity is *not a property of actions* on a Kantian view. Dignity is a property of all and only those entities that have humanity, and while we can fail to respect a person's dignity, this does not undercut their dignity or make them undignified. For Kantians, dignity is a freestanding source of a moral constraint, not something to be exemplified, promoted, or realized. While we may (or may not) show respect for a person's dignity, and a person may (or may not) show respect for her own dignity (MM 6:436), dignity itself is not something shown or expressed. To use Rosen's terms, Kantian dignity is something we respect by *observing* it.[13]

4.5 Conclusion

Let us return to the question that motivated our investigation of Kantian dignity: Do Kant's claims about dignity add anything significant to his ethical theory, or should we conclude, following Schopenhauer, that Kant's conception of dignity, like those conceptions that followed it, is a meaningless "shibboleth" with no "real basis" in morals?[14]

In one respect, I am sympathetic to the thought that dignity is a notion that Kant could have done without. As we observed in Section 4.1, dignity is a popular, but vague, notion. Kant's ethics is sometimes misunderstood because his notion of dignity is confused with other notions of dignity. Perhaps Kant could have avoided being misunderstood by not using the notion of dignity. That said, I have tried to show that Kant's own notion of dignity is precise, and while it has some similarities to other common notions of dignity, it is distinguished from them in linking dignity to an inalienable, unearned, unchanging property of human selves: their humanity or rational agency.

But perhaps Kant should have jettisoned dignity because it does not seem to add much to the underlying logic of his ethics. As we noted in Section 4.4, Kant closely associates dignity with the Formula of Humanity, to the extent that he effectively equates treating rational agency as an end in itself with respecting someone's dignity. There does not seem to be, therefore, a separate category of moral wrong consisting in failing to respect someone's dignity. Rather, failing

[13] Rosen, Dignity: Its History and Meaning, pp. 57–58.
[14] Arthur Schopenhauer, *On the Basis of Morality* (Hackett, 1965).

to respect someone's dignity and treating their rational agency merely as a means rather than as an end in itself are simply alternative descriptions of the property that makes wrong acts wrong on a Kantian view. Thus, to whatever extent Kant succeeds in showing that the Formula of Humanity is one expression of the supreme principle of morality, and to whatever extent he succeeds in showing that his taxonomy of duties rests on the Formula of Humanity, he would not be any more or less successful in these regards had he deployed the notion of dignity instead of humanity in this principle.

Still, even if dignity does not add significant substance to Kant's ethics, I maintain that Kant's use of the notion of dignity is *rhetorically* useful, in two key respects.

First, by invoking the contrast between price and dignity, Kant helps to underscore his credentials as a non-consequentialist ethical theorist. As we noted in Chapters 2 and 3, both of the main versions of Kant's Categorical Imperative – the Formula of Humanity and the Formula of Universal Law – are non-consequentialist principles because they sometimes require us to perform an action despite the fact that the action is not the one which has the best consequences when compared to alternative courses of action. The Categorical Imperative thus differs from fundamental moral principles such as the principle of utility. And in drawing the contrast between price and dignity, Kant helps us to see how the Categorical Imperative is not a principle requiring us to promote or maximize some good. Rather, 'priceable' goods and the good of rational nature (which alone has dignity) are incommensurable. On Kant's view, we may permissibly trade priceable goods for other priceable goods, but we may not simply give ourselves away for goods that have price (MM 6:462). As we saw, Kantianism and utilitarianism are rival value monisms: For Kant, rational agency alone has intrinsic moral significance, whereas for utilitarians, happiness or well-being alone has intrinsic moral significance. But Kant's ethics also sees rational agency as subject to a different scale of evaluation: For utilitarians, trading a smaller quantity of well-being for a greater quantity of well-being is not only rational, it is morally obligatory. In contrast, for Kant, our dignity is not to be sacrificed for what has price, even including happiness. Utilitarianism's monism is thus thoroughgoing: On this view, there is a single intrinsic value and all quantities of this value are to be measured morally on a single scale, whereas for Kant, there is a single intrinsic value, and it is not be exchanged for goods on another moral scale.

Second, by invoking dignity, Kant emphasizes the egalitarian and *comparative* aspects of his ethical theory. As we noted in Section 4.3, Kant held that all individuals who are rational agents have dignity and have it to the same degree. Dignity is not the special province of the skilled, the virtuous, or the well born. Hence, whatever else might distinguish human agents, they are not distinguishable in terms of differences in dignity. Kant is therefore especially sensitive to behaviors that involve one individual appearing to subjugate herself to another or being asked to subjugate herself to another. The duty to treat ourselves with dignity can be recognized, according to Kant, in examples such as these:

> Be no man's lackey. – Do not let others tread with impunity on your rights. – . . . do not be a parasite or a flatterer . . . or a beggar. – . . . Kneeling down or prostrating oneself on the ground . . . is contrary to the dignity of humanity; for you then humble yourself, not before an *ideal* represented to you by your own reason, but before an *idol* of your own making. (MM 6:436–437)

In Kant's mind, such conduct is contrary to our dignity because it amounts to making ourselves appear servile to others. In a moral community where all have dignity of the same kind and in the same measure, gestures such as prostrating oneself before another or begging imply a hierarchy between individuals that Kant finds odious. Kant was acutely aware of the ways in which such social customs reinforce comparative judgments that some human beings are better or more worthy of respect than others. To treat ourselves in these ways, or to demand that others treat themselves in these ways, shows contempt (MM 6:463). The admonition to treat rational agency as an end in itself is what we might call a non-comparative demand, a demand that we treat someone in accordance with their inherent status or nature. The admonition to respect their dignity is a comparative demand, a demand that we not treat some as if they have an inherent status or nature that others lack. Morality demands not only that we respect each other's dignity; it also demands that we respect dignity equally, making possible an "aristocracy of all."[15]

The enlightened individual, Kant thought, not only deploys her own reason and thinks for herself. She also insists that her own inherent worth, and the worth of all other rational agents, be respected on the same grounds. The mutual recognition of dignity is thus the lynchpin of a community of moral equals.

Further Reading

Michael Rosen's Dignity: Its History and Meaning (Harvard, 2012) offers an excellent historical overview of how various religious and ethical traditions have come to shape how we understand the notion of dignity. Riekeder Graaf and Johannes Jmdelden, "Clarifying appeals to dignity in medical ethics from an historical perspective," *Bioethics* 23 (2009): 151–160, is similarly useful. Aurel Kolnai, "Dignity," *Philosophy* 51 (1976): 251–271, is one of the first systematic philosophical attempts to make sense of dignity. Thomas Hill is

[15] Rawls, Lectures on the History of Moral Philosophy, p. 306.

among the Kantian philosophers who have investigated Kant's conception of dignity most thoroughly. See in particular his "Humanity as an end in itself," *Ethics* 91 (1980): 84–99. Stephen Darwall shows how dignity functions as an interpersonal or social moral ideal in "Why Kant needs the second-person standpoint," in T. Hill (ed.), Blackwell Guide to Kant's Ethics (Wiley-Blackwell, 2009), pp. 138–158. Oliver Sensen, Kant on Human Dignity (de Gruyter, 2011) is a comprehensive account of Kant on dignity that reaches different interpretive conclusions than I have in this chapter. Jyl Gentzler, "What is a death with dignity?," *Journal of Medicine and Philosophy* 28 (2003): 461–487, investigates the different notions of dignity at play in end-of-life ethics debates.

5 Freedom, Reason, and the Possibility of the Categorical Imperative

Chapters 1 through 3 sought to describe the five criteria Kant believed the supreme principle of morality must satisfy and to indicate how his own Categorical Imperative, expressed either as the Formula of Universal Law of the Formula of Humanity, satisfies these self-imposed criteria. Our emphasis thus fell on what Kant called the 'analytical' task of ethical theory – that is, on outlining the *content* of morality: the supreme principle of morality, the various moral duties, how Kant recommends we reason about ethical questions, etc. We primarily relied on the first two sections of Kant's Groundwork to complete this task, with texts such as the Metaphysics of Morals entering the scene principally to fill in the details in Kant's taxonomy of duties.

However, we were only in a position to provide a tentative defense of the Categorical Imperative in relation to Kant's fifth criterion, that the supreme principle of morality must *be a principle conformity to which requires only that we are practically rational beings*. Both Kant and many of his critics have recognized that criterion [5] raises special challenges for his attempt to demonstrate that the Categorical Imperative is morality's supreme principle. Kant lays out these challenges as he transitions from section II of the Groundwork to section III. The first two sections of that work, Kant states, sought to outline "the generally conceived concept of morality," the upshot of which is that the Categorical Imperative is the supreme principle of morality (G 4:444–445). Kant is confident that he has identified morality's supreme principle, so that "whoever holds morality to be something and not a chimerical idea without any truth must admit the principle of morality brought forward" (G 4:445). But for all this, Kant worries that morality might yet turn out to be a "phantom." Showing that morality is not a phantom, Kant says, requires a "synthetic" investigation of our rational powers, a task to be addressed in section III.

Precisely what concerns Kant here is far from obvious. Here is what lies behind Kant's anxiety: Recall Kant's remark that the aim of the Groundwork is "the search for and establishment of the *supreme principle of morality*" (G 4:392). Suppose that sections I and II of the Groundwork were a success.

If so, then Kant succeeded in arguing that the Categorical Imperative satisfies the first four of his self-imposed criteria:

The supreme principle of morality must

[1] provide plausible explanations of moral obligations we already recognize,

[2] be an imperative that it is rationally necessary for us to adopt, that is, a categorical imperative,

[3] be whatever principle governs the choices of the morally good will, and

[4] be a non-consequentialist principle, i.e., it must not make the rightness or wrongness of actions depend on the value of actions' consequences.

Kant's success on this score entails that his "search for" morality's supreme principle is complete: He found that principle in the Categorical Imperative. Nonetheless, Kant himself harbors doubts that he has 'established' the Categorical Imperative as the supreme principle of morality. There is, in Kant's mind, a gap between *articulating* morality's supreme principle and accounting for its *authority* over us:

> [Kant] thinks that we can say what morality demands of us but still ask whether it is reasonable for us to accept its requirements. Thus, he believes that further questions about the authority of the moral law remain after we have a more explicit picture of what it contains.[1]

Assuming that the Categorical Imperative is morality's supreme principle, why should we suppose that we ought to try to act as the Categorical Imperative bids us act? Kant seemed to recognize that a full vindication of his ethics requires answering this latter question. It is not enough to show what morality *would* require of us *if* it applied to us. Kant must also show that morality in fact *does* apply to us.

You may worry in particular about one challenge Kant faces in bridging the gap between morality's content and its authority, a challenge arising from criterion [5]. The possibility of conforming our maxims to the Categorical Imperative seems to require that certain psychological or metaphysical truths hold true of us. Recall that the Categorical Imperative asks us both to respect humanity as an end in itself and to act only on maxims that can be consistently willed as universal laws. The supreme principle of morality thus does not derive its rational authority from our inclinations or happiness. (If it did, this principle would generate a hypothetical rather than a categorical imperative, as well as being a consequentialist principle to boot.) The possibility of acting on morality's supreme principle thus requires that our choices and actions are not

[1] Andrews Reath, "Value and law in Kant's moral theory," *Ethics* 114 (2003): 136.

simply determined by our strongest inclinations or desires. But what if that is not the case – what if we, like other parts of nature, are subject to laws of nature, and in particular, that our choices and actions are determined by our inclinations or desires? What if the extant facts about us as individuals – the biological facts about our brains and bodies and the biographical facts about our upbringings and social environment – generate desires or inclinations that inevitably and invariably determine our ends? That, from Kant's point of view, would be a catastrophe for morality. We would have a clear understanding of what morality is, but every reason to doubt that moral dutifulness or virtue is a state toward which it is possible for us to aspire. Morality would turn out to be a "phantom," our belief that we are subject to moral duty an "empty delusion and a chimerical concept" (G 4:402). As Kant puts it later in section III, a full vindication of his ethics therefore requires some reason to believe that the Categorical Imperative is "possible" – that is, not simply that it expresses what morality would require of us if it applied to us, but that it actually does apply to us (G 4:453).

Showing how the Categorical Imperative is possible is therefore a crucial task for Kant's ethics as a whole. If Kant cannot give persuasive reasons in defense of the possibility of the Categorical Imperative, then his accomplishments as an ethical theorist will have been purely *theoretical*. He will have demonstrated to us what morality consists in – what its underlying principle is, how its fundamental ideas are interrelated, how it 'hangs together' in the broadest sense. But he will have fallen short of illustrating that morality deserves to be treated with the seriousness or authoritativeness with which morally conscientious people treat it. Hence, absent compelling reasons for believing that the Categorical Imperative is (in Kant's vernacular) "possible," morality turns out to be like a language whose grammar we can codify but that we cannot really speak.

The principal objective of this chapter is therefore to elaborate and assess Kant's efforts to justify the 'possibility' of the Categorical Imperative. It will be a departure from previous chapters in several ways. First, making sense of Kant's arguments for the possibility of the Categorical Imperative requires that we engage more deeply with Kant's moral psychology and his metaphysics, two areas of his philosophy that we have heretofore mostly avoided because of their notorious obscurity. It requires in particular delving into Kant's views regarding human freedom. As a result, this chapter is likely to be the most dense and difficult in this book. To fully grasp the issues at hand, readers would benefit from familiarity with Kant's major works in metaphysics, especially his Critique of Pure Reason. However, I will endeavor to lay out the challenges that the possibility of the Categorical Imperative presents to Kant, as well as how he tries to meet those challenges, in ways that presuppose minimal knowledge of Kant's views in metaphysics. Second, we will be consulting texts to which we have made only passing reference so far. Kant appears to provides a different answer to the question of how the Categorical Imperative is possible in the Groundwork than he provides in his Critique of Practical Reason.

We will begin by outlining a claim on which Kant's approaches to this task depends. We then turn to the different strategies Kant deploys in undertaking this task. The first, found primarily in the Groundwork, relies on a thesis about freedom as a presupposition of deliberation and action. The second, found primarily in the Critique of Practical Reason, relies on what Kant called "the fact of reason" – namely, our awareness of being subject to the Categorical Imperative. The first strategy, I argue, addresses the task in question directly, but requires the acceptance of controversial claims from Kant's metaphysics. The second is obscure and is unlikely to address the task in ways that satisfy Kant or his critics. I conclude by proposing that Kant's best strategy for vindicating the possibility of the Categorical Imperative is to lower the bar for its vindication by showing that our freedom can be defended but not explained.

5.1 The Reciprocity Thesis

To understand Kant's attempt to demonstrate the possibility of the Categorical Imperative, we will start in the middle, with the crucial thesis that animates Kant's effort to vindicate morality's authority over us.

Near the beginning of Groundwork section III, Kant asserts that "a free will and a will under moral law are one the same" (G 4:447). Kant expresses a similar claim in his Critique of Practical Reason when he states that "freedom and unconditional practical law reciprocally imply each other" (C2 5:29). These are the clearest statements of what is often called Kant's *Reciprocity Thesis*:

> A person is subject to the moral law (i.e., to the Categorical Imperative) if and only if that person's will is free.

As we shall see, proving the Reciprocity Thesis will not by itself demonstrate the possibility of the Categorical Imperative. But it is a key premise in Kant's demonstration, so some analysis of the Reciprocity Thesis, as well as an elaboration of how Kant defends it, are essential.

The Reciprocity Thesis claims that all and only those persons who are subject to the moral law are free, and vice versa. Before turning to Kant's defense of the Reciprocity Thesis, we need to clarify its vocabulary, and, in particular, to clarify what Kant means here by a person's will being free. The opening paragraphs of section III of the Groundwork are a good place to start: "*Will*," Kant declares, "is a kind of causality of living beings insofar as they are as rational, and *freedom* would be that property of such causality that it can be efficient independently of the alien causes *determining* it." (G 4:446) We touched upon the notion of a good will in Section 1.6, but said little there to fill in Kant's understanding of the will.[2] Beings like us have wills, which means that we possess a kind of causal power. We are not simply inert, passive entities, affected by the world but not affecting it in any way. We are instead beings that can act and bring about change in the world. Recall that Kant understood action to have a means–ends structure. Our acts are the means by which we seek to cause the world to conform with our chosen ends.

But what does saying that this causal power is *free* amount to? Kant proceeds to distinguish between two senses in which our wills might be free. The notion of freedom just described – being "efficient independently of the alien causes determining it" – Kant dubs "negative." For our wills to be negatively free would mean that our choices and actions can be "efficient," i.e., possess causal efficacy. Unfortunately, Kant is not explicit in the Groundwork about what these "alien causes" are which, if they determined our choices, would entail that we are not 'negatively' free. The will's causal power does not, Kant says, operate in accordance with "natural laws" or "natural necessity." Furthermore, he explains elsewhere that negative freedom is "independence" from our choices being determined by a "desired object" (C2 5:33) or by "sensible impulses" (MM 6:213). Hence, to be negatively free would mean that we are not determined in our choices and actions by "natural necessity," by the inclinations and desires we have thanks to the fact that we are embodied beings, parts of the natural world subject to laws that give rise to our desires and inclinations. This sense of freedom is 'negative' in that if our wills possess it, then there is something that does *not* determine our wills and its choices: our inclinations and desires.

Yet, to deny that a certain sort of fact causally determines our choices does not tell us what *does* determine our choices. Crucially for Kant, the freedom that matters for morality is not purely negative, not simply a freedom *from* our inclinations or desires. Rather, there is a deeper form of freedom possible for wills such as ours. As Kant understood causation, it always takes place in accordance with 'laws.' Anytime a given cause produces a given effect, there is some law – some overarching principle – that explains why the cause produced the given effect. Our wills have causal power. Hence, Kant argues, there must be some law that accounts for our wills having causal power. A "lawless" will would, Kant says, be an absurdity, so there must be a law or laws "of a special kind" to govern the choices of a rational will (G 4:446).

[2] An additional complication here is that Kant uses two different terms, each of which are typically translated as 'will.' The first, *Willkür*, is our capacity to choose among alternatives. The second, *Wille*, is our ability to identify and set ends. Most of what I say in this chapter about 'will' concerns the former.

The question at hand is what law accounts for the causal power of our wills, as Kant says, (a) "insofar as they are rational," and (b) given that this law is not that our choices are determined by our inclinations or desires. The only possibility, Kant surmises, is that this law is found in the will itself – that the will, by virtue of being rational, has the property of "autonomy," of "being a law to itself" (G 4:447, C2 5:33). To be positively free, then, is to act on a principle grounded in the will's own distinctive rationality. Positive freedom is the "ability of pure reason to be of itself practical" (C2 6:214) – that is, to be guided in its choices by a law of its own devising. Our wills, being rational, are distinctive because not only can we conform our choices to principles or laws, but we can act from an awareness or "representation" of a principle or law (G 4:412, 4:427). We are positively free to the extent that (a) we act on the basis of reasons and maxims we recognize as authoritative for ourselves, and (b) we can subject these reasons and maxims to the will's own principle, namely, the Categorical Imperative ("to act on no other maxim than that which can also have as object itself as a universal law," G 4:447). For Kant, the freedom needed for us to be moral agents – for the Categorical Imperative to be 'possible' in Kant's sense – is therefore not a freedom based on the absence of constraint. It is not a negative freedom to do what we wish. It is instead a positive freedom based on our capacity to choose and act in accordance with rational principles that function as 'laws' to us. And if we are positively free and autonomous in this sense, we are subject to the rational demands expressed in the Categorical Imperative. Freedom for Kant is thus best understood as a kind of *self-determination* – as our capacity to exercise our rational agency to guide our own choices and actions.

An important implication of the Reciprocity Thesis is that anytime a person acts on a morally impermissible maxim, that act is free in one sense but unfree in another. Let us focus on an example to elaborate this claim. (The example is adapted from C2 5:156.)

Luis and Donald have been friends for many years – clear back to their high school days, when both were actors in the school theatrical productions. Donald often invites Luis for daylong fishing excursions. These excursions typically end with dinner at an expensive restaurant overlooking the pier. But now their friendship faces an unanticipated obstacle: Luis learns that Donald has been charged with embezzling money from his employer. Worse still, it turns out that Luis will be asked to testify at Donald's upcoming trial. Part of the prosecution's circumstantial evidence is likely to be Donald's possessing large amounts of cash, and unfortunately, Luis has witnessed Donald displaying bulky wads of cash: renting a fishing boat, purchasing equipment, buying rare wines to accompany their dinners. Luis doesn't know if Donald is guilty – but he does know that if he testifies truthfully about Donald's spending habits, Donald is more likely to be convicted of the charges. Luis enjoys Donald's company and knows he would miss their fishing trips. It also pains him to imagine Donald incarcerated for months or years on end – bored, terrified, or resentful. When the day of Donald's trial arrives, Luis is called to the witness stand. Under prosecution questioning, Luis denies that he ever saw Donald make large cash purchases.

Luis acted wrongly in lying about Donald's spending habits, a conclusion Kant would almost certainly agree with. His maxim, something akin to *I will lie under oath about a friend's actions to protect him from punishment*, cannot be consistently universalized, as Kant's Formula of Universal Law requires. In order to achieve his end – protecting Donald from punishment – his maxim must be one others do not share with him. For his lie will only be effective in achieving his end if others suppose that witnesses under oath do not lie to protect their friends.

But, more importantly for our purposes, there is an important sense in which Luis acted *freely* when he lied – though he would also have acted no less freely had he told the truth. First, in lying to protect his friend, Luis presumably acted on his strongest inclination or desire. Not only would he be happier if Donald were to avoid punishment, Donald would be happier as well. Luis thus shows sympathy for Donald's predicament. But it was not inevitable, according to Kant, that Luis lie in order to advance his strongest inclination or desire. Luis' choice and action were not *determined* by his strongest inclination or desire. Rather, as Kant sees it, Luis freely *incorporated* into his maxim his desire to save Donald from punishment. And had he told the truth, he would have freely opted not to act on this desire but instead to act from respect for morality and for other rational agents who rely on the truthfulness of his testimony in order to decide Donald's guilt or innocence.[3] Either way, his inclinations or desires do not necessitate how he acts. Luis' lie thus illustrates how we rational agents are negatively free. However, Luis' maxim does not express or exhibit his positive freedom: He does not in fact act on the basis of the Categorical Imperative, and so the rule that guides his action (i.e., his maxim) does not reflect the rational will's own law. We might say, then, that Luis' negative freedom made it possible for him to act as he did, whereas his failure to exercise his capacity for positive freedom made it the case that his act was morally impermissible. Had Luis chosen not to lie, then his act would be indicative of both negative *and* positive freedom.

If it seems puzzling how an action can be both free and unfree, or how an action can be made unfree by virtue of its maxim being morally impermissible, we should recall a similar parallel in Kant's understanding of practical rationality. As we noted in Chapter 3, all our voluntary actions rest on our maxims, which express our reasons for action. In this respect, all our actions are rational – that is, they reflect the reasons we take to justify our acting as we do. But only some of our maxims are morally permissible – that is, only some

[3] Henry Allison, *Kant's Theory of Freedom* (Cambridge, 1990).

maxims are rationally consistent once universalized. A morally impermissible maxim is thus rational in the first sense but irrational in the second. In the former sense, rationality is a *condition* of action. In the latter sense, rationality can be an *achievement* of action. Jennifer Uleman elaborates the parallel with free action succinctly:

> Just as there is for Kant a sense of rationality according to which rationality pervades all action *and* a sense of rationality according to which rationality is something to achieve ... so there is a sense of freedom according to which freedom pervades all choice and all action, *and* a sense of freedom according to which freedom is something to achieve ... Just as determination by pure reason is the pinnacle of 'achievable' (non-inevitable) rationality, so complete freedom, or determination only on internal grounds, would be the pinnacle of 'achievable' (non-inevitable) freedom.[4]

We are, for Kant, inevitably negatively free, our choices being "underdetermined by the grounds or reasons" presented to the will by our inclinations or desires. But we only sometimes exhibit or express our positive freedom – namely, when our choice of maxims is determined by the fundamental law of our own reason.

Note that Kant has not yet *argued* that we are free in either sense. But his analysis of the negative and positive freedom necessitates a modification to our earlier statement of the Reciprocity Thesis:

> A person is subject to the moral law (i.e., to the Categorical Imperative) if and only if that person's will is *positively* free (or 'autonomous.')

With that modification in place, we can see that we have already encountered Kant's reasons for accepting the Reciprocity Thesis. On the one hand, our being positively free means that we are 'laws' to ourselves and are rationally required to act only on maxims that satisfy this moral law, the Categorical Imperative. Let us call this claim [F]:

> [F] If a person's will is positively free, then that person is subject to the Categorical Imperative.

Conversely, the Categorical Imperative serves as morality's supreme principle for us only if it we can act on maxims other than those grounded in our strongest or most immediate inclinations. We act from duty, and not merely in accordance with it, when our maxims are grounded in respect for their universalizability and for rational agency as an end in itself. Our being subject to the Categorical Imperative thus entails that we are positively free – that is, we can act on considerations derived from our being 'laws' to ourselves. Let us call this claim [C]:

4 *An Introduction to Kant's Moral Philosophy* (Cambridge, 2010), p. 63.

[C] If a person is subject to the Categorical Imperative, then that person's will is positively free

[F] and [C] together entail Kant's Reciprocity Thesis.

5.2 Kant's Challenge, Part I: Acting Under the Idea of Freedom

The Reciprocity Thesis does not establish the possibility of the Categorical Imperative by itself. For note that it does not tell us anything about whether any of us are subject to the moral law or whether any of us are positively free or autonomous. It merely states that these two facts are co-extensive: Anyone subject to the moral law is also positively free, and anyone positively free is subject to the moral law. But that relation holding true is entirely compatible with no one being positively free or being subject to the moral law. (Compare: The statement 'A creature is a minotaur if and only if it possess a bull's head atop a human body' is true, but does nothing by itself to suggest the existence of minotaurs.)

What Kant needs in order to demonstrate the possibility of the Categorical Imperative is to argue successfully that either *we are subject to the moral law* (which would entail that we are positively free) or that *we are positively free* (which would entail that we are subject to the moral law). Throughout his career, Kant wrestled with how best to address this question, sometimes adopting the former strategy, sometimes the latter. Since the latter strategy predominates in the Groundwork, let us first consider how in that text he argues for our positive freedom.

For Kant, only rational beings can be subject to moral demands. Hence, if he can show that "freedom" can be proven to belong "to the activity of all beings whatever that are rational and endowed with a will," he will have shown that the moral demands of the Categorical Imperative apply to us insofar as we are rational beings – that is, that the Categorical Imperative is "possible" (G 4:448). Kant argues that negative freedom is presupposed in the very activity of rational choice. Any being with a rational will necessarily acts, as he puts it, "under the idea of freedom": "every being that cannot act otherwise than *under the idea of freedom* is just because of that really free in a practical respect . . . to every rational being having a will we must necessarily lend the idea of freedom also, under which alone he acts" (G 4:448). That we who have rational wills cannot but act "under the idea of freedom" shows that we are, Kant concludes, "really free in a practical respect." Kant does not state directly whether the "freedom" under whose "idea" we act is negative or positive. However, Kant later describes the reasoning of G 4:448 as involving an "inference from freedom to autonomy" (G 4:453). Since "autonomy" is roughly equivalent to positive freedom, it appears that "freedom" in this argument means negative freedom: that because we must act "under the idea of freedom," we are therefore negatively free, and because we are negatively free, we are also positively free, which, along with the Reciprocity Thesis, entails that we are subject to the moral law and that the Categorical Imperative is possible for us. Kant's argument, then, appears to be that because our negative freedom is presupposed in the activities of our rational wills – that is, it is *presupposed* in the very act of choice – we are justified in ascribing such positive freedom to ourselves.

> We have finally traced the determinate concept of morality back to the idea of freedom; but we could never prove the latter as something real in ourselves and in human nature; we saw only that we must presuppose it if we want to think of a being as rational and endowed with consciousness of his causality with respect to actions, that is, with a will. (G 4:448–449)

This argument raises several puzzles. We must act under the idea of freedom, according to Kant. What does this obscure claim mean? "All human beings think of themselves as free," Kant notes (G 4:455). But in what sense is our thinking ourselves free unavoidable or necessary – and why would that show that we are free?

One clue here is Kant's addendum that the unavoidability of acting under the idea of freedom shows that we are free "in a *practical* respect." This suggests that acting under the idea of freedom is necessary when we consider our choices from a practical point of view – not from the standpoint of an outsider observing, cataloging, or investigating our behavior, but from the standpoint each of us occupies when we decide what to do. From that standpoint, we cannot but see our choices as self-determined, as choices that *we* make rather than that are foisted upon us by some force or power outside our rational wills. Christine Korsgaard illustrates this thought by asking us to imagine that you are the subject of a scientific experiment wherein your choices and actions are determined by an electronic device inserted into your brain:

> The device is not going to bypass your thought processes and make you move mechanically, but rather to work through them; it will determine what you think. Perhaps you get up and decide to spend the morning working. You no sooner make the decision than it occurs to us that it must have been programmed. We may imagine that in a spirit of rebellion you then decide to skip work and go shopping. And then it occurs to you that that must have been programmed. The important point here is that efforts to second guess the device cannot help you decide what to do. They can only prevent you from making any decision. In order to do anything, you must simply ignore the fact that you are programmed, and decide what to do – just as if you were free.[5]

Korsgaard takes this thought experiment to show that from the familiar standpoint of rational deliberation, we must see our choices as stemming from the

[5] "Morality as freedom," in her *Creating the Kingdom of Ends* (Cambridge, 1997), pp. 162–163.

free choice of our wills, *even when we have compelling reason to believe that they do not.* Acting under the idea of freedom – that is, deliberating and choosing *as if* we are free – is a fundamental feature of what it is to be a rational agent. We cannot help but "regard our decisions as springing ultimately from principles that we have chosen, and justifiable by those principles. We must regard ourselves as having free will."[6] That we are free, negatively and hence positively, is thereby presupposed in the very fact of rational choice. And from that practical standpoint, that we may not be free in our choices cannot even be intelligibly countenanced.

Has Kant thereby shown that we are free? A first point of contention is whether the idea of freedom must be presupposed in any rational choice. Is it possible for a being to see itself as making choices and initiating action without seeing those choices and actions as free – to see those choices and actions as being determined not by their own wills, but by their strongest inclinations or desires? I readily grant to Kant (and Korsgaard) that we *ordinarily* choose and act under the idea of freedom. Yet there are instances of choice and action where it does not seem incoherent, even from the chooser's point of view, to engage in deliberation, choice, and action while still seeing their choices as determined by their strongest inclinations or desires. Imagine a person in the throes of a powerful drug addiction who is trying to refrain from using her favored drug. Suppose that on one occasion she nevertheless uses the drug. She might well describe her using the drug as a choice, one wherein she was unable to resist its allure and her will 'gave in.' That would amount to conceptualizing her using the drug as a choice, in Kantian terms, made under the idea of freedom. But it does not seem impossible to imagine the addict as denying that she had any choice in that matter. She may conclude that though it *seemed* 'up to her' whether to succumb to her addiction, her brain was under the powerful grip of neurochemically induced cravings that led her to choose to use the drug. In that case, her self-understanding is at odds with Kant's claim that we necessarily see our choices as actions under the idea of freedom.

I do not take such examples to offer decisive objections to Kant's claim that we necessarily choose under the idea of freedom. After all, one might claim that the addict's addiction makes her an agent but of a *non*-rational sort, incapable of choosing other than as her neurochemistry determines her to choose. It might also matter that retrospective examination of choice seem more amenable to deterministic explanation than does choosing 'in the moment.' Nevertheless, they exert pressure on Kant's thesis that we necessarily act under the idea of freedom. For it is not obviously incoherent to see ourselves as merely *seeming* to act under this idea – that, for all we can tell, our choices flow from rational deliberation and decision instead of from our strongest inclinations – while

6 "Morality as freedom," p. 163.

maintaining that our choices are ultimately determined by what Kant called "natural necessity" (G 4:456).

Kant's likely reply to such worries is to re-emphasize that acting under the idea of freedom does not prove the existence of freedom "as something real in ourselves and in human nature" – only that we are free "in a practical respect." There are, Kant thought, two standpoints from which we may understand ourselves. Throughout Kant's metaphysics, he articulates a contrast between two 'worlds' or standpoints. Most commonly he describes this as a contrast between *phenomena* and *noumena*. But he also describes it in terms of a contrast between an intelligible world and a sensible world, between a world of understanding and a world of sense, or between things in themselves and appearances. Much ink has been spilled over what this contrast comes to and how Kant motivates it. Unfortunately, we will only be able to give passing attention to this distinction, and, in particular, to how Kant utilizes it to argue for our being positively free.

We take, Kant says, a "different standpoint when by means of freedom we think of ourselves" as possessing causal powers than "when we represent ourselves in terms of our actions as effects that we see before our eyes" (G 4:450). When we adopt the latter standpoint, we view ourselves as parts of a larger, observable system of nature. This system, the system of phenomena or sense appearances, can be investigated by science, and, in particular, we can discover causal laws that govern this system. Thus, to see our selves, including our rational wills, as phenomenal is to see them as part of a system of nature governed by these causal laws. These causal laws explain the states of our bodies and minds, including our inclinations and desires. From this 'sensible' or 'empirical' standpoint, the choices of the will are as explicable in terms of causal laws as are the tides, gravity, or the growth of plants. But Kant insists that we must also posit, 'beyond' these appearances, a world of understanding or of things in themselves. Things in themselves are not observable and cannot be investigated by observational means. To conceptualize ourselves as part of this "intelligible" or "intellectual" world (G 4:451–452) is to posit that we exist as rational, self-governing beings whose will is unaffected by the phenomenal world governed by causal laws. It is from this standpoint that rational beings understand the "causality" of their wills under the idea of freedom, that, as independent from the causes that determine appearances in the sensible world. Neither standpoint on our selves and our wills can be eliminated, according to Kant, nor can we reduce one to the other:

> A rational being counts himself, as intelligence, as belonging to the world of understanding, and only as an efficient cause belonging to this does he call his causality a *will*. On the other he is also conscious of himself as part of the world of sense, in which his actions are found as mere appearances of that causality [i.e., the causality found in the world of sense]. (G 4:453)

In thinking about our choices and actions, we can similarly view these through either the lens of phenomenal appearances or the lens of things in themselves. Were we only members of the world of things in themselves, we could not fail to act on reason's own law. We would necessarily act only on morally permissible maxims. But because we are in effect members of both domains, we can opt to be influenced by the inclinations that arise insofar as, and because, we belong to the phenomenal world governed by the laws of nature.

The distinction between noumena and phenomena is central to the larger aims of Kant's 'theoretical' philosophy, or metaphysics. Kant famously argued that once we distinguish between the world of things in themselves and the world of appearances, certain long-standing controversies in philosophy (including God's existence, the immortality of the soul, the nature of time and space) are shown to be the product of excessive philosophical ambition. Philosophers thought their arguments on these matters could home in on the fundamental truths of metaphysics, but (Kant argued) such truths concern things in themselves, to which we have no cognitive access and therefore no knowledge. Kant concludes that we can have abundant knowledge of the world of appearances, while the world of things in themselves must remain essentially unknowable. (We will discuss a very different set of arguments for God's existence and the soul's immortality when we take up Kant's practical postulates in Section 8.8.)

A full consideration of Kant's metaphysics, and the noumenal/phenomenal distinction especially, is beyond the scope of this book. Our immediate concern is whether invoking this distinction helps Kant in his effort to show that we are in fact free and thereby vindicate the Reciprocity Thesis.

Armed with this distinction, Kant proposes that there is no contradiction between seeing ourselves and our choices as causally determined parts of the natural, phenomenal world and seeing ourselves as acting under the idea of freedom, independent of the causes that govern the observable world. From the phenomenal standpoint, our choices and actions are not free but causally determined. From the noumenal standpoint, our choices and actions result from our free choices. That seems contradictory, according to Kant, only if we fail to note that we speak of ourselves as determined and free in different senses. Even if we are determined and unfree from a phenomenal or 'theoretical' standpoint, we are free 'in a practical respect' or from a practical standpoint. And when we engage in deliberation about what to do, we are in effect adopting that practical standpoint, a standpoint from which we in fact act under the idea of freedom. There is at least no contradiction, Kant argues, in supposing that we are practically free: "Philosophy must therefore assume that no true contradiction will be found between freedom and natural necessity in the very same human actions, for it cannot give up the concept of nature any more than that of freedom" (G 4:456). Consider again the drug addict mentioned above: When deciding whether to take her favored drug, the addict adopts a prospective or practical standpoint on her choice, a standpoint wherein she understands her choice as positively free. After the fact, she adopts the retrospective or theoretical standpoint, wherein she attempts to identify a causal explanation of her choice referring to the workings of her brain, etc. But, Kant may argue, there is no contradiction between her adopting these different standpoints at different times to one and the same choice; they simply reflect distinct approaches to thinking about our own agency.

With this argument, Kant takes himself to have shown that our positive freedom is at least *possible*. For we are at least entitled to assume that we are free from a practical point of view even as, from another point of view, we see our choices as determined products of natural laws. Granted, if Kant's argument appealing to acting under the idea of freedom is sound, it reduces the tensions between the two standpoints we take on our choices and actions. But note that despite Kant's language of showing that the Categorical Imperative is "possible," his real target with this argument should be to show that the supreme principle of morality is *actual* – that is, that the Categorical Imperative really does apply us to because we are free. Yet even if positive freedom is possible, we cannot thereby infer its actuality. That our being free from a practical standpoint would not contradict our being determined from a phenomenal standpoint gives us no positive evidence for our being free. And we may, for reasons articulated above in connection with Korsgaard's thought experiment, harbor the suspicion that our freedom is in fact an illusion, even as we operate within the practical standpoint where we choose and act *as if* we are free. And it is hard to see how Kant's appeal to our having unavoidably to choose under the idea of freedom can rebut such suspicions.

5.3 Kant's Challenge, Part II: The Fact of Reason

Kant seems to pursue a very different strategy to defend the Reciprocity Thesis in the Critique of Practical Reason. Indeed, the strategy deployed there opposes the strategy he adopted in the Groundwork.

Kant begins by asking "from what our *cognition* of the unconditionally practical *starts*, whether from freedom or practical law" (C2 5:29). Here Kant draws our attention back to the Reciprocity Thesis. Assuming that we are subject to the moral law if and only if our wills are positively free, do we 'cognize' the moral law by first cognizing our positive freedom, or do we 'cognize' our positive freedom by first cognizing the moral law? The argument of the Groundwork, appealing to the necessity of acting under the idea of freedom, at least from a practical standpoint, follows the first tack.

Surprisingly, in the Critique, Kant seems to deny that such a strategy can succeed. Our freedom is not something of which we can be conscious, Kant argues. Negative freedom, the absence of determination by causal laws, cannot be observed, nor can our freedom be "reasoned out from antecedent data" such as our "consciousness of freedom" (C2 5:31). Here Kant effectively denies that any appeal to our experience or awareness of freedom, presumably including the seeming unavoidability of acting under the idea of freedom, can establish that we are free. Kant thus explicitly rejects the strategy he embraced earlier in the Groundwork.

The alternative is to appeal to our being subject to the moral law as the basis for concluding that we are positively free (C2 5:47–48). That is the alternative Kant pursues in the Critique. Our experience of being subject to morality's demands is adequate to show that we are free:

> It is therefore the *moral law*, of which we become immediately conscious (as soon as we draw up maxims of the will for ourselves), that *first* offers itself to us and, inasmuch as reason presents it as a determining ground not to be outweighed by any sensible conditions and indeed quite independent of them, leads directly to the concept of our freedom. . . . morality first discloses to us the concept of freedom. (C2 5:29–30)

Here Kant's thought is that our moral experience – our awareness of the moral law, of the demand to abide only by universalizable maxims, etc. – leaves no doubt that we are subject to the Categorical Imperative. Given this experience of morality's demands, we must concede that we have the freedom, negative and positive, necessary to abide by those demands. As Kant says, "the moral law, and with it practical reason, [have] come in and forced this concept [freedom] upon us" (C2 5:30). The authority morality has over us can be given no deeper account, according to Kant. Our "consciousness of this fundamental law" – that is, of the Categorical Imperative and its requirements – is simply "a fact of reason" (C2 5:31). The moral law is thus "given, as it were, as a fact of pure reason of which we are a priori conscious and which is apodictically certain" (C2 5:47).

Kant's defenders and critics have long been puzzled by this argumentative strategy. Kant presents his reasoning abruptly and with little elaboration of what this "fact of reason" is exactly. In terms of his Reciprocity Thesis, Kant appears to be arguing that because we are subject to the Categorical Imperative, we are positively free. The principal weakness of this strategy is that it will neither persuade Kant's critics nor answer the problem of morality's authority in the terms Kant himself lays out.

To see why, recall that Kant's Reciprocity Thesis expresses a conjunction of two claims:

[F] If a person's will is positively free, then that person is subject to the Categorical Imperative.

[C] If a person is subject to the Categorical Imperative, then that person's will is positively free.

As we have seen, if the Reciprocity Thesis is true, and Kant can show that either of these two claims are true, then the other claim will follow. The primary strategy of the Groundwork invokes claim [F] and the Reciprocity Thesis to show that we are subject to the Categorical Imperative:

[Reciprocity Thesis] A person is subject to the Categorical Imperative if and only if that person's will is positively free.

[F] Therefore, if a person's will is positively free, then that person is subject to the Categorical Imperative.

[i] Because a person must, from a practical standpoint, act under the idea of freedom, a person's will is positively free.

[ii] Therefore, that person is subject to the Categorical Imperative (i.e., the Categorical Imperative is 'possible.')

I raised concerns about claim [i] in the previous section. Those concerns notwithstanding, that strategy had the advantage of at least being responsive to what worries Kant's critics (and, arguably, what worries Kant himself as he transitions between Groundwork sections II and III). What might render morality a 'phantom' is that we lack the freedom necessary to act as the Categorical Imperative bids – namely, the capacity to defy "natural necessity" so as to act on the basis of our recognition of the moral law instead of on our strongest inclinations or desires. Kant and his critics are worried that our sense that we are bound by the Categorical Imperative would be undermined if, as it turns out, we are not (positively) free. They are *not* worried that our sense that we are (positively) free would be undermined if, as it turns out, we are not bound by the Categorical Imperative. They doubt whether morality has the metaphysical basis (our positive freedom) it seems to need in order for the Categorical Imperative to be 'possible.' They do *not* doubt whether our positive freedom entails the Categorical Imperative. In other words, the implicit reasoning of the second Critique

[Reciprocity Thesis] A person is subject to the Categorical Imperative if and only if that person's will is positively free.

[C] Therefore, if a person is subject to the Categorical Imperative, then that person's will is positively free.

[iii] Our being subject to the Categorical Imperative is a "fact of reason."

[iv] Therefore, that person's will is positively free

avoids, rather than confronts, the worry that drives Kant and his critics. Kant appreciates the threat of circular reasoning here, showing that we are free because we are bound by the Categorical Imperative while showing that we are bound by the Categorical Imperative because we are free (G 4:450). But not just any way of breaking out of this circle will serve Kant's argumentative purposes and satisfy his likely critics. He seems to need to vindicate [F] rather than [C]. For the primary doubts we might have about the Reciprocity Thesis arise from [F] rather than from [C].

The 'fact of reason' strategy thus holds little promise in showing that criterion [5] – that morality's supreme principle be one conformity to which requires only that we are practically rational beings – has been vindicated. That strategy instead amounts to claiming that criterion [5] is satisfied simply because criteria [1]–[4] are. Such a strategy seems to rest content with merely identifying morality's supreme principle while falling short of truly 'establishing' that principle.

5.4 Explanation Versus Defense

Sections 5.2 and 5.3 offered doubts about the effectiveness of Kant's attempts to demonstrate the 'possibility' of the Categorical Imperative. The Groundwork strategy described in Section 5.2, appealing to acting under the idea of freedom, is relevant to the primary worries Kant and his critics have about the Categorical Imperative's possibility but is open to objection. The strategy of the Critique of Practical Reason, described in Section 5.3, does not seem relevant to these worries in any case. Yet before concluding that Kant fails outright to demonstrate the Categorical Imperative's possibility, we should consider precisely what would count as success in that regard.

At least in the Groundwork, Kant sometimes describes his task as providing a 'deduction' or 'proof' of morality's authority (G 4:445). However, in the Critique, Kant explicitly disavows that the moral law is amenable to a "deduction" (C2 5:47–48). A similar modesty can also be found in the Groundwork when Kant denies that freedom can ever be proven. At most, reason must "regard itself" as free and autonomous (G 4:448).

Such remarks suggest that, notwithstanding the difficulties Kant had in propounding a proof or deduction of our freedom, Kant may have had a less ambitious goal in mind. There is some reason to think that Kant held that, at most, the *possibility* of our freedom – and hence the 'possibility' of the Categorical Imperative – can be shown. In other words, perhaps human freedom is not the sort of property whose existence we can hope to prove. But if we have grounds for believing it possible, that may be sufficient to assuage any doubts about morality's authority. Here I will briefly articulate how this final strategy might proceed.

Key to this strategy is Kant's claim that our freedom is amenable to *defense* but not to *explanation*. Let us consider at length Kant's explanation of this claim:

> reason would overstep all its bounds if it took upon itself to *explain how* pure reason can be practical, which would be exactly the same task as to explain *how freedom is possible*.
>
> For we can explain nothing but what we can reduce to laws the object of which can be given in some possible experience. Freedom, however, is a mere idea, the objective reality of which can in no way be presented in accordance with laws of nature and so too cannot be presented in any possible experience . . . Now, where determinations by laws of nature ceases, there all *explanation* ceases as well, and nothing is left but *defense*, that is, to repel the objections of those who pretend to have seen deeper into the essence of things and therefore boldly declare that freedom is impossible. (G 4:458)

Kant makes two important claims regarding freedom in this passage: First, it cannot be explained. Second, it can nevertheless be defended. Let us consider each in turn.

Our freedom, Kant states, cannot be explained, and, indeed, for us to try to do so would "overstep" the bounds of reason. In this passage, Kant provides two conditions that must be met for something to be open to explanation: (a) We must be able to observe it in experience, and (b) it must be explicable in terms of "determinations by laws of nature." Freedom is not something we experience, Kant alleges here. Now, Kant cannot mean that we do not 'experience' freedom in the sense that we do not take ourselves to be free in our choices and actions. That we do take ourselves to be free in this way is the entire point of his appeal to our acting "under the idea" of freedom. His thought appears instead to be that freedom is not an "object" of "possible experience" inasmuch as we do not encounter it in our sensory awareness. Our freedom is not a directly observable fact about us. It has no length, width, color, fragrance, flavor, mass, velocity, or audible pitch. Any explanation of our freedom, Kant argues, would require that our freedom be, or stand in some logical relation with, data acquired through sensory observation. Since freedom is not observable in these ways, explaining such freedom is a "subjective impossibility" (G 4:459).

Moreover, an explanation of freedom would have to be explicable in terms of laws of nature. Here Kant's thinking is more elusive. But here is my own speculation as to what Kant is gesturing at: Consider again our example of Luis, who opts to lie under oath about his friend Donald's financial activities. Suppose that we attempted to explain how Luis' choice to lie under oath was free. How could we explain that such a choice was free? We might appeal to certain background psychological, biological, or social laws that together work in concert to influence Luis' choice. Let us simply call all of these laws L. We can imagine explaining Luis' act with the following line of reasoning:

> Luis' choices are governed by L. Given L, and various other facts about Luis and his circumstances, Luis chose to lie under oath.

The trouble here is that appealing to L seems incapable of providing an explanation of how Luis *freely* chose to lie under oath. If Luis chose to lie because of L, then his choice was determined by L. He lacked the independence from "alien influences" or "natural necessity" that are the hallmarks of negative freedom and moral responsibility, according to Kant.

Kant is making a deep point here about explanation: Explanation, by appealing to the 'mechanical' laws of nature that govern empirically observable facts, forecloses freedom on the part of what is being explained. "Experience lets us cognize only the law of appearances and hence the mechanism of nature, the direct opposite of freedom" (C2 5:29). Our freedom, Kant says, is a kind of "absolute spontaneity" (C2 5:48, 5:99; G 4:452). Not only do our wills operate without prior determination by causal laws, their freedom consists in the possibility of self-directed moral choice. For in order for a will to be free from a moral perspective, it also has to be up to us whether we abide by the Categorical Imperative. A free rational will is bullied neither by its inclinations and desires nor by the rational demands imposed by morality. It must, in other words, be possible both that we abide by morality's demands and possible that we not so abide. And which option we choose must ultimately be inexplicable, i.e., not explicable in terms of deterministic laws, lest our choice be unfree. Freedom merely "signifies a 'something' that is left over when I have excluded from the determining grounds of my will everything belonging to the world of sense" (G 4:462). In any explanation of human choice and action, freedom therefore leaves behind an explanatory remainder, according to Kant.

Explanation, in contrast, necessarily appeals to causal laws. So, *given what freedom would have to be in order for us to be subject to the Categorical Imperative*, our freedom cannot be explained. If so, then Kant's attempts to provide a proof or deduction of that freedom, making use of the Reciprocity Thesis, cannot succeed *even on Kant's own terms*. From an explanatory standpoint, how we are free must remain a mystery, but only because freedom is the sort of property that is necessarily precluded from explanation in the first place. Freedom functions for Kant as a basic power, and "all human insight is at an end as soon as we have arrived at basic powers or basic faculties; for there is nothing through which their possibility can be conceived" (C2 5:46–47). Attempts to explain freedom thus misfire. In other words, freedom is what we must resort to in order to comprehend how our wills can act on anything other than causal laws.

Yet even if our freedom cannot be explained, it can be defended. Recall Kant's claim (which, in Section 5.2, I conceded was controversial) that the question of our freedom cannot be decided on theoretical or metaphysical grounds – that any philosophical effort to do so runs aground because it attempts to apply our rational powers beyond their proper provenance, to objects outside possible experience. Suppose that Kant is correct in this, so that freedom can be neither proven nor disproven precisely because it could not be an object of possible experience. Our freedom would nevertheless remain a possibility, Kant reasons. Freedom's possibility can thus be defended against those who claim to know with metaphysical certainty that we are *not* free – those who, in Kant's words, "pretend to have seen deeper into the essence of things and therefore boldly declare that freedom is impossible" (G 4:458).

In my estimation, Kant's best option for defending morality's authority is therefore not to seek to prove our practical freedom, but to deny its provability, thereby preserving its possibility and its immunity from disproof. Given Kant's own philosophical commitments, this is arguably the best avenue to ensure that morality can enjoy the "tranquility and security from the external attacks that could make the land on which it wants to build a matter of dispute" (G 4:457).

5.5 Conclusion

Criterion [5] generates problems for Kant's ethics because, unlike criteria [1]–[4], it is not a strictly ethical claim. It is not a claim about what morality is, but about its applicability to us. Like any theory of ethics, Kant's must fit into the world as we know it. A theory of ethics should not rest on false or dubious claims about reality, including human nature. This is a particularly acute challenge for Kant's ethical theory because the principle Kant identifies as morality's supreme principle implies a strong form of motivational or rational freedom: that we are able to act on something other than our strongest desires or inclinations, and, because of this 'negative' freedom, are capable of acting on a law that our rational wills generate ourselves. That Kant adopted different strategies throughout his lifetime to meet this challenge is an indication that he grasped how steep a challenge this is. But the best Kantian solution, I have argued, is to make the challenge somewhat less steep: to admit that our freedom can be neither demonstrated nor explained, but nor can its impossibility be demonstrated or explained either.

Further Reading

This chapter has only scratched the surface of the difficult issues raised by Kant's understandings of freedom, will, morality, and their interrelations. Some resources that shed further light include Karl Ameriks, "Kant's deduction of freedom and morality," *Journal of the History of Philosophy* 19 (1981): 53–79; Thomas E. Hill, "Kant's argument for the rationality of moral conduct," *Pacific Philosophical Quarterly* 66 (1985); Henry Allison, Kant's Theory of Freedom (Cambridge, 1990); Christine Korsgaard, "Morality as freedom," in her Creating the Kingdom of Ends (Cambridge, 1997), pp. 159–187; Andrews Reath, "Kant's critical account of freedom," in G. Bird (ed.), A Companion to Kant (Wiley-Blackwell, 2006), pp. 275–290; Jennifer Uleman, An Introduction to Kant's Moral Philosophy (Cambridge, 2010), chapter 4; and Tamar Schapiro, "Foregrounding desire: A defense of Kant's incorporation thesis," *Journal of Ethics* 15 (2011): 147–167. Pauline Kleingeld, "Moral consciousness and the 'fact of reason,'" in A. Reath and J. Timmermann (eds.), Kant's *Critique of Practical Reason*: A Critical Guide (Cambridge, 2010), pp. 55–72, is an excellent entry point for controversies about how to understand Kant's "fact of reason." A number of the essays in Paul Guyer's Kant on Freedom, Law, and Happiness (Cambridge, 2000) address Kant's understanding of freedom. For varied views on Kant's metaphysics and the noumena/phenomena distinction, see (among many others) Rae Langton, Kantian Humility: Our Ignorance of Things in Themselves (Oxford, 2001); Henry Allison, Kant's Transcendental Idealism (Yale, 2004); and Michelle Grier, Kant's Doctrine of Transcendental Illusion (Cambridge, 2007).

Part II

6 Objections to the Formula of Universal Law

Part I of this book tried to make the positive case for Kant's ethical theory, illustrating how it makes sense of a number of plausible ideas about morality. However, it is often said that a philosophical theory is only as good as the best objection it can withstand, and since Kant's death over two hundred years ago, his theory of ethics has been subject to many objections (in all honesty, more objections than we can pursue here). Yet there are certain objections to Kant's ethics that tend to recur, and so Kant's ethics will be all the more credible if its defenders can at least provide strong replies to the most resilient and perennial of these objections. This is the principal aim of Part II of this book. It groups these objections into three broad categories and gives a spirited but (I hope) fair-minded defense of Kant's ethics against these objections.

In this chapter, we consider some popular objections to Kant's Formula of Universal Law. Probably no moral principle has been more heavily criticized. This chapter addresses three objections concerning the Formula of Universal Law that tend to recur in critical writings on Kant's ethics. The first alleges that because we are handicapped in determining what attitudes or maxim a person in fact acts upon on a given occasion, we cannot draw specific conclusions about whether a person's maxim is morally permissible, and, by extension, about whether the person's action is morally permissible or not. The second objection claims that even if we do know what maxim a person is acting upon, the Formula of Universal Law generates implausible verdicts about particular actions. The third objection is that Kant's Formula of Universal Law implausibly commits us to a clumsy moral absolutism according to which every act that belongs to a certain general kind (lying, for example) is impermissible or, alternatively, obligatory (keeping one's promises, say). For the sake of terminological convenience, I will call the first objection the *identification* objection, the second the *wrong answers* objection, and the third the *absolutism* objection.

6.1 The Identification Objection

This objection begins from a commonplace observation about human conduct. When a person engages in a particular behavior, there will nearly always be many ways to describe that behavior which are, to outside observers at least, accurate. Suppose a student raises her hand while seated at a desk. We might call her raising her hand, the observable movement of her body, her *behavior*. Depending on what other facts hold true, it is possible that any of the following descriptions might account for the student's action:

- she is responding to a teacher's question
- she is preparing to ask the teacher a question
- she is trying to distract the teacher while another student tries to leave class without the teacher's notice
- she is preparing herself for tomorrow's exam
- she is currying favor with the teacher
- she is trying to humiliate a rival student
- she has become tired during the teacher's lecture and is stretching in order to keep herself awake

Kantians will claim that what matters from a moral perspective is not the individual's behavior as witnessed by outside observers. Kantians hold that what we are attempting to assess when we assess conduct morally, whether the conduct of ourselves or that of others, is not a person's behavior but her *action* – what, in some larger sense, the person *wills* that in turn results in her observable behavior. More specifically, as we saw in Section 3.1, Kantians believe that a person's *maxim* determines what she does (whether the student's raising her hand amounts to responding to a question, trying to distract the teacher, etc.).

Take one of Kant's best-known examples, the shopkeeper who charges the same prices even to children and "inexperienced customers" (G 4:397). From a Kantian perspective, we cannot ascertain the moral status of the shopkeeper's actions simply by looking at his behavior. That he charges consistent prices to his customers does not tell us everything necessary to know in order to use Kant's Formula of Universal Law to morally evaluate his actions. Recall that this version of the Categorical Imperative requires us to act only on those maxims that can be consistently universalized, where (as we interpreted it in Section 3.6) this amounts to refraining from acting on any maxim the rationality of which (more specifically, the individual's likely success in achieving the end contained in her maxim) depends on others not sharing that maxim with her. Some of the maxims on which the shopkeeper could act will meet this criterion and therefore be morally permissible: for example, "I will always charge the same prices to all my customers so that the inexperienced are not disadvantaged in their dealings with me." Other maxims that would lead the shopkeeper to charge consistent prices may well not be morally permissible: for example, "I will always charge the same prices to all my customers in order to maintain my reputation as a honest entrepreneur." As this contrast illustrates, one and the same behavior – charging consistent prices to one's customers – can result from different maxims. But only the behavior can be immediately observed. The other components of the shopkeeper's maxims, including his end, etc., cannot. Thus, Kant's critics contend, we cannot know what we need to know in order to morally evaluate the shopkeeper's action – namely, the maxim that underlies it.

Note that it is not a person's *motive* that is at issue here. The worry is not that we cannot know whether a person adopts a maxim out of "good will," or whether she acts from duty or merely in accordance with it. If whether a person's action is morally permissible depends on its maxim (see Sections 2.1–2.2), then if a person's maxim cannot be known, then the moral permissibility of her action cannot be known either. The difficulty is in knowing whether our maxims are consistent with the moral law, not with whether their adoption by us is motivated *by* that law.

Kant only seems to exacerbate this worry with his views concerning our own capacity for ethical self-knowledge. Our knowledge of our own moral attitudes and judgments, according to Kant, is imperfect and extremely limited. No one "can fathom the depths of his heart, as to be able to attain through self-observation, an entirely reliable cognition of the basis of his maxims which he professes, and of their purity and stability" (R 6:63). The unreliability of our judgments regarding our own maxims entails that even when we seem to behave in morally admirable ways, we cannot rule out the possibility that our end was rooted in love for the "dear self" rather than some other end. Worse still, we are profoundly susceptible to self-deception: "We like to flatter ourselves by falsely attributing to ourselves a noble motive, whereas in fact we can never, even by the most strenuous self-examination, get entirely behind our covert incentives" (G 4:407). To Kant's eyes, not even the person whose behavior is in question is in a position to know precisely what maxim explains that behavior. Neither the shopkeeper nor his customers seem to be able to know for certain if he charges equitable prices for love of reputation, or honor, or for some other end.[1]

To summarize the identification objection: According to Kantian ethics, whether a person's action is right or wrong depends on the maxim of that action. But while we can observe a person's behavior, we cannot know well enough what maxims underlie and explain that behavior. Hence, even if Kantian ethics succeeds in telling us what we need to know in order to morally evaluate a person's actions, we are unable in the end to know whether a person's actions are right or wrong. So even if Kant succeeds in giving us the correct account of right action, that account is of limited practical value

[1] As Owen Ware ("The duty of self-knowledge," *Philosophy and Phenomenological Research* 79 (2009): 671–698) observes, Kant's claim that we are incapable of moral self-knowledge makes his assertion that we have a duty to know ourselves puzzling indeed. See also the earlier discussion of lying and the duty to examine ourselves with integrity (Section 2.7).

because we lack the knowledge necessary to know when, on Kant's account, a person has acted rightly or wrongly.

A certain caution is in order when considering how to answer the identification objection. It would be wrongheaded, I think, to dismiss out of hand Kant's worries about self-deception and the opacity of our knowledge of our maxims. It is often easier to convince ourselves of our own virtue than it is to exhibit the virtue of moral probity. Furthermore, we can clearly err when we attempt to interpret *others*' moral conduct. Hence, any attempt to answer this objection by showing that we always succeed in identifying individuals' maxims – that we are in effect *infallible* in our judgments about what moral attitudes people have, including ourselves – would be misguided. That claim simply does not square with the facts. Fortunately, answering the identification objection does not require defending that claim. Instead, it will suffice if we can show that we *often* have knowledge of individuals' maxims – or, at the very least, that such knowledge is *possible*.

We have a number of sources of evidence about our own maxims. The first of these is *reflection*: deliberately considering what our beliefs and motives are. As a method for gaining knowledge of our own moral outlook, such reflection is not likely to be an especially reliable method. For one, our maxims are not like mental sensations. I cannot, simply by paying attention to the workings of my own thoughts, ascertain the maxims upon which I am acting in the way that, for example, I can figure out just by paying attention to the working of my own thoughts that I am in pain, that I am thirsty for lemonade, or that I am perceiving the color yellow. And ever since Freud hypothesized the existence of the unconscious, the notion that the reasons that lead us to act are just as they appear to us at first glance is no longer credible.

And Kant was particularly wary of reflection, since (as we noted above) he believed that self-deception commonly leads us to appraise our own choices more charitably than they deserve to be. And it is when we reflect, asking ourselves "what maxim am I exhibiting in my actions?" that we are most likely to be excessively charitable. After all, none of us want to be seen as morally deficient, even in our own eyes, but as far as reflection is concerned, there is nothing to 'check' our tendency toward self-deception. After searching his soul, our shopkeeper can well conclude that his maxim was to charge customers fair prices in order not to disadvantage the naïve or inexperienced. But it is hard to see how to avoid the worry that even the most probing acts of reflection can be self-serving, in which case the shopkeeper may simply be wrong about his own maxims. Moreover, even if an individual discovers through reflection a maxim that renders her action morally permissible, it does not follow that she acted (or will act) on that maxim. Simply recognizing or entertaining a maxim is not the same as its moving us to act.

So clearly reflection is not a particularly reliable way to arrive at knowledge of a person's maxims. This is not to say that such reflection tells us nothing about her maxims. But it needs to be augmented with other kinds of evidence if we are to arrive at well-reasoned conclusions concerning what our maxims are.

One other source of evidence concerning our maxims is what we might call our *moral self-appraisals*. Each of us is equipped with what Kant called "moral feeling," "the susceptibility to feel pleasure or displeasure merely from being aware that our actions are consistent with or contrary to the law of duty" (MM 6:399). Not only are we able to deliberate about what moral duty asks of us, we also undergo emotional responses – feelings of pleasure or displeasure – stemming from our judgments about whether we have done our duty and why. These emotional responses constitute evidence about what maxims we act upon.

For instance, suppose that after agonizing over whether to overcharge naïve customers, our shopkeeper decides to continue with his policy of charging the same prices to all his customers. But, following this decision, our shopkeeper could well feel *guilt*. What might his guilt tell us about the maxims behind his decision? Guilt represents a kind of unstated judgment of oneself, a judgment to the effect that one has violated a moral standard that one tacitly accepts. If Kant's ethics is on the right track, the standard in question is Kant's Categorical Imperative (or some version thereof). To feel guilt, then, is the result of having found oneself guilty in the "inner court" of conscience. In the shopkeeper's case, his guilt is an indication that the reason or maxim that led him to charge the same prices to all was not a morally permissible one.

Of course, guilt is not infallible. Sometimes a person fails to feel guilt when she ought to, or, conversely, feels guilt when she ought not to. (Kant himself might have disagreed with this, since he held that the verdicts of conscience are infallible – that an "erring conscience is an absurdity"; MM 6:401.) Still, the presence of the negative self-appraisal of guilt is informative about what a person's maxims are. Conversely, sometimes a person will enjoy positive self-appraisals that suggest what maxims she acts upon. Kant held that when we fulfill our duties, we experience a form of moral self-respect or self-esteem (MM 6:402). This is not, as Kant saw it, a kind of smug self-satisfaction, a holier-than-thou feeling of superiority. Rather, in subjecting our choices to the requirements of the Categorical Imperative, we exhibit what Jeanine Grenberg has called the Kantian attitude of "proper humility."[2] In acting morally, we show ourselves to be both "capable and dignified," able to value our own practically rational natures by both exhibiting rationality and showing respect for our own rational agency.

[2] *Kant and the Ethics of Humility* (Cambridge, 2005), p. 133f.

As with guilt, feelings of positive moral self-appraisal are likely to be fallible: Sometimes a person fails to feel moral self-esteem or proper humility when she ought to, or, conversely, has these feelings when she ought not to. But this fallibility notwithstanding, our moral self-appraisals provide us a body of evidence from which we can ascribe maxims or reasons to ourselves. For our moral self-appraisals are conscience's way of indicating our moral self-worth in our own eyes.

Finally, it is worth keeping in mind that the evidence we have regarding the maxim of a *particular* action can extend beyond the circumstances of that choice of action. We human agents are not completely consistent in our choices, but nor (typically) are our choices utterly unpredictable and unpatterned. Our moral choices are likely to exhibit some consistency over time. Thus, in trying to discern a person's maxim in one situation, it can be helpful to consider their choices and conduct in other morally similar situations. Talbot Brewer offers the following example:[3] Suppose that you stop to help someone whose car has broken down on the side of a highway. You might scrutinize your own maxim: Why did you bother to help? You might then notice that you stopped to help when you had a companion with you in your vehicle. In fact, you notice that you have consistently helped others in need only when doing so would likely enhance your reputation for "goodness and humanity" in the eyes of others. This observation should thus lead you to interpret your own conduct in a somewhat unflattering light: The maxim that led you to help is something like "I will help strangers in need when I stand to improve my reputation for generosity by so doing."

Brewer's example illustrates that the entire pattern of our choices and actions across time can help us to identify the maxims that motivate our actions on a given occasion. (It is worth noting that Kant sometimes refers to these larger patterns of choice as maxims, thus suggesting that maxims form a hierarchy, with more general maxims at the top and maxims in the sense we have been investigating, the maxims of specific choices and actions, at the bottom.[4]) By identifying this pattern, the maxims we act upon on specific occasions come into view more clearly and serve as "a check against self-flattering (or, for that matter, self-deprecating) distortions in our understanding of our current evaluative outlooks."[5]

Kant deserves credit for being among the few philosophers to fully appreciate the difficulties of moral self-knowledge. He recognized, in ways that few philosophers before or since have recognized, that we are prone to self-deception – that in many respects, it is easier to seem morally good in our

[3] "Maxims and virtues," *Philosophical Review* 111 (2002): 557.

[4] For an explanation of this hierarchy, see Jens Timmermann, "Kant's puzzling ethics of maxims," *Harvard Review of Philosophy* 8 (2000): 39–52.

[5] "Maxims and virtues," p. 559.

own eyes than it is to actually be morally good. This is why the moral duty of self-perfection includes a duty of self-knowledge. For we are prone to interpret our own motives and maxims in unduly charitable ways.

Fortunately, though, answering the identification objection does not require showing that we are infallible in identifying the maxims we in fact act upon. For it seems obvious that our own moral psychology is not transparent, even to us. But at the same time, our moral psychology is not totally opaque to us either, and we have several sources of evidence from which to infer what our maxims likely are: reflection on our own reasons or motives, our moral self-appraisals, and our patterns of moral behavior over time. These sources do not ensure we know what our maxims are, but nor do they leave us helpless in discerning the maxims that explain our actions.

6.2 The Wrong Answers Objection, Part I: False Positives

Some critics allege that Kant's Formula of Universal Law sometimes implies that intuitively permissible actions are impermissible and vice versa – that Kant's principle yields wrong answers about certain actions.

For instance, Kant's Formula of Universal Law sometimes appears to condemn seemingly innocent actions because the maxims associated with those actions cannot be consistently universalized. Suppose that a person entertains and acts upon the following maxim:[6]

(Tennis Maxim 1) To improve my backhand, I will play tennis with Katrina on the public courts every Wednesday at 4 pm.

Again, to evaluate whether acting on this maxim is morally permissible, we must determine if it can be consistently universalized. As we interpreted this requirement in Chapter 3, it means that the maxim is morally permissible if the person could achieve the end specified in her maxim were everyone to share this maxim with her. If not, then acting on this maxim is irrational in the sense that successfully achieving the maxim's end requires that the person will her own acting on that maxim while willing that others not adopt that maxim. In this case, our tennis enthusiast cannot achieve her end if others share this maxim with her. For one, unless the community in question is exceedingly small, it would be impossible for everyone to play on the public courts every Wednesday at 4 pm. Furthermore, not everyone can play with Katrina either. Universalizing this maxim thus yields a contradiction: In order for it to be rational for our tennis player to act on this maxim, she must will this maxim for herself but reject it for others. Yet it seems unlikely that acting on such a maxim

[6] Barbara Herman attributes this example to T.M. Scanlon, "Moral deliberation and the derivation of duties," in *The Practice of Moral Judgment* (Harvard, 1993), p. 138.

is in fact wrong. Such a maxim putatively represents a "false positive" – i.e., a maxim that Kant's Formula of Universal Law finds to be morally impermissible but is not in fact impermissible. The Formula of Universal Law thus seems to generate verdicts about the morality of particular actions that are at odds with our considered moral judgments: It is not wrong to play tennis with Katrina every Wednesday at 4 pm on the public courts. Hence, if the Formula of Universal Law tells us otherwise, this is powerful evidence against its being the supreme principle of morality.

A plausible answer to the problem of false positives emerges when we analyze our tennis player's maxim:

(Tennis Maxim 1) To improve my backhand, I will play tennis with Katrina on the public courts every Wednesday at 4 pm.

Why does this maxim generate a contradiction? A large part of the reason is that it contains highly specific information. The tennis player does not simply desire to play tennis. She desires to play with a specific person at a specific location at a specific time. This specificity explains why her maxim cannot be consistently universalized: If anyone else were to act on that same maxim, neither person would be able to achieve her ends by acting on that maxim. Hence, it seems likely that a reformulation of the maxim that abstracts away from those specifics might well be consistently universalized and could therefore allow Kant to avoid such false positives.

To see what such a maxim would like, we should remind ourselves that a maxim is not just any principle that might be used to justify a course of action. Maxims are always someone's maxims, and, as we saw in Section 3.1, they express or represent a person's *reasons for acting* on a given occasion.[7] If they did not express our reasons for acting, then the Formula of Universal Law, as a test of which maxims it is morally permissible for us to act upon, would not make any sense. For, as we have interpreted that Formula, maxims are impermissible when, in order to be successfully acted upon, they require the individual in question to will both the maxim and its negation. A maxim is thus a candidate for a rationally (and morally) permissible principle of action only because the person whose maxim it is sees the maxim as expressing what she believes are sufficient reasons for acting in a particular manner in a particular situation.

Yet many apparent false positives seem to result from attributing a maxim to someone that is very unlikely to express her actual reasons for action. Consider our tennis player again. As we noted, Tennis Maxim 1 ends up as a false positive because it contains highly specific information. But I would argue

[7] Onora O'Neil (previously Onora Nell), *Acting on Principle: An Essay on Kantian Ethics* (Columbia University Press, 1975), p. 13.

that this highly specific information may not track or reflect her reasons for acting. Her reasons, in other words, are almost certainly more generic: She plays with Katrina because Katrina is a skilled partner who can reliably hit shots to her backhand side. She plays every Wednesday at 4 pm because this is the only day of the week her work schedule permits it. Furthermore, Wednesdays at 4 pm are, for whatever reason, an hour when the public courts tend not to be especially busy. Her playing every Wednesday at 4 pm with Katrina is her *specific* intention, but that intention probably rests on a more general intention or policy: to play tennis with a skilled partner when the public courts are available and her work schedule permits it.

That, I would suggest, is a better expression of her reasons for acting as she does than Tennis Maxim 1. One way to test this would be to note the answers our tennis player might provide to hypothetical questions we might pose to her.[8] For example, if we asked the tennis player, "Would you be willing to play tennis Friday at 9 am if the courts were available and it matched your work schedule?' and she responded affirmatively, then we know that there is nothing special about Wednesday at 4 pm so far as her reasons for action go. Instead, she subscribes to some more general maxim specifying the conditions under which she wishes to play tennis, and it is just happens to be true that playing at Wednesday at 4 pm satisfies those conditions. Her maxim would therefore be

(Tennis Maxim 2) I will play tennis with a skilled partner when the public courts are available and my work schedule permits it.

But note that this maxim, unlike Tennis Maxim 1, does not violate Kant's Formula of Universal Law. Can our tennis player achieve her end by acting on this maxim if others share this maxim with her? Yes. For nothing precludes other tennis buffs from playing with *other* skilled players when *their* work schedules allow it and when the public courts are available to *them*, even when our tennis player acts on this maxim.

This example illustrates how false positives for Kant's Formula of Universal Law can arise when individuals' maxims are represented as resting on far more specific reasons for action than those we typically act upon. By and large, our decisions to do X on some occasion C reflect some broader pattern of reasons we take ourselves to have, and these broader patterns are better candidates for grounding our maxims than the highly specific intentions we adopt on particular occasions. I conclude, then, that in cases such as these, we do not have a genuine false positive, but a misrepresentation of the individual's likely maxim.

[8] This approach mirrors what Richard Galvin calls the "isolation test" for determining someone's maxim. See "The universal law formulas," in T.E. Hill (ed.), *Blackwell Guide to Kant's Ethics* (Wiley-Blackwell, 2009), p. 61.

Here proponents of the objection may concede this point but still wonder: What if her maxim was, in fact, that specific, that she was in fact acting on Tennis Maxim 1 – would the Formula of Universal Law condemn it? It may seem like playing tennis every Wednesday at 4 pm is morally innocent. But I counter that it only appears morally innocent because of our awareness of the kinds of more general considerations captured in Tennis Maxim 2: Playing tennis at 4 pm each Wednesday, etc., is not objectionable so long as courts are readily available, etc. If our tennis player insisted that she must play every Wednesday at 4 pm with Katrina, and she appealed to no additional, more general reasons, then we would have to conclude that her acting on Tennis Maxim 1 is wrong.

This result may seem odd. But in fact, this result underscores that Kant's Formula of Universal Law essentially mandates that we act on principles that can serve as the common underpinnings of cooperation. To ask us to act only on maxims whose success in acting on them is compatible with others sharing those maxims with us is to appeal to an ideal of hypothetical cooperation – to ask us to govern our behavior on terms that other agents can openly share with us. In insisting that she play with Katrina at 4 pm, etc., our tennis player is being uncooperative, demanding that she be able to pursue her own ends in the way she desires, heedless of the ends that other rational agents have and the ways they desire to pursue them. (In terms of Kant's Formula of Humanity, she fails to respect others as equal rational agents.) Granted, this impermissible maxim does not rise to the level of a moral outrage. Our uncooperative tennis player is neither a thief nor a killer. But she is acting contrary to Kant's Formula of Universal Law, and in so doing exhibits a failure to understand a central tenet of Kantian ethics: Morality is something that we rational agents do together, and to insist upon one's own ends taking precedence over others is, in a very general or formal way, the essence of immorality.

Hence, some 'false positives' are in fact falsely positive – acts that Kant's Formula of Universal Law seems to condemn but in fact ought not. Other 'false positives' are positives, but (we have reason to think) not falsely so.

6.3 The Wrong Answers Objection, Part 2: False Negatives

Some of Kant's critics believe that the Formula of Universal Law generates implausible results of a different kind – namely, 'false negatives,' in which acts that are clearly morally impermissible turn out to be morally permissible.

Consider R.M. Hare's infamous example of the conscientious Nazi.[9] The conscientious Nazi is deeply committed to harassing Jews and members

[9] *Freedom and Reason* (Oxford, 1977), pp. 170–174.

of other non-Aryan groups. His reason for this is that such harassment discourages such individuals from protesting policies that discriminate against them. In fact, he is so committed to this practice of harassment that he would be willing to be harassed if he were a Jew or a non-Aryan. The conscientious Nazi's maxim might be

(Nazi Maxim 1) To discourage non-Aryans from protesting, I will harass them whenever the opportunity presents itself.

Again, on our understanding of Kant's Formula of Universal Law, it requires an individual to act only on maxims which, if others shared that maxim with him, would enable him to achieve the end specified in his maxim. In the case of the conscientious Nazi, if others shared that maxim with him, then he could successfully realize his end of discouraging non-Aryans from protesting discriminatory policies. Hence, his maxim, once universalized, reveals no apparent inconsistency or contradiction in his attitudes. All the more, the conscientious Nazi will be far more likely to achieve his objective if others were to share this maxim with him. For a community in which all are committed to harassing non-Aryans is much more likely to discourage protests by non-Aryans than a community in which only the conscientious Nazi is thus committed. But surely this kind of harassment is a serious moral wrong. The conscientious Nazi example thus appears to be a "false negative" – i.e. an instance of a maxim that Kant's Formula of Universal Law finds to be morally permissible but is in fact impermissible.

We can work our way toward a response to the false negative problem by building off observations made in connection with the false positive problem. As we noted above, false positives seem to result when maxims contain too much information and, in particular, information extraneous or incidental to the individual's reason for action. In contrast, maxims that generate false negatives seem to *omit* morally crucial information. Again, the conscientious Nazi is not stymied in his pursuit of the end of discouraging non-Aryans from protesting government policies if his maxim is universalized. Quite the contrary! Yet it seems morally tone deaf to suppose that the apparent consistency of his maxim is any defense of the conscientious Nazi's conduct. Hence, his stated maxim neglects something morally important about the harassment of non-Aryans, an added ingredient or element which, were it included, would bring to light the wrongfulness of acting on Nazi Maxim 1. Recall again that maxims express an individual's reasons for acting in a particular circumstance. With false positives, we encountered maxims that contain information that often does not seem relevant to the individual's reasons for acting. With false negatives, we encounter maxims that omit information relevant to what a person has moral reasons to do. With false positives, the maxims often misdescribe the individual's reasons for action and hence misdescribe her maxim. With false negatives, the maxims may well describe the individual's reasons for action and hence accurately describe her maxim. The problem is that the maxim itself fails to take adequate account of morally important features of what the individual intends to do by acting on that maxim.

How can we elaborate what is absent from such maxims and thereby address these troublesome false negative examples? To answer this question, we must confront a long-standing challenge to Kant's ethics that has come to be known as *the problem of relevant maxim descriptions.*[10] As we have seen, one and the same behavior can be justified by appeal to multiple maxims. The problem we just observed about false negatives is that some maxims seem to omit morally crucial information: information that might well transform the maxim from a morally permissible one into a morally impermissible one. The problem of relevant maxim descriptions is the problem of finding "a principled way of specifying which features of an action are morally relevant and thus should be mentioned in the description of the action"[11] – i.e., in the individual's maxim. The conscientious Nazi's maxim does not incorporate a morally crucial feature or fact. But what feature or fact is that? Answer that question, and we will have the basis for an answer not only for the problem of relevant maxim descriptions, but also for the problem of false negatives.

Nazi Maxim 1 is not morally objectionable because of any inconsistency that emerges when we attempt to universalize this maxim. Rather, its wrongfulness stems from the very end and the means it involves: attempting to stifle the political voices of non-Aryans through harassment. In trying to stifle the dissent of non-Aryans, the conscientious Nazi not only fails to show beneficence, he attempts to stifle their rational agency as well. That the non-Aryans may well have objections to being subject to discriminatory treatment does not seem to register with the conscientious Nazi. Their rational agency is thus not a constraint he respects. Their rational agency serves as merely an inconvenient obstacle to his realizing his ends. In terms of Kant's Formula of Humanity (which demands that we treat rational agency always as an end in itself and never merely as a means), the conscientious Nazi's policy of harassment is wrong precisely because it takes no account of non-Aryans as rational agents.

That acting on Nazi Maxim 1 violates the Formula of Humanity offers us a hint as to how best to answer the false negatives objection. To this point, we have analyzed Kant's Formula of Universal Law and his Formula of Humanity largely separately. Yet we noted (in Section 3.11) that there is some reason to believe that Kant was correct when he claimed that these formulas of the

[10] For worthwhile discussions of this problem, see O'Neill, Acting on Principle, and Mark Timmons, "Decision procedures, moral criteria, and the problem of relevant descriptions in Kant's ethics."

[11] Timmons, "Decision procedures, moral criteria," p. 398.

Categorical Imperative are equivalent, "only so many formulations of precisely the same law" (MM 4:435).

My proposal for how to deal with the false negatives problem assumes that even if Kant was incorrect in asserting the equivalence of these formulas, we should nevertheless interpret his ethical theory on the assumption that these two Formulas are substantively related. In this instance, this interpretive strategy means that we should fault the conscientious Nazi for acting on a maxim that does not acknowledge the humanity, or rational agency, of the non-Aryans he chooses to harass. In other words, Nazi Maxim 1 passes Kant's universalization test only because it does not take the rational agency of some individuals into moral account. In this respect, the Formula of Humanity provides "raw material" for maxims,[12] and moral agents can err by acting on maxims that overlook the raw material that, according to Kantian ethics at least, is most morally salient – namely, considerations relating to rational agency. My proposal concedes that Nazi Maxim 1, as stated, passes Kant's Formula of Universal Law as we elaborated that Formula in Chapter 3. However, if his maxim had incorporated the moral significance of humanity or rational agency, it would fail to pass Kant's Formula of Universal Law.

Let us see how to work out this proposal in more detail. Nazi Maxim 1, I have argued, omits considerations that are relevant to the morality of his actions – more specifically, considerations about the rational agency of non-Aryans. Compare Nazi Maxim 1 to

(Nazi Maxim 2) In order to attain the rational assent of non-Aryans to my political aim of marginalizing non-Aryan rational agents, I will harass them whenever the opportunity presents itself to discourage them from protesting their marginalization.

Unlike Nazi Maxim 1, Nazi Maxim 2 does not seem innocuous, either from the perspective of the Formula of Humanity or, more importantly for our purposes, that of the Formula of Universal Law. Acting under Nazi Maxim 2, the conscientious Nazi seeks to achieve an end (the rational assent of non-Aryans to his political aim of marginalizing them) through means (harassing those same non-Aryans) that may well succeed in securing that end. However, in such a case, his success would not be the result of others, and in particular non-Aryans, sharing that maxim with him. As we have interpreted the Formula of Universal Law, it demands that an individual act only on maxims which, if others shared that maxim with her, would enable the individual in question to achieve the end specified in the maxim by acting on that maxim. In the case of Nazi Maxim 2, the conscientious Nazi only appears to secure his end of

[12] Timmons, "Decision procedures, moral criteria," p. 391.

attaining non-Aryans' rational assent to their own marginalization. For the very means he uses in achieving his end preclude non-Aryans from sharing his maxim: His presumed intention in harassing non-Aryans is to compel them to accede to their own political marginalization, but not by rationally assenting to it. Rather, the conscientious Nazi can secure his end by acting on this maxim only through the threats, bullying, etc., that constitute harassment. If he acts successfully on Nazi Maxim 2, it will be precisely because non-Aryans do not share this maxim with him.

By including facts about the rational agency of those affected by acting upon it, facts that are not expressed in Nazi Maxim 1, Nazi Maxim 2 manifests the kind of rational contradiction that Kant's Formula of Universal Law condemns. Hence, Nazi Maxim 2 offers us a solution to the 'false negatives' problem. The conscientious Nazi's original maxim, Nazi Maxim 1, does not fail Kant's universalization test. But Nazi Maxim 2, which incorporates morally salient facts about the rational agency of those affected by its being acted on, does fail Kant's universalization test. And insofar as Kantianism demands that maxims reflect all the morally salient facts about the rational agency of those affected by its being acted upon, Nazi Maxim 2, which does not generate a 'false negative,' is the better representation of the conscientious Nazi's actions.

Kant's critics might worry that my response to the 'false negative' worry does not so much address it as sidestep it. After all, according to Kant, the moral status of a person's actions is determined by the maxim she takes to justify her actions. In the case of the conscientious Nazi, that seems to be the morally permissible Nazi Maxim 1. So is it not simply irrelevant that Nazi Maxim 2, which the conscientious Nazi did *not* act on, is morally impermissible? If the moral status of a person's action is determined by her maxim, then the moral status of some maxim which was not hers appears irrelevant to the moral status of what she in fact did.

I readily grant that in claiming that the conscientious Nazi acts wrongly because he acts on Nazi Maxim 1 *instead* of Nazi Maxim 2, I am modifying an important element of the received picture of Kant's ethics. On the received picture, all that matters to the morality of a person's action is whether the maxim of her action – the maxim she in fact acts upon – can be universalized without contradiction. I grant that Nazi Maxim 1 can be so universalized, but claim that the immorality of the conscientious Nazi's actions stems from his *not* acting on Nazi Maxim 2. This claim makes Kant's maxim-based morality more complicated, and, in general, we should prefer simpler theories to more complicated ones. But in this case, I believe that this greater complexity is offset by a more plausible Kantian theory overall. As we saw in Section 3.6, many apparently immoral maxims will display their morally objectionable features when we try to universalize them. We find, for instance, that false promising is morally objectionable because in order to pursue one's end by way of a false promise, others have to not share the false promisor's maxim. Part of living morally has to do, then, with what maxims we act upon and whether those maxims can be rationally acted upon when shared with others.

But another part of living morally is recognizing what matters from a moral point of view. As we have seen, Kantians believe that what fundamentally matters from a moral point of view is rational agency. And it would be remarkable indeed if an individual could live a morally good life by adopting maxims that, like Nazi Maxim 1, manage to be rationally consistent while being seemingly indifferent to the moral importance of rational agency. Here our earlier analogy with consistency of belief comes into play again. As we noted in Section 3.8, to have inconsistent beliefs is a sign of irrationality. So too, we suggested, was having inconsistent stances toward one and the same maxim – both willing that it be universalized and that it not be universalized. But it has often been pointed out that having consistent beliefs is no assurance that those beliefs will be true. Imagine, for instance, someone who, thanks to a brain injury, has an impaired sense of smell. She might, for instance, be able to smell only some odors. According to one common classificatory scheme, there are six basic odors: flowery, foul, fruity, spicy, burnt, and resinous. A person who could only detect the first three – flowery, foul, fruity – could well have a consistent set of beliefs about what the world smells like. That is, her beliefs about the smells of different substances would not be contradictory. However, her inability to detect spicy, burnt, or resinous odors would entail that she would nevertheless have false beliefs about the smells of cinnamon, ashes, or pine. Namely, she would believe these to be odorless. In this respect, her beliefs regarding how the world smells would be erroneous despite being logically consistent with one another. In an important way, someone with such an impaired sense of smell is cut off from olfactory reality. For in order to have true beliefs about that reality, one must be able to detect all the salient features of that reality. Merely having consistent beliefs is necessary but not sufficient for one's beliefs to be true.

In a similar vein, a person whose maxims were rationally consistent in the way that the Formula of Universal Law requires could nevertheless be cut off from moral reality. In theory, all of her maxims might be such that if universalized, she could act rationally on those maxims to achieve her ends. However, as the example of the conscientious Nazi illustrates, she might fail to take into account what (according to Kantians at least) constitutes the fundamental fact about moral reality – namely, the distinctive value of rational agency – and as a result she may act on a morally wrongful maxim that is nevertheless rationally consistent. And just as having consistent beliefs is necessary but not sufficient for one's beliefs to be true, having maxims that are rationally consistent is necessary but not sufficient for one's actions to be morally justified. The conscientious Nazi thus suffers from a kind of moral blindness, an inability to detect or to be rationally engaged by the value of rational agency. By contrast, a morally virtuous agent's maxims are not only rationally consistent; they also reflect her grasping fully the moral significance of rational agency. For her, rational agency is morally salient, whereas it is not for the conscientious Nazi.[13]

Let us review the response given to the wrong answers objection. As we have seen, this is in fact a pair of objections. The first is that Kant's Formula of Universal Law generates false positives, condemning seemingly innocuous actions whose maxims cannot be universalized. There I suggested that the maxims that generate false positives are often not good candidates for agents' maxims because they incorporate more specific facts or considerations than are necessary to make sense of those maxims as expressing the agents' reasons for action. And where the agents' reasons for action do rest on these very specific facts, we have good reason to think that agents do not act rightly when they insist on being able to act on the basis of these specific facts. The second is that the Formula of Universal Law generates false negatives, failing to condemn conduct (such as the conscientious Nazi's harassment of non-Aryans) that is obviously immoral. To answer this objection, I proposed a revision to the standard picture of Kant's Formula of Universal Law. A maxim can violate this Formula by failing to be universalizable or by being universalizable only because the maxim does not respond to the value of rational agency. Maxims of the latter sort, once revamped to be adequately responsive to the value of rational agency, turn out to be non-universalizable as well.

6.4 The Equivalence of the Categorical Imperative Formulas

Addressing the 'false negatives' objection by appealing to how maxims can fail to incorporate the core Kantian value of rational agency has the added benefit of enabling us to elaborate further on a vexing issue in Kantian ethics – namely, the relations among the different formulations of the Categorical Imperative and their supposed equivalence. As we noted in Section 3.10, there are good reasons to think that the Formula of Universal Law and the Formula of Humanity are *practically* equivalent – that is, that any action deemed permissible by one Formula will be found similarly permissible by the other Formula, and any action deemed impermissible by one Formula will be found similarly impermissible by the other Formula. In other words, these Formulas have *co-extensive* implications regarding the morality of our

[13] Barbara Herman, "The practice of moral judgment," offers the best known account of the role of moral salience in a Kantian picture of ethics.

actions. That we can derive much of Kant's taxonomy of duties from either Formula is good evidence for this practical equivalence.

However, it is less clear that that these Formulas are *metaphysically* equivalent. By this I mean that is disputable whether the properties referred to in these two Formulas are one and the same. On its face,

that an act treats rational agency as an end in itself

and

that an act's maxim can be consistently universalized

seem to be different properties of the same act. One reason for denying their metaphysical equivalence is that we can credibly doubt whether an act that has one property has the other. That is not the case with properties that are related 'analytically,' as Kant would have put it. In contrast, *being a bachelor* and *being an unmarried male* are such that we cannot credibly doubt that anything with one of these properties has the other and vice versa.

That said, Kant sometimes appears to assert that these two properties are metaphysically equivalent, or close to it:

> to say that in the use of means to any end I am to limit my maxim to the condition of its universal validity as a law for every subject is tantamount to saying that the subject of ends, that is, the rational being itself, must be made the basis of all maxims of actions, never merely as a means but as the supreme limiting condition in the use of all means, that is, always at the same time as an end. (G 4:438)

I suggested earlier that, in this passage, Kant gestures at how these two properties are linked by the notion of justification to others: In refraining from acting on maxims that require for their instrumental rationality that others not share those maxims with us, we also treat others' humanity as an end in itself. Both principles direct us to treat rational agency, particularly that of others, as an ally with whom we are obligated to partner in pursuing.

Our response to the 'false negatives' objection brings into relief additional connections between the two Formulas. I have in effect argued that a necessary condition on a maxim's being permissible, from the standpoint of the Formula of Universal Law, is that it incorporate or take account of the rational agency of those who would be effected by its universalization – that Nazi Maxim 1 is morally permissible because it fails to do so despite 'officially' passing the Formula's universalization test. At G 4:438, Kant says that "the subject of ends" or "the rational being itself must be made the basis of all maxims." I propose that being the "subject of ends" – that is, being a rational agent or an end in itself – "must be the basis of all maxims" suggests a condition not on the moral permissibility of maxims, but on their being *eligible for moral evaluation in the first place.* A linguistic analogy is helpful here: The Formula of Universal

Law places limits on which maxims it is permissible to perform – namely, those that can be consistently rationally willed. The Formula itself is thus a 'formal' principle in that it does not make reference to any specific maxims or specific ends. The *syntax* of a natural language limits how different components of speech can be combined (which elements are nouns, verbs, etc., and where these may to be located within sentences). The Formula of Universal Law, we might say, provides moral deliberation its syntax – that is, its rules governing which combinations of ends, acts, circumstances, etc., one can act upon. But a natural language needs more than a syntax. It also needs a vocabulary, a *semantics* that provides it the relevant components of speech that are in turn structured into sentences. The Formula of Humanity, I propose, provides moral deliberation part of its semantics – that is, it requires that moral deliberation have rational agency as one of its 'components.' The original Nazi Maxim 1, we might say, is syntactically well-formed but semantically amiss, according to Kantian ethics, precisely because it does not take rational agency as morally 'meaningful.' Yet this does not make the formal or 'syntactic' test generated by the Formula of Universal Law superfluous or redundant. It simply needs supplementation by the 'semantic' test generated by the Formula of Humanity to produce morally permissible maxims.

The lesson of the 'false negatives' objection is therefore that it can matter morally *why* a maxim passes this test. The most apt way to criticize Nazi Maxim 1 is thus not to say that this maxim is morally impermissible because it cannot be universalized (indeed, arguably it can). Rather, this maxim is morally impermissible because it does not take into account the fundamental factor – rational agency, and the effect of a maxim's universalization on rational agency – that renders a maxim eligible to be subject to the Formula of Universal Law. To impose such a condition on maxims is far from a trivial move: The Formula of Universal Law has typically been treated as a 'formal' principle, one for which there are no substantive constraints maxims must meet in order to be subject to its universalization test. On the view, I propose, the Formula of Humanity provides a substantive constraint, not so much on whether a maxim passes the universalization test, but on whether it is suitable to be tested. The "subject of ends" is thus the "basis" of all maxims inasmuch as rational agency must be accounted for in order for a maxim to even be evaluable in terms of its "universal validity." The Formula of Humanity implicitly determines which maxims can be tested for their universal validity, not whether they pass that test.

6.5 The Absolutism Objection

The final objection to Kant's Formula of Universal Law we will consider is that it implies a very implausible kind of moral *absolutism*. At a number of points in his ethical writings, Kant appears to claim that the Categorical Imperative entails that certain types of actions are always wrong (or conversely, always obligatory). Perhaps the most notorious example of this is an essay of Kant's entitled "On a Supposed Right to Lie from Philanthropy." There Kant states that "truthfulness in all declarations" is "a sacred command of reason prescribing unconditionally, one not to be restricted by any conveniences" (SRL 8:427). Kant asserts that not only are harmless lies wrong, but we are also culpable for whatever consequences, good or bad, might ensue even when we lie for seemingly morally compelling reasons. For instance, if by lying one might prevent "someone just now bent on murder from committing the deed," then this lie violates a duty – a duty of "truthfulness in statements that one cannot avoid" – that we owe to everyone no matter how advantageous or beneficial the lie may be. Unsurprisingly, Kant's lying essay is often understood to support an 'absolutist' stance on lying: that any lie, no matter the circumstances, is morally impermissible.

Readers of Kant's ethical texts can find other passages that appear to endorse other absolutist stances, such as that suicide is always wrong. As Kant's critics see it, if Kant's ethics implies this kind of absolutism, then so much the worse for Kant's ethics. No doubt absolutist understandings of morality are very influential in Western culture. This can perhaps be traced to the prominence of Judeo-Christian ethical ideals. The Ten Commandments, for example, appears to be a list of absolute prohibitions against killing, stealing, and the like. And we often suppose that someone who is unwilling to perform actions of a certain type is somehow more 'principled' than a person who 'bends the rules' in the belief that these absolute rules admit of justified exceptions. However, I am inclined to agree with Kant's critics that *if* Kant's ethics implies this kind of absolutism about action types, then this is a serious deficiency in Kantian ethics. For a moment's reflection will illustrate the philosophical difficulties associated with this kind of absolutism. Consider, for example, the phenomenon of *moral conflict*. The Ten Commandments directs us not to bear false witness and to honor our parents. Suppose that your parents are involved in a legal dispute and ask you to give false testimony in a legal hearing, testimony that may lead the dispute to be decided in their favor. Honoring one's parents is typically interpreted to mean that one must be obedient to one's parents. But in this situation, fulfilling this commandment requires violating another: the commandment not to bear false witness. Absolutism of this kind thus confronts an apparent problem in adjudicating moral conflict. Kant's own 'murderer at the door' example appears to be another example of moral conflict. There the general moral injunction against lying clashes with another moral duty that Kantians should presumably take seriously: As we saw in Chapter 2, the Kantian duty of beneficence sometimes entails that we have a duty to rescue others from harm or death. I have argued that Kantianism places rational agency at the center of morality. Presumably, the moral importance of rational agency means that we are to protect rational agents from lethal threats, including threats posed to them by other rational agents. By lying in an attempt to stop a murder, we are responding appropriately to the special value that rational agents have in Kantian morality. And while we may regret that a lie may be necessary to prevent the destruction of a rational agent, if any lie is morally justified, lying to prevent such a murder is.

So, in general, it just does not seem plausible to think every act of a given kind is wrong (or obligatory). The thought that there are *no* exceptions to these principles – that there are no conceivable circumstances, for example, in which lying is morally permissible – seems far-fetched. Hence, rather than defending absolutism, I will respond to this objection by illustrating that Kant's ethics neither endorses nor logically implies this sort of absolutism.

Part of my response is textual: Nowhere does Kant advocate absolutism outright, and while Kant often seems attracted to absolutist positions about various act types, in other passages, he rejects absolutism about those same act types. And in those passages where Kant defends absolutism, his Categorical Imperative, the supreme principle of morality, plays little if any role. Nor can absolutism be inferred from what Kant says about perfect duties and the obligations they generate.

The other part of my response is philosophical: Proper attention to the structure of maxims shows that the moral permissibility of acting on a given maxim depends on more than simply the kind of action the maxims justifies (lying, ending one's life, breaking a promise, etc.). Rather, it also depends on the circumstances specified in the maxim and the end the individual aims to achieve by acting on the maxim. As a result, a particular maxim that, for example, it would not be morally permissible to act upon could be permissible if the circumstances or the end specified in the maxim were changed. Hence, an act of lying, say, that would be impermissible in a given set of circumstances or when performed in order to achieve a given end may not be impermissible if performed in a different set of circumstances or in order to achieve a different end. So, not every act of a given kind is wrong because not every maxim specifying the performance of an act of that type will fail Kant's universalization test.

Before replying to this objection, I should note that there is an obvious sense in which Kant (and many other moral philosophers besides) are absolutists. As we noted in Chapter 1, Kant intends his Categorical Imperative to be the supreme principle of morality, a principle that applies to all rational agents regardless of what particular ends or aims they may have. In this respect, there is a single kind of act that Kant believes it is always wrong to perform. He is, we might say, an 'absolutist' about acts whose maxims violate the Categorical

Imperative. But the absolutism objection claims that certain act types are necessarily wrong according to Kant's ethics, where we mean by an act type the more mundane idea that all lies, all promise breakings, etc., are wrong.

No doubt the picture of Kantian morality as absolutist, as propounding exceptionless moral principles, has some basis in Kant's writings. Alasdair MacIntyre interprets Kant's rationalistic morality in this absolutist way:

> "Reason ... lays down principles which are universal, categorical, and internally consistent ... principles which both can and ought to be held by all, *independent of the circumstances and conditions*, and which could consistently be *obeyed by every rational agent on every occasion*."[14]

Yet this sort of absolutism, I shall now argue, is not a position best ascribed to Kant.

For one, there are certainly passages in Kant's writings in which he seems to favor absolutism about one type of act or another. But we should be hesitant to take these passages as expressing Kant's views on these matters period, for in other passages Kant adopts a noticeably less absolutist tone. While he sharply condemns lying in "On a Supposed Right to Lie," he is far more forgiving about lying elsewhere. For instance, in his Lecture on Ethics, Kant at first seems to espouse absolutism: "Every lie is objectionable and deserving of contempt, for once we declare that we are telling the other our thoughts, and fail to do it, we have broken the *pactum* [i.e. the social contract], and acted contrary to the right of humanity." But Kant immediately makes an exception to his stance, an exception applicable to cases such as the 'murderer at the door':

> But if, in all cases, we were to remain faithful to every detail of the truth, we might often expose ourselves to the wickedness of others, who wanted to abuse our truthfulness. If everyone were well-disposed, it would not only be a duty not to lie, but nobody would need to do it, since we have nothing to worry about. Now, however, since men are malicious, it is true that we often court danger by punctilious observance of the truth, and hence has arisen the concept of the necessary lie. (LE 27:448)

Lying to the would-be murderer looks like just such a "necessary lie," a morally permissible utterance whose truth would be abused by the would-be murder, enabling him to succeed in achieving his morally wrongful aims. Likewise, Kant readily grants that polite lies, lies made in contexts where people do not ordinarily expect truthful statements and so are not deceived by lies, are not morally troubling (MM 6:431).

With respect to lying, then, the evidence for Kant as an absolutist, morally opposed to each and every lie, is equivocal. So too for Kant's remarks about suicide, an act type where many have interpreted Kant as an absolutist. In the Lectures on Ethics, for instance, Kant says that suicidal individuals are no

[14] *After Virtue* (University of Notre Dame Press, 1981), p. 43, emphases added.

better than animals, the moral equivalent of rotting flesh with "no inner worth" (LE 27:344, 372). We ought to react to suicide, Kant claims, with "revulsion or hate," even when it is motivated by grief or depression. (LE 27:372). For no matter how much suffering a person confronts, she must always choose life over death: "neither the greatest advantages, nor the highest degree of well-being, nor the most excruciating pains and even irremediable bodily sufferings can give a man the authority to take his own life, to escape from anguish and enter earlier upon a hoped-for higher happiness" (LE 27:628). Elsewhere, though, Kant takes a softer line on suicide. He expresses admiration for heroic suicides, such as that of Cato the Younger. And while he does not waver in condemning suicides intended to avoid further misery, he seems to take seriously the possibility that a person's duty of self-preservation may permissibly be violated in order to fulfill duties to others. For example, Kant asks whether a person who contracts rabies from a mad dog has a duty to take his life in order not to infect others (MM 6:424). (We shall have much more to say about suicide in Section 6.2.)

Thus, it is not so simple to ascribe absolutist views to Kant. With respect to certain moral questions, Kant sometimes espouses absolutism while sometimes distancing himself from absolutism. This fact naturally invites speculation about why Kant seems to waver in this regard. My own guess is that Kant sometimes wanted to defend absolutism to certain audiences or in certain authorial contexts even though he was probably not a genuine absolutist.

A further reason to interpret Kant this way is that the Categorical Imperative, which we know was Kant's supreme moral principle, often plays little if any role when Kant defends absolutist views. For instance, "On a Supposed Right to Lie" does not directly refer to any version of the Categorical Imperative to defend its absolutist stance on lying. The point here is that Kant does not seem to argue, or even hint, that absolutism is a logical consequence of the Categorical Imperative in any of its formulations. Taken together, that (a) Kant does not appear to be a consistent absolutist, and (b) he often does not rest apparently absolutist conclusions on the Categorical Imperative, raises the question of the depth or sincerity of Kant's commitment to absolutism. For if Kant really did believe that the Categorical Imperative implies the kind of absolutism his critics find objectionable, we would expect him not to waver on his absolutism. After all, for Kant, the Categorical Imperative is the supreme principle of morality, and Kant was probably too capable a philosopher to think that the supreme principle of morality both implies and does not imply absolutism about action types. As I see it, sometimes Kant felt free to theoretically improvise, defending particular moral conclusions without grounding them in his own core moral principle, especially when he wanted to underscore the seriousness of moral wrongs such as lying or suicide. But his absolutism is far from consistent and not well grounded in the Categorical Imperative.

Another textual reason to think that Kant was an absolutist about at least some act types rests on how Kant describes perfect duties. As we noted, what characterizes the duties Kant called 'perfect' is that they require the performance of particular actions (in contrast to imperfect duties, which require the adoption of certain ends but do not require that one always act to further or to realize those ends). If truth telling, promise keeping, etc., are perfect duties, that would seem to imply absolutism – that is, that it can never be morally permissible not to tell the truth, to break a promise, etc. However, as we have already seen, Kant acknowledges 'exceptions' to the perfect duties of truth telling and self-preservation – or, perhaps more accurately, that there are instances in which the performance of acts of this type is not our duty. Moreover, nowhere does Kant explicitly state that perfect duties are exceptionless. Indeed, in the one passage where Kant discusses whether perfect duties admit of exceptions, Kant states that they admit of "no exception in favor of inclination" (G 4:421). 'Inclination' is a technical term in Kant's ethics, but, generally speaking, an inclination is any motive of action besides the motive to do what duty requires. Inclinations would thus include such motives as self-interest, the pursuit of pleasure, etc. Acting on inclinations is neither morally good nor morally bad except insofar as acting on them can prevent a person from fulfilling her duty. Thus, in saying that perfect duties admit of no exception for the sake of inclination, Kant is implicitly allowing that moral considerations can sometimes result in justifiable exceptions to perfect duties. More exactly, a given perfect duty may admit of exception for another perfect duty. Such is the case, I would propose, in the 'murderer at the door' scenario. This situation presents an apparent conflict of perfect duties: One must not lie, but one also has an obligation to prevent an innocent person's death. Kant seemed to believe that any apparent conflict of duties must ultimately be resolvable, and, all the more, that a genuine moral dilemma is impossible. For when an individual is in a situation in which "two grounds of obligation" present themselves, it will turn out that one or the other of these grounds will not be sufficient to generate an obligation and will turn not to be a duty (MM 6:224). As we noted above, Kant would seem to endorse lying to the would-be murderer as an instance of what he called a "necessary lie" in his Lectures on Ethics, a lie to someone who would "abuse our truthfulness" in order to act maliciously. Between the two "grounds of obligation" in the 'murderer at the door' scenario, Kant appeared to hold that the obligation to save an innocent person is applicable whereas the duty not to lie is not.

I shall have more to say in a moment about how lying in this scenario could be justified in light of Kant's Formula of Universal Law. The crucial point now is that Kant not only did not say that perfect duties are exceptionless, he in fact allowed for exceptions to them in order to fulfill other duties.

As I see it, Kant's critics have brought to their interpretation the assumption that Kant's ethics is absolutist and have consequently misunderstood what makes a duty perfect: What makes a duty perfect is that, *when one is subject to the duty*, it requires the performance of a particular action. But this is consistent with there being situations in which we are not morally obligated to fulfill an apparent perfect duty. What makes a duty perfect, therefore, is *what* it requires of us – the performance of a particular action on a given occasion – not *when* we are subject to it.

Finally, even if Kant himself was led to absolutist conclusions, it is not apparent that his ethical theory, and in particular the Formula of Universal Law, implies any such absolutism. Recall again the basic ACE structure of a Kantian maxim:

(ACE) I will do act **A** in circumstances **C** to achieve end **E**

Suppose that Kantianism implies absolutism about lying. This would require that every maxim of the following form

I will lie in circumstances C to achieve end E

fails to survive the test imposed by the Formula of Universal Law – namely, that the rationality of the agent acting on the maxim to secure the end sought in that maxim cannot depend on others not sharing that maxim with her. Or, put slightly differently: Kantianism is absolutist about the wrongfulness of lying if and only if for all values of C and for all values of E, acting on the maxim "I will lie in circumstances C for end E" is morally impermissible.

However, it seems rather unlikely that every such maxim is morally impermissible. Return again to the 'murderer at the door' example that Kant's critics have found so troubling. Perhaps there are some maxims involving lying to the murderer that it would be impermissible for an agent to act on. At the same time, though, there appear to be maxims involving lying to the murderer that do survive the Formula of Universal Law's universalizability test. Consider this maxim:

I will lie when asked by a would-be murderer for his victim's whereabouts in order to prevent an immoral killing.

This maxim does not seem at all problematic from a Kantian perspective. Let us apply the detailed procedure outlined in Chapter 3 to see why this is so. First, we identify the universalized counterpart of this maxim:

Anyone will lie when asked by a would-be murderer for his victim's whereabouts in order to prevent an immoral killing.

The person contemplating lying in this situation must will acting on her maxim on the assumption that others share it with her – i.e., she must both will the maxim and its universalized counterpart in acting to secure the end described in the maxim. We must ask, "does her achieving her end – preventing an immoral killing – by acting on this maxim require that others not share that end with her?" In this case, the answer is 'no.' If others were to share this maxim with her, she would face no obstacles in trying to prevent the immoral killing by lying to the would-be murderer. This maxim is therefore a morally permissible one.

The preceding reasoning shows that Kantian ethics is not committed to absolutism about lying. Of course, we have not shown that Kantian ethics is not committed to absolutism about some other act types. Perhaps every promise-breaking maxim (of the form "I will break a promise in C to achieve E") or every suicide maxim (of the form "I will intentionally end my life in C to achieve E") will turn out to be morally impermissible. However, the example of lying shows that if Kantian ethics is absolutist, it is not absolutist in general and not because of any central feature of Kant's ethical theory. Rather, Kant's ethics is at most absolutist about certain act types which, no matter the circumstances in which acts of that types are performed or the ends for which acts of that type might serve as means, are embedded in maxims that cannot be consistently universalized.

However, even this possibility seems far-fetched: How likely is it that *every* maxim of the form "I will do an act of type T in circumstances C to achieve end E" will turn out to be morally impermissible? We must keep in mind here the incredible array of circumstances in which acts of a given type can be performed, as well as the incredible array of ends one might seek to achieve by performing acts of a given type. (Try to think of all the situations in which it might seem justified to lie.) Again, while we have demonstrated definitively that Kantianism is not committed to absolutism about lying, it could still be the case that there are act types about which Kantianism is absolutist.

Nevertheless, the sheer improbability that every maxim prescribing acts of a given type is morally impermissible according to the Formula of Universal Law shifts the burden onto to those who wish to associate Kantianism with absolutism. After all, in order to show that Kantianism is not absolutist with respect to some given act type T, all the non-absolutist defender of Kant's ethics (such as myself) must do is show that there is at least one set of circumstances, and/or some end, which render a maxim prescribing an act of type T morally impermissible. In contrast, the absolutist interpreter of Kant's ethics must show that every such maxim is impermissible. She must show, for instance, that

> *I will do an act of type T in C1 to achieve E1* is impermissible
> *I will do an act of type T in C2 to achieve E1* is impermissible
> *I will do an act of type T in C3 to achieve E1* is impermissible
> *I will do an act of type T in C1 to achieve E2* is impermissible
> *I will do an act of type T in C1 to achieve E3* is impermissible
> etc.

In fact, she must show that maxims prescribing an act of type T are impermissible *for every conceivable combination of C and E.* Of course, I have not shown this to be impossible. But I believe it more reasonable to believe that this is impossible than it is to believe that at least one such maxim will turn out to be permissible. At the very least, the defender of the absolutist reading of Kantian ethics has a much greater burden to bear than the opponent of the absolutist reading.

My reply to the absolutism objection has been both textual and philosophical. The textual evidence for Kant as an absolutist is equivocal and slight. He also explicitly allows for exceptions to perfect duties for the sake of other perfect duties. Furthermore, once we attend to how a maxim is structured, we see how Kant's ethical theory does not imply absolutism about lying and how unlikely absolutism about any given act type is. We can thus answer the absolutism objection by paying more careful attention to the underlying logic of Kantian moral thinking, without having to augment the theory to deal with exceptional circumstances such as the 'murderer at the door.'[15]

6.6 Conclusion

In this chapter, we have addressed several objections to Kant's Formula of Universal Law:

- the identification objection: that we are unable to identify the maxims on which individuals act and are therefore unable to rely upon the Formula of Universal Law to morally evaluate human conduct
- the wrong answers objection: that the Formula of Universal Law implies implausible answers about the morality of certain maxims, sometimes implying that morally permissible maxims are impermissible (false positives), other times implying that morally impermissible maxims are permissible (false negatives)
- the absolutism objection: that the Formula of Universal Law results in an unlikely form of absolutism about acts such as lying or suicide

Ultimately, none of these objections raise insurmountable difficulties for Kant's defenders. Suitably and subtly interpreted, the Formula of Universal Law does not imply absolutism nor does it imply the wrong answers critics have supposed. And while we are far from infallible in our beliefs about our own maxims and the maxims of others, we nevertheless have several sources of

[15] For more on this dispute, see Christine Korsgaard, "The right to lie: Kant on dealing with evil," *Philosophy and Public Affairs* 15 (1986): 325–349, and my "The constitutive approach to Kantian rigorism," *Ethical Theory and Moral Practice* 16 (2013): 439–448.

evidence from which we can make reasonable inferences about the maxim a person acts on in a given situation.

In my estimation, these objections are mistaken, in part, because Kant's critics have often brought to their reading of Kant the expectation that he will defend a kind of theory of morality philosophers call *deontologism*. Philosophers differ in how they use this word. Sometimes the word designates any *non-consequentialist* theory of morality – that is, any theory which denies that right and wrong depend solely on how good the consequences of various courses of action are. As we saw in comparing Kantianism with utilitarianism, Kant did not believe that right actions are necessarily those that have the best overall consequences or results. It may sometimes be wrong, for instance, to break a promise or to subject someone to medical treatment without her consent even if doing so has the best consequences overall. The demand to respect rational agency constrains how we may pursue good consequences. As the Kantian political philosopher John Rawls often put it, the right takes priority over the good. Hence, Kantianism is 'deontological' in this sense. However, there is a different sense of 'deontologism' that does not apply to Kantianism. In this sense, a deontological moral theory holds that right actions are those that conform to rules specifying the performance or non-performance of certain act types. A deontological theory thus says that there are certain act types T, such as intentional killing or promise breaking, that can be described in morally neutral language and which it is always wrong to perform (as in the case of intentional killing) or always obligatory to perform (as in the case of promise breaking). The morality of the Biblical Old Testament, the Ten Commandments, is a deontological theory in this regard.

However, Kantianism is not a deontological theory in this latter sense. Of course, Kantian ethics is rule-based in that (unlike intuitionism or particularism) it rests on a single moral rule: the Categorical Imperative. Moreover, one version of that rule, the Formula of Universal Law, tests maxims, which are themselves a kind of rule. Yet as we have seen, a maxim is not a rule along the lines of 'always X' or 'never Y.' First, a maxim also incorporates the circumstances of an action and the end for which the action is performed. Second, a maxim is not just any rule. A person's maxim is the principle she takes to justify what she does on a given occasion. It expresses, we have said, her reasons for action. This chapter has illustrated the centrality of maxims to Kantian ethics. For the common thread in our responses to the three objections to the Formula of Universal Law is that this Formula tests maxims, and careful attention both to the structure and justificatory role of maxims enables us to see why these objections are misplaced.

The stereotypical picture of Kant's ethics as focused around act-based rules stated in simple to apply, morally neutral language is wrong, and, regrettably, the source of a great deal of misunderstanding. Kant's ethics is an ethics of principles or maxims. It explains right and wrong action in terms of the moral permissibility of acting on various maxims. This fact has some surprising implications. For instance, one and the same act – or, as we put it earlier, one and the same behavior – can be permissible if performed on the basis of one maxim, but impermissible if performed on the basis of another. A particular lie may be permissible because it was performed by a person acting on the basis of maxim M, but impermissible if performed on the basis of maxim N. This may seem strange at first blush. But it underscores that Kantians see morality as fundamentally principle-based and interpersonal: not simply about how we treat rational agents, but also about why we treat them as we do. Each of us of course wants to be treated well by others. The reasons that motivate how others treat us are essential to our perception of that treatment. We do not merely want to *seem* respected as rational agents. We want to *be* respected as rational agents. The difference between these hinges on a person's reasons for how she acts – in short, on the basis of her maxims she takes to justify how she acts.

Much of the force of the objections raised in this chapter can thus be blunted with careful attention to central tenets of Kant's own ethical writings. However, to answer the 'false negatives' problem, we introduced a philosophically salutary modification into Kant's views. Taking our cue from Kant's assertion that the Formulas of Universal Law and of Humanity are equivalent, we proposed that some maxims manage to be universalizable only because they omit the very facts about rational agency that Kantianism places front and center. An agent who acts on such a maxim acts wrongly despite her maxim satisfying the universalizability test found in the Formula of Universal Law. This is not a trivial modification to orthodox understandings of Kantian ethics. This modification also enables Kantian ethics to take into account that morality is not just a matter of the considerations agents do act upon, but also the considerations they fail to act upon.

Further Reading

Some of the argumentative strategy I use in this chapter has been greatly influenced by Mark Timmons. See in particular his "Decisions procedures, moral criteria, and the problem of relevant descriptions in Kant's ethics," cited above, and chapter 8 of his book Moral Theory: An Introduction (Rowman & Littlefield, 2013). The essays in Barbara Herman's Practice of Moral Judgment (Harvard University Press, 1993), especially "Leaving deontology behind" and "Moral deliberation and the derivation of duties," do much to dispel the impression of Kant as a deontologist in ethics. The 'murderer at the door' examples, and the ethics of lying more generally, have attracted a great deal of scholarly attention. See in particular Christine Korsgaard, "The right to lie:

Kant on dealing with evil," *Philosophy and Public Affairs* 15 (1986): 325–349; Sally Sedgwick, "On lying and the role of content in Kant's ethics," *Kant-Studien* 82 (1991): 42–62; James Mahon, "Kant on lies, candor, and reticence." *Kantian Review* 7 (2003): 102–133; and my own "The murderer at the door: What Kant should have said," *Philosophy and Phenomenological Research* 79 (2009): 17–46.

7 Three Problems in Kant's Practical Ethics

So far, we have largely investigated the *theoretical* underpinnings of Kant's ethics: his criteria for the supreme principle of morality, the Categorical Imperative in its different formulations, his taxonomy of duties, and so on. However, Kant also weighed in on many divisive ethical issues, and for some critics Kant's views regarding some of these issues are sufficiently alarming to cast doubt on the Kantian ethical enterprise as a whole. The goal of this chapter is to investigate why Kant reaches controversial conclusions about such issues and whether the conclusions he reaches, or the arguments deployed in support of these conclusions, cast doubt on Kant's ethical theory. The three issues we will investigate are sexuality, suicide, and the treatment of non-human animals. In selecting these three issues, I do not mean to suggest that there are not other issues where Kant reaches controversial conclusions, most notoriously the moral standing of women and non-whites.[1]

My approach in this chapter is to show that the controversial conclusions Kant reaches in these arenas do have some basis in Kant's ethical theory. However, in order to reach these specific conclusions, Kant appeals to premises that are either unrelated to the commitments that define a Kantian ethical outlook or are implausible in their own right. Hence, a reasonable version of Kantian ethics need not endorse the controversial conclusions Kant himself reached. Moreover, in propounding such conclusions, Kant inadvertently obscured the important moral insights these arguments contain.

[1] There can be little doubt that many of Kant's writings express appalling and misguided sentiments regarding women and non-whites. These writings include his essays "Observations on the Feeling of the Beautiful and the Sublime" (1764), "Of the Different Human Races" (1775), and "On the Use of Teleological Principles in Philosophy" (1788), as well as his primary work on human psychology and human nature, Anthropology from a Pragmatic Point of View (1798). A taste of these views can be found at MM 6:279 and MM 6:314–315. A brief introduction to Kant's views on race and gender can be found in Allen Wood, *Kantian Ethics* (Cambridge, 2008), pp. 6–12. As with much in the study of Kant, Kant's views are more complicated than they first appear. His views seemed to have changed over time, particularly as regards race. Pauline Kleingeld's work is seminal here. See her "Kant's second thoughts on race," *Philosophical Quarterly* 57 (2007): 573–592 and *Kant and Cosmopolitanism: The Philosophical Ideal of World Citizenship* (Cambridge, 2011).

7.1 Sex and Marriage

Despite having many forward-looking ideas, Kant was (like any philosopher) the product of his time and place. In Kant's case, the time and place in question was eighteenth-century Germany, and, more specifically, the Lutheran movement known as Pietism. We will not say much here about Kant's religious beliefs, but the Pietist movement shared much of its doctrine with Puritanism. Indeed, Kant shared with the Puritans a deep suspicion, even hostility, toward sexuality that his contemporary readers generally do not share.

At the heart of Kant's views of sexuality is an analysis of sexual desire. In Kant's eyes, sexual desire is fundamentally a selfish desire, a desire to attain pleasure through physical engagement with a person's body: "Sexual union is the reciprocal use that one human beings makes of the sexual organs and capacities of another" for the purpose of enjoyment (MM 6:277). Furthermore, Kant saw sexual desire as perhaps the most powerful of human desires. But Kant's suspicion of sexual desire does not stem merely from its irrepressibility or ardor. Rather, Kant thought of sexual desire as rooted in a desire to treat persons not as rational agents but merely as things to be used for our own hedonistic purposes. According to Kant, sexual desire is not a desire for a person or for that person's good. Because sexual desire is directed at using a person's body to sate one's desire for physical pleasure, it is inimical to the attitude of respect for persons as rational agents. Acting on sexual desire thus invites the possibility of treating oneself and others not as full human agents but as animals:

> When a man wishes to satisfy his desire, a woman hers, they stimulate each other's desires; their inclinations meet, but their object is not human nature but sex, and each of them dishonors the human nature of the other. They make of humanity an instrument for the satisfaction of their lusts and inclinations, and dishonor it by placing it on a level with animal nature. (LE 27:385)

This passage indicates how central *objectification* is to Kant's analysis of sexual desire.[2] As the name suggests, to objectify someone is to see her only as an object. Objectification involves seeing a person as a tool rather than as an entity with agency or interests of its own. Kant seemed to believe that it belongs to the very nature of sexual desire that it objectifies persons – that sexual desire just is a desire to use another person or her body, and is thus incompatible with treating a person as a rational agent.

In fact, Kant detects three kinds of objectification in sexual desire and sexual activity. Suppose that A sexually desires B. First, if A acts on a sexual desire for B, A seeks to use B's body for her pleasure, thus treating B merely as

[2] See Martha Nussbaum, "Objectification," *Philosophy and Public Affairs* 24 (1995): 249–291, for an account of this notion.

a means. Second, if B acquiesces to A's desire for sexual contact, then B treats herself merely as a means for A's pleasure. In giving "oneself up to the other" for sexual contact, B "makes himself into a thing, which conflicts with the right of humanity in his own person" (MM 6:278). Third, in acting on her sexual desire for B, A treats her own power of rational choice merely as a means for her own physical gratification. A thus violates her duties to herself. Hence, in typical sexual encounters, the instigator of sex acts wrongly by treating his or her partner merely as a means, the partner wrongs herself by acceding to sexual contact, and the instigator acts wrongly by treating himself or herself merely as a means.

Kant thus saw sexual desire as a motivation at odds with the moral demands imposed by his Formula of Humanity. To act on a sexual desire is to act on a motive inextricably linked to treating persons merely as means, rather than as ends in themselves, as the Formula of Humanity requires. For these reasons alone Kant saw human sexuality as a morally perilous domain, one rife with the potential for exploitation, debasement, and abuse.

However, Kant further distinguishes between natural and "unnatural" uses of our sexual capacities. Homosexual sex, masturbation, and bestiality are contrary to our natural sexual instincts, according to Kant. Such activities are "unmentionable vices" that must be "repudiated completely" (MM 6:277). Homosexual sex, masturbation, and bestiality are such profound wrongs to our humanity so as to degrade ourselves "below the level of animals" (LE 27:391).

Unsurprisingly, Kant's antidote to all of these sexual vices is heterosexual marriage. In marriage, a man and a woman acquire a right to the use of another's sexual capacities. Indeed, Kant thought of marriage as an act in which each partner agrees to serve as an object for the other partner's use and enjoyment. The act of marriage is thus akin to acquiring property in another person. As we noted in Chapter 2, Kant's Formula of Humanity opposes treating one another as things to be owned or consumed. Hence, Kant is careful to emphasize that marital partners do not *literally* acquire one another as items of property:

> the natural use that one sex makes of the other's sexual organs is *enjoyment*, for which one gives itself up to the other. In this act, a human being makes himself into a thing, which conflicts with the right of humanity in his own person. There is only one condition under which this is possible: that while one person is acquired by the other *as if it were a thing*, the one who is acquired acquires the other in turn. (MM 6:278)

Kant concludes that this act of mutual 'acquisition' is the only act capable of removing the moral stain of sexual desire and activity – that marriage alone makes it possible for sex partners to avoid treating one another merely as things.

in this way each reclaims itself and restores its personality. But acquiring a member of a human being is at the same time acquiring the whole person, since a person is an absolute unity. Hence it is not only admissible for the sexes to surrender to and accept each other for enjoyment under the condition of marriage, but it is possible for them to do so *only* under this condition. (MM 6:278)

Kant further infers that "if a man and a woman want to enjoy each other's sexual attributes they *must* necessarily marry" (MM 6:278). Adultery and extramarital sex are thus ruled out on moral grounds as well.

Needless to say, few of Kant's modern readers share his rather restrictive views about the ethics of sex. Kant's views are not, by today's lights, 'sex positive.' Defenders of Kantian ethics are understandably tempted to dismiss Kant's views on sexual ethics as reflections of his own less enlightened, and morally judgmental, era. However, I believe that Kant's writings on sexual ethics contain an important insight about human sexuality that we neglect at our peril and so we must engage with them, rather than dismiss them as historical anachronism. I will argue, first, that nothing in Kant's ethical commitments requires the condemnation of "unnatural" sex acts such as homosexuality, bestiality, and masturbation. In a more positive vein, I will try to show that though Kant's analysis of sexual desire identifies a genuine danger associated with sexual desire, human rational agents can nevertheless engage in sexual contact in ways respectful of their own rational agency and the rational agency of others.

Let us start, then, with the categories of sexual activity Kant designates as "unnatural." We saw earlier, in Section 2.7, how Kant used the Formula of Humanity to argue that behaviors such as suicide, neglecting one's physical health, excessive drinking, etc., can be immoral. These behaviors undermine, or make it impossible, for us to maintain and successfully exercise our rational agency. Kant seems to have thought that sexual desire and activity imperil rational agency in a similar way. By instigating, or agreeing to, sexual activity, we treat our rational agency merely as a means to the pleasure of ourselves and others. Suppose we grant to Kant, for the moment at least, his claims about the nature of sexual desire and its relation to rational agency. Even so, Kant does not seem to have a clear basis for singling out the supposed "unnatural" sexual vices of homosexuality, masturbation, and bestiality as especially egregious examples of the misuse of our rational agency. Those engaging in homosexual sex, masturbation, or bestiality presumably treat themselves as things no less than those engaging in consensual sex with other opposite sex humans. Admittedly, masturbation and bestiality do not also make use of another *person's* sexual capacities and so do not treat other persons merely as things. Still, whatever reasons Kant had for holding that homosexuality, bestiality, and masturbation violate duties we owe to ourselves as rational agents, those same reasons apply to heterosexual sex, which (in the context of marriage at least) Kant deemed morally permissible.

Moreover, as commentators have pointed out, Kant does not seem to have such a rationale for singling out these supposedly "unnatural" sexual vices for special criticism.[3] Kant's ethical writings are littered with references to nature's purposes or ends. For instance, he claims that the natural purpose or end of our sexual capacities is reproduction and the continued existence of the human species (MM 6:424). Still, even if morality required that we not act *contrary* to the natural purposes for which our sexual capacities were apparently designed, it would not follow logically that homosexuality, bestiality, and masturbation were immoral. For while these behaviors do not enable procreation, they also do not stymie it. Those who engage in these behaviors do not preclude themselves, or others, from engaging in sexual acts on other occasions that are conducive to reproduction. Furthermore, Kant did not hold that all sex must be procreative in order to be morally permissible (MM 6:277). Thus, the fact that indulging in the unnatural sexual vices does not lead to reproduction does not morally taint it.

More importantly, Kant did not seem to think that any moral conclusions can be straightforwardly inferred from claims about nature's purposes or ends, including the natural purpose of sexual desire. We cannot, in other words, conclude from the fact (supposing it to be a fact) that the natural purpose or end of our sexual capacities is reproduction that sexual activity must aim at reproduction in order to be morally permissible. For instance, immediately after announcing that masturbation is "contrary to morality in its highest degree" (a claim that supposedly "occurs to everyone immediately"!), Kant concedes that "it is not so easy to produce a rational proof that unnatural, and even merely unpurposive, use of one's sexual attribute is inadmissible as being a violation of duty to oneself" (MM 6:425). Hence, even Kant recognized that his own theory of value does not entail that the purposes or ends for which nature designed our sexual capacities determine the morally permissible ways of using those capacities. As a being capable of setting rational ends for herself, a human being "must owe the use of his powers not merely to natural instinct but rather to the freedom by which he determines their scope" (MM 6:444). As free rational agents, we give nature its purposes – it does not give us our purposes. The presumed natural purpose of the human foot is to enable us to stand upright. But it hardly seems wrong to repurpose our feet for other ends (dancing, kicking a football, etc.).

So to appeal, as Kant does, to the alleged unnaturalness of homosexuality, bestiality, and masturbation in order to establish their moral wrongfulness is therefore to appeal to deeply un-Kantian premises. Finally, in the case of homosexuality, the very institution that Kant believes sanctions sexual

[3] See especially Lara Denis, "Kant on the wrongness of 'unnatural' sex," *History of Philosophy Quarterly* 16 (1999): 225–248.

conduct – marriage – seems able to perform the same function regardless of the genders of the partners. Being an opponent of homosexuality, Kant hardly seemed to countenance the possibility of same sex marriage. But if (as Kant believed) marriage restores or re-establishes the personhood of opposite sex individuals in the face of heterosexual desire, there is no reason to think marriage could not also restore or re-establish the personhood of same sex partners in the face of homosexual desire. As Kant sees it, marriage codifies a kind of equality between the partners. But there is no reason to believe that such equality is any less possible within same sex marriage than within opposite sex marriage.[4]

Kant therefore does not have a principled basis, grounded in his own ethical thought, for singling out the purportedly unnatural sexual vices as particularly wrong from a moral perspective. Still, this conclusion does not directly address Kant's reasons for being suspicious of sexual desire and activity in general. If Kant is correct, sex (whether "unnatural" or not) inherently treats us merely as means.

Is it possible, though, for sex to be rendered morally innocuous on a Kantian view? Some Kantians have thought that *consent* goes a long way in removing the danger Kant associates with sex.[5] As we have observed, Kant believed that respect for rational agency requires that we respect individuals' choices, particularly about matters relating to their most basic interests. This is why, for example, Kant's Formula of Humanity provides the basis for the medical principle that individuals can only be subject to medical interventions if they provide informed consent to those interventions. Similarly, sexual activity bears on our most basic interests (whether to reproduce, which close personal relationships we will maintain, etc.) Hence, it might appear that so long as participants in sexual activity provide voluntary and informed consent to that activity, Kantianism has no basis for morally opposing such activity.

To its credit, this attempt to soften Kant's position correctly identifies a consideration – rational consent – that will be important to any Kantian view of the morality of sex. Indeed, Kant clearly found rape and other forms of non-consensual sex to be outrageous wrongs, to the point of claiming that those facing rape should die trying to resist rather than submit to it (LE 27:371). Furthermore, intimate relationships are an arena where manipulation, coercion, deception, and other tactics designed to induce others into sex are unfortunately common. Yet this appeal to consent will not entirely answer Kant's worries

[4] Matthew Altman, *Kant and Applied Ethics* (Wiley-Blackwell, 2011), chapter 6, defends a similar Kantian rationale for same sex marriage.

[5] See Onora O'neill, "Between consenting adults," *Philosophy and Public Affairs* 14 (1985): 252–277, and Thomas Mappes, "Sexual morality and the concept of using another person," in T. Mappes and J. Zembaty (eds.), *Social Ethics* (McGraw-Hill, 1992), pp. 203–216, for consent-based approaches to Kantian sexual ethics.

about sexual desire and activity. For even when sex is consensual, it will still be true, according to Kant at least, that the sex partners are consenting to their mutual objectification, and it is this objectification that Kant believes makes sex so morally perilous. For Kant, agreeing to sexual objectification is morally akin to selling oneself into (temporary) slavery. Even if one could acquire valuable goods, such as money for one's family, by selling oneself into slavery, doing so amounts to treating oneself as no better than a tool to be put to use for other's ends. In the case of sex, the partners treat themselves and one another as tools to provide sexual pleasure. Yes, doing so without consent is wrong on a Kantian view. But even sex with mutual consent does not overcome Kant's basic objection to sexual objectification.[6]

In my estimation, a more plausible way to render sex more morally palatable from a Kantian point of view is to question the psychological claims to which Kant appeals. The central question facing Kantian sexual ethics is "How can we treat each other with the dignity we deserve as rational persons when, in sexual terms, we are out to use each other for the sake of some end, be it our own pleasure or reproduction?"[7] Suppose Kant is right that sexual desire is objectifying inasmuch as it involves a desire to make use of a body (one's own or another's) in order to attain pleasure. Kant seemed to suppose that this desire is fundamentally incompatible with treating a person as a rational agent with ends of his or her own. But this should be questioned. A comparison: Suppose a woman with a chronic disease agrees to participate in a clinical trial of an experimental drug. On the basis of laboratory testing, the drug seems like a promising treatment for her diseases. Her participation is voluntary, informed, and consensual. The researchers who conduct the trial do use her body as a means to their ends (the hoped-for approval of the drug). She too hopes the drug will prove effective and so is using her own body, and authorizing its use by others, to serve her ends (finding an effective treatment for her disease). In essence, the patient is objectifying her body, and allowing it to be objectified, for the purpose of advancing medical knowledge. But she is also serving her own ends, as well as those of the medical researchers. This situation thus seems to parallel sex in just the ways that morally troubled Kant: An individual consents to her body being treated as an object, albeit for purposes of scientific study, rather than for pleasure. Yet it would be striking if this arrangement violated Kant's Formula of Humanity by treating the patient merely as a thing, as something conceived merely as a means. In this example, the patient is objectified while also being treated as a full rational agent with interests of her own.

[6] Alan Soble, "Sexual use and what to do about it: Internalist and externalist sexual ethics," *Essays in Philosophy* 2 (2001): 1–19.

[7] Altman, Kant and Applied Ethics, p. 142.

This example illustrates that Kant was probably wrong when he supposed that objectification and respect for rational agency are necessarily opposed. It is possible to objectify a person *and* respect her rational agency. Respecting a person is best understood as a disposition to respond to her rational agency For instance, the medical researchers are morally required to honor the patient's request to discontinue her involvement in the drug trial. But while the researchers are measuring her vital signs, examining her blood chemistry, and so on, they are treating her as an object of scientific study. Their 'objectifying' of her and their respecting her as a rational agent co-exist. In objectifying the patient, the researchers treat her as a means, but in being responsive to her concerns, not merely so.

The same seems possible for sex: In the throes of sexual arousal, no doubt few are thinking about their partners primarily as rational agents. More likely, they are, as Kant supposed, fixated on their partner's bodies as sources of pleasure. They are objectifying one another (and themselves) in the moment, so to speak. But this is wholly compatible with them responding to one another's rational agency as the circumstances dictate. If one of the partners indicates that the sex act in which they are engaged is physically or emotionally uncomfortable, it would be disrespectful of the other to continue with that act, no matter how pleasurable it might be to him. If he is morally decent, his attention will advert from his desire to his respect for his partner's rational agency.

What Kant's analysis of sexual desire misses, therefore, is that background context matters: Even if sexual desire is inherently objectifying, the wrongfulness of that objectification is mitigated, and perhaps even eliminated, if it occurs in a wider context of respect for humanity. Consent is one especially important component of that wider context. Another, I propose, is the relationship between the partners. Martha Nussbaum has argued that within intimate relationships objectification can be combined with equality and respect between the partners.[8] Appreciating this fact enables us to see why Kant was correct in believing that marriage can be a powerful antidote to sexual objectification, but wrong to suppose that sexual activity is only morally permissible within marriage. Recall how Kant thought that marriage transformed sexual activity. By marrying, partners give one another access to their respective bodies to be enjoyed sexually. Kant saw marriage as akin to acquiring another's body for one's use. Ordinarily, acquiring another person's body would be morally objectionable. We are not to serve as possessions to one another. But Kant maintained that because the acquisition was reciprocal (i.e., the partners acquire each other), marriage makes their sexual relationship morally permissible. In marrying B, A acquires B insofar as A now has access to B's body for consensual sexual use. And in marrying A, B acquires A insofar as B now has

[8] Nussbaum, "Objectification," p. 251.

access to A's body for consensual sexual use. This establishment of reciprocal or mutual ownership makes it the case that spouses "regain" possession of themselves. (LE 27:388) For instance, B re-acquires himself because B has acquired A by marrying A, and A has acquired B in marrying B. Sexual conduct becomes morally permissible within marriage because it is no longer true that each partner is treating himself like the other's property to be used and discarded, in Kant's disconcerting image, "as one throws away a lemon after sucking the juice from it" (LE 27:384).

Kant's attempt to show that marriage alone can morally validate sex is ingenious, but it is a failure. For one, Kant depicts marriage as a transaction in which property rights are established and exchanged. Marital partners acquire mutual possession of one another that renders sex between them morally permissible. However, this line of reasoning contradicts Kant's claim that the only things fit to serve as property are corporeal things. "[S]omeone can be his own master but cannot be the owner *of himself* . . . since he is accountable to the humanity is his own person" (MM 6:270). But if neither marital partner owns herself – that is, if neither can have a property right in herself – then it is impossible for them to exchange property rights to one another via marriage. I cannot give you a right to what I myself lack a right to. Hence, Kant's understanding of how marriage renders sexual contact permissible because the partners are making use of what they possess and acquire is at odds with the limits that Kant sets on property rights.

Moreover, even if we could acquire property rights in one another, Kant does not believe that we can treat each other as if we are property. Marital partners cannot sell one another, remove organs from each other, etc. – all of which would be morally permissible if the partners were one another's property. Kant's defenders may claim that I am taking him too literally. For he does not say that marital partners are each other's property, but that the rights they acquire via marriage are rights "as if" to a thing. So perhaps Kant did not mean for us to think of these rights as precisely analogous to property rights. Nevertheless, Kant's strategy of showing that marriage makes sexual contact morally permissible rests on suspect attempts to analogize marital rights to property rights, an analogy that his own views about property undermine.

Kant's appeal to property is also unnecessary, for Kant has a different route by which to show that marriage provides a context in which sexual contact is morally permissible. Kant describes marriage as establishing a "household" with a unified will and interests. The interests of the household flow from the interests of the marital partners (MM 279). Thus, by marrying, partners agree to take special responsibility for advancing one another's ends by providing companionship, emotional and financial support, etc. Marriage is thus a form of reciprocal commitment: Each partner is legally bound to treat the other as a rational agent with ends of his or her own in ways that preclude the partners being bound to anyone else in the same way. In other words, marriage establishes duties between the partners that they do not have toward anyone else. This commitment is thus not so much a transfer of existing rights, property or otherwise, as an exercise wherein new moral rights are created. Namely, marriage provides each partner the right to make claims on the other's beneficence. Among these claims will presumably be claims to sexual pleasure or other goods associated with sex. Marriage thus makes sexual contact morally permissible because it creates a moral context wherein the partners have moral duties to another that legitimate such contact. Sex within marriage involves a morally permissible form of making one's body available for the other's use and pleasure.

Yet it is difficult to see why long-lasting relationships that do not involve marriage could not have commitment of the same type or degree. Thus, Kantian morality need not preclude non-marital sex. At the same time, though, marriage represents a Kantian ideal of committed relationships. For marriage adds to existing romantic commitment a legal sanction: Marital partners can be made to suffer legal consequences if they do not fulfill their duties to one another. By marrying, partners restrict their own freedom, since they cannot marry anyone else. But they also indicate an especially high level of commitment precisely because marriage imposes duties the non-fulfillment of which become legally wrong and hence costly. While non-marital sexual is not necessarily wrong, marriage creates a context, and a set of material incentives, that mandates and reinforces a deep commitment between the partners.

In the end, Kant deserves credit for seeing the threat that sexual desire poses to rational agency. Sex and sexual desire *can* be objectifying, and thus have the potential to undercut our humanity. But Kant overlooked the possibility that sexual desire need not be objectifying in particular contexts of human relationship and interaction. By recognizing this – and by jettisoning Kant's confused claims about the "unnaturalness" of certain sex acts – we can recover the seed of a more reasonable Kantian sexual ethics.

7.2 Suicide

As harsh as Kant's language concerning sex is, his language concerning suicide is often harsher. In the Lectures on Ethics, for example, Kant says that because those who commit suicide treat themselves as little better than animals. They are, he says, "carrion" (LE 27:372) with no "inner worth" (LE 27:344). According to Kant, suicide should inspire "revulsion" or "hate," even when we might sympathize with the suffering that prompts it. For, according to Kant, even the individual beset by "grief, worry, and depression" engages in a crime against her body, a "*crimina carnis*," if she seeks to take her own life (LE 27: 372–375).

In the Groundwork, Kant presents an argument for this position concerning the morality of suicide that appeals to the Formula of Universal Law. Supposedly, a maxim to end one's life "when its continuation threatens more evil than it promises pleasure" cannot be consistently universalized because this maxim, being based on "self-love," is incompatible with the self-preservation that our instinct of self-love is naturally intended to promote (G 4:422). Most scholars have found this argument unconvincing, for reasons similar to those for which we found Kant's argument about "unnatural" sex unconvincing: Even if our natural instinct to love ourselves exists in order to promote our self-preservation, it is up to us as rational agents to decide how, and whether, to act on that instinct, just as it is up to us as rational agents to decide how, and whether, to act on the instincts that drive sexual desire and attraction. Suicide may be "unnatural" in the sense Kant had in mind in the Groundwork, but that does not seem to render it morally objectionable, even on Kantian terms.

However, the Formula of Humanity appears to provide a stronger footing for Kant's opposition to suicide. Recall that the Formula of Humanity requires that we always treat 'humanity' – i.e., rational agency – as an end in itself and never merely as a means. As we saw in our discussion of duties to self in Chapter 2, Kant clearly intended the Formula of Humanity to be self-regarding as well as other-regarding. We have duties to develop our talents, perfect our moral character, etc., because we owe respect to ourselves as rational agents, no less than we owe respect to other rational agents. Kant saw suicide as representing a practical contradiction, using one's power of rational choice to destroy the very power of rational choice that gives a person her moral value or worth (G 4:435). When a person ends her life because she believes she will have a better life overall by doing so, she treats her rational agency as a means to her own happiness instead of treating her rational agency as worthy of inherent respect. Suicide, particularly self-interested or *prudential* suicide, thus treats one's humanity merely as a means and thus flouts the "the first, though not the principal, duty of a human being to himself as an animal being": the duty of self-preservation (MM 6:422).

Before considering what many of Kant's critics find distressing about his views concerning the ethics of suicide, it is crucial that we not misunderstand or exaggerate those views. As we noted in Section 6.5, suicide is an issue where Kant often expresses absolutist tendencies. Thus, we might think that critics are worried that Kant's opposition to suicide allows for no exceptions. However, it is not clear that Kant was an absolutist about suicide. For one, Kant's position does not require that we *merely* preserve life. In other words, the duty of self-preservation is a duty concerning ourselves as "animal beings" but one we owe to ourselves as moral beings. By preserving our bodies we preserve the instrument through which we are able to exercise our rational agency. As rational agents, we need our bodies to perceive the world around us and to instigate plans of action that realize our chosen ends. We are thus required to preserve our lives in order to preserve our rational agency. But there can be unfortunate situations in which the continued preservation of the body does not serve our rational agency in any way. For instance, sometimes no medical treatment can cure a person's fatal illness. In such a case, the Kantian duty of self-preservation seems inapplicable. Similarly, a person in a permanently comatose condition, one in which she is and never again will be a rational agent, has no duty of self-preservation. Furthermore, Kant takes seriously the possibility that our duty of self-preservation may sometimes take a back seat to other moral duties. Martyrs seeking to save their countries and those who have been bitten by a rabid dog have duties to others that they can fulfill through suicide. Whether such suicides are morally permissible is, for Kant, an open "casuistical" question (MM 6:423).

Thus, Kant was not suggesting that failing to preserve one's life, or even acting to end one's life, is always morally impermissible. The more worrisome aspect of Kant's position is that *prudential* suicide – i.e., the intentional ending of one's life in order to prevent future misery – is necessarily morally impermissible. Notice that Kant does not argue that many seemingly prudential suicides are in fact imprudent. That is a legitimate worry about suicidal behavior, given that many suicidal individuals suffer from depression or other conditions that compromise their rational capacity to deliberate about the value of their futures. Kant instead argues for the stronger claim that what one's future is like – whether it will be happy or not – is simply irrelevant to the moral justification of suicide. Recall Kant's claim that "neither the greatest advantages, nor the highest degree of well-being, nor the most excruciating pains and even irremediable bodily sufferings can give a man the authority to take his own life, to escape from anguish and enter earlier upon a hoped-for higher happiness" (LE 27: 628). On Kant's view, then, no amount of extraordinary suffering or hardship can morally justify suicide. To destroy one's rational agency (by destroying the body in which such agency is realized) for future happiness is to trade what, according to Kant, is priceless or unconditionally valuable for what has price or conditional value: "disposing of oneself as a mere means to some discretionary end is debasing humanity in one's person" (MM 6:423). Thus, no matter how bleak the future may seem, to end one's life to avoid that future is to treat one's rational will, the very source of a person's value or worth, as a means to happiness.

On its face, there is something unforgiving, even cruel, about Kant's position. To believe that individuals owe it to themselves to stay alive even when, after the most careful and considered deliberation, they have rationally determined that their lives would be better if they were curtailed seems insensitive, utterly disregarding the suffering or degradation that many suicidal individuals report. And, as we have noted, central to Kant's ethics is the notion that we rational agents and our choices deserve respect. Why, then, does Kant believe that the decision to end one's life is not worthy of respect? As with Kant's sexual ethics, Kant's stance on suicide contains an insight that, in my estimation, cannot be easily dismissed. I will try to elaborate that insight and indicate one way in which one might try to defend a slightly more lenient Kantian position on suicide.

As we noted, Kant locates the wrongfulness of suicide in the fact that it violates a duty of self-preservation owed to oneself. However, this fact should not obscure that the same considerations that Kant offers for the immorality of suicide – that when it treats our rational agency as means to our well-being we fail to respect rational agency – also apply to the killing of others. In other words, the very reasons a Kantian would give for what makes *homicide* wrong are equally applicable to suicide. Consider this pair of scenarios:

[1] Boris' teenaged children stand to inherit a great deal of money if Boris' nephew Charles dies before Boris' children do. Boris loves his children very much and wants the very best for them, including top-notch schools and university educations, no matter the financial cost. Boris hatches a plan to kill Charles before his children reach adulthood.

[2] Boris' teenaged children stand to inherit a great deal of money if Boris dies. Boris loves his children very much and wants the very best for them, including top-notch schools and university educations, no matter the financial cost. Boris hatches a plan to kill himself before his children reach adulthood.

Few would dispute that Boris is wrong to kill Charles in scenario [1]: From a Kantian perspective, his killing Charles treats Charles and his rational agency as little more than an obstacle to Boris acquiring the means (considerable wealth) sufficient to his chosen ends (expensive educational opportunities for his children). What about scenario [2]? One reason why we might not find Boris' suicide in [2] as morally objectionable as his killing Charles in scenario [1] is that we typically think that benevolent conduct is morally laudable. And certainly we cannot deny the incredible self-sacrifice Boris' suicide represents. Yet from Kant's point of view, it is hard to decipher any moral significant differences between the homicide in [1] and the suicide in [2]. In both cases, Boris treats a rational agent merely as a means in order to advance his (i.e., Boris') happiness. The only apparent difference here is that the agent he treats merely as a means in [2] is himself. But why, Kant might ask, should that make any moral difference? One does not evade the duty to treat rational agents as ends in themselves just because the rational agent in question is oneself.

From a Kantian perspective, then, homicide and suicide are morally *symmetrical*. The very same considerations that make killing another agent wrong will generally apply to self-killing, and vice versa. The symmetry between homicide and suicide makes the task of justifying prudential suicide tougher for those ethicists sympathetic to a Kantian point of view. They must provide an argument that breaks this symmetry by showing that suicide is sometimes permissible even when homicide is not. After all, if a justification for prudential suicide also justified prudential homicide, demonstrating that it is morally permissible to kill another person whenever doing so would be beneficial to the killer, that would seem to be a *reductio ad absurdum* of any justification of prudential suicide.[9]

Many contemporary Kantians would claim that this symmetry can be broken by appealing to the value of *autonomy*. In 1997, a group of American philosophers, all of them sympathetic to Kantian ethical thinking, proposed such an argument in a brief to the United State Supreme Court:

> Each individual has a right to make the "most intimate and personal choices central to personal dignity and autonomy." That right encompasses the right to exercise some control over the time and manner of one's death. . . . no official can prescribe what shall be orthodox in politics, nationalism, religion, or other matters of opinion or force citizens to confess by word or act their faith therein. A person's interest in following his own convictions at the end of life is so central a part of the more general right to make "intimate and personal choices" for himself that a failure to protect that particular interest would undermine the general right altogether. Death is, for each of us, among the most significant events of life. Most of us see death – whatever we think will follow it – as the final act of life's drama, and we want that last act to reflect our own convictions, those we have tried to live by, not the convictions of others forced on us in our most vulnerable moment.[10]

The authors of this "Philosophers' Brief" were of course primarily making a legal rather than a moral argument. Nevertheless, we can detect in their reasoning certain key Kantian themes. They invoke "autonomy" and "dignity" to argue that fundamental choices about the course of our lives, including the time and manner of our own deaths, are up to us. How we die should reflect our convictions, presumably including when death is prudentially justified for ourselves. Put in more familiar Kantian language, respect for rational agency entails that others may not interfere with how we treat our own bodies, a right that extends to the right to die under some circumstances. If this appeal to autonomy can be made sound, then Kantians will have found a way to break the apparent symmetry between suicide and homicide: Suicide can be morally

[9] Here we might recall the first criterion to which Kant subjects the supreme principle of morality: that it provides plausible explanations of moral obligations we already recognize. An argument that showed that because prudential suicide is sometimes morally justified, prudential homicide is likewise morally justified would seem to flout this criterion.

[10] Ronald Dworkin et al., "Assisted Suicide: The Philosophers' Brief," *New York Review of Books* March 27, 1997. Available at: www.nybooks.com/articles/archives/1997/mar/27/assisted-suicide-the-philosophers-brief/.

permissible because we are autonomous over our *own* lives, whereas homicide is morally impermissible precisely because others are autonomous over *their* lives.

However, there are two reasons why Kant himself would reject the reasoning of the Philosophers' Brief. First, the Brief aims to show that others do not have a right to *prevent* a person from making "intimate and personal choices central to" her "dignity and autonomy." Though Kant does not address this question, I suspect he would agree that other people, including the state, do not have the moral right to *prevent* rational agents from ending their lives. But for Kant, the source of the moral prohibition against suicide is that it violates a duty to *oneself*, the duty to preserve our rational natures insofar as we are animal beings. Thus, even if others are not permitted to stop us from ending our lives, there exists a moral obligation we bear against ourselves not to end our lives.

Second, Kant and the authors of the Brief do not use the notion of 'autonomy' in the same sense. For the Brief authors, our "autonomy" and "dignity" are a source of moral *permissions*. Because we are autonomous, we are morally permitted to make choices regarding our interests or welfare free from interference from others. For the most part, Kant would agree with that sentiment: Our being autonomous permits us (within the limits set by our moral obligations) to pursue our rationally chosen ends free from others' interference. However, our autonomy cannot serve as a source of permissions unless, according to Kant, there are limits to that autonomy rooted in the Categorical Imperative. Indeed, for Kant, 'autonomy' nearly always refers not to the capacity to make choices regarding our own interests or welfare, but to our 'positive' freedom, our being subject to the rational demands set by morality. "Autonomy" is the "ground of the dignity of human nature and of every rational nature" (G 4:436), that "property of the will," according to Kant, by which the will provides itself the Categorical Imperative as the moral law or the "sole principle" of morality (G 4:433, 4: 440; C2 5:33). Our autonomy is thus the source of morality and of moral requirements that limit how we may pursue our own interests or welfare. To end our lives is to treat the very source of morality – our autonomy or our rational agency – merely as a means to our own interests and welfare, and that is no more permissible than it is to treat *others*' autonomy or rational agency merely as a means to our own interests or welfare.

Kant thus saw suicide as representing a practical contradiction: using one's power of rational choice to destroy the very power of rational choice that gives a person her moral value or worth. David Velleman has recently argued against the right to die on similar Kantian terms. Velleman concedes that autonomy is a source of moral permissions – in particular, that because people are autonomous, we should defer to their judgments about what is good for them, or, to put it in more Kantian language, what ends they ought to adopt. But Velleman argues that this deference makes sense only if there is something good or valuable about a person apart from her interests, a fact about her that makes *her* valuable.

> what's good for you wouldn't matter if you didn't matter. . . . what's good for a person is worth caring about only out of concern for the person, and hence only insofar as he is worth caring about. A person's good has only hypothetical or conditional value, which depends on the value of the person himself.[11]

It is incoherent, according to Velleman, to treat a person's autonomy, the source or rationale for deferring to her autonomous judgment about what is good for her, as something over which she has authority. If a person is permitted to choose her profession or whom to marry because she is autonomous, she cannot autonomously renounce her autonomous agency. A person's autonomy "isn't something that he can accept or decline, since it isn't a value *for* him; it's a value *in* him, which he can only violate or respect." Hence, a person who engages in suicide is failing to value her own autonomy properly. She is treating her own autonomy "like a stick of dynamite, which realizes its nature by blowing itself up."[12]

Velleman's neo-Kantian argument contains an important insight. If the fact that we are autonomous is what mandates respect for our rational choices, then the choice to destroy ourselves is the choice to destroy the very thing that serves as the source of respect for our choices. That, Kant and Velleman maintain, is incoherent. Respect for our choices must ultimately be based in something that is valuable independent of our choices – our autonomy.

To show that prudential, or self-interested, suicide could be permissible on a Kantian view requires, as we have seen, showing how suicide is morally distinguishable from homicide. I do not see any path by which Kant, or anyone espousing a recognizably Kantian ethical perspective, could argue that prudential suicide is *in general* morally permissible while homicide is not. The respect for rational agency, and in particular the claim that we are not morally permitted to subordinate our rational agency to the contingent ends that constitute our happiness, bars Kantians from a permissive moral stance on killing. However, there is a path by which some self-concerning suicides could be morally permissible from a Kantian perspective.

Imagine a severely and persistently depressed person, someone who cannot find satisfaction or fulfillment in any activities or pursuits. This individual is not merely a *pessimist* regarding her well-being. Her reality is not that she has ends or purposes she has willed – that is, ends she is rationally committed to pursuing, but believes these ends stand little chance of being realized. She is instead a *nihilist* regarding her own ends or happiness. A nihilist does not have

[11] "A right of self-termination?" p. 611. [12] "A right of self-termination?" p. 625.

any personal ends she cares about and so has no basis for choosing which ends to pursue. A nihilist has not given up on pursuing ends she cares about. She has given up on her ends, and on the having of ends, altogether. In Kantian terms, she recognizes the force of no hypothetical imperatives. Her desire to end what would feel like a pointless, hollow, disillusioned life would be understandable. But even here Kant must dig in his heels. Suicide in this instance, Kant would likely say, wrongfully prioritizes the ends that constitute her happiness, which has price, over her rational agency, which has dignity. Her rational agency retains its value independently of what she may use it for – rational agency is a source of unconditioned value even for those who find themselves without any ends to be pursued with that rational agency. Or so Kant would say.

Yet note that Kant's reason for morally opposing suicide does not straightforwardly apply to nihilistically motivated suicide. Our depressed nihilist is not opting for *her* ends over her rational agency, for she does not have the sorts of ends that make her rational agency valuable to her. Her situation is akin to a structural degradation or collapse of her rational agency instead of an inversion of the proper relationship between her agency and her ends. She may well be capable of respecting others as ends in themselves, but she has no ends of her own that she wills. And in such a case, I suggest that her suicide is nevertheless in her interests in that she literally has no interest in continuing to live. There is nothing, however remote its possibility, to live for. Thus, the nihilist cannot engage in the morally illicit exchange – her rational agency for her contingent ends – that Kant condemns. Her suicide lacks the features that make it wrong on a Kantian view: She is not disrespecting her humanity, treating it merely as a means to her happiness or other discretionary ends.

If (as I believe) nihilistic suicide is not necessarily morally impermissible, then it seems as if Kant erred in thinking that all self-interested suicide is morally impermissible. Where exactly does Kant's argument err? Kant's mistake, I contend, was to believe that our rational agency is valuable irrespective of its relationship to our happiness – that our rational agency confers upon us priceless dignity regardless of whether we also have ends the commitment to, and pursuit of which, constitute our happiness. I propose that rational agency should instead be seen as having *contrastive* value[13] – that is, rational agency's value consists not in its having dignity per se, but in its having *dignity rather than price.* Our dignity derives from our rational agency rather than from our contingent ends. However, our rational agency lends us dignity only if we also have such ends. For nihilistic agents who lack such ends, their rational agency does not confer upon them priceless dignity precisely because nothing about them has price. Hence, it is not morally impermissible for them to destroy their own rational agency via suicide.

[13] On contrastivism, see Martijn Blaauw, *Contrastivism in Philosophy* (Routledge, 2012).

There is, then, a modified basis for concluding that *some* prudentially justified suicides, those undertaken by genuinely nihilistic agents, do not treat our agency merely as a means to our happiness and are therefore not morally impermissible. And so in what we might think of as 'the worst cases' – those in which individuals have lost all hope of finding any ends worth pursuing – this modified Kantian view can embrace the moral permissibility of suicide. Note that I have not shown that all prudential suicides are morally permissible. Still, many suicidal persons show signs of the helplessness and hopelessness I have attributed to nihilists.[14]

Of course, 'merely' pessimistic suicides would remain morally impermissible even on this modified Kantian view.[15] Again, I do not see any path by which Kantians can adopt a permissive view on suicide's morality, given the dignity or incomparable value that Kant ascribes to our rational agency. Yet in condemning suicide, Kant rightly saw a moral parallel between self-killing and the killing of others, a parallel that we should not dismiss out of hand. But if agency's value depends on its being valuable to its possessor rather than valuable *simpliciter*, it does seem possible to intentionally end one's life, and do so for one's own gain or benefit, in ways that are consistent with respect for the value of rational agency.

7.3 Non-human Animals

We turn now to Kant's views regarding the moral treatment of non-human animals. Here Kant held views that, when compared to those of his eighteenth-century peers, are enlightened. Kant opposed the "violent and cruel treatment" of animals, including their being painfully killed, worked beyond their natural capacities, subjected to experimentation "for the sake of mere speculation, when the end could be achieved without these" (MM 6:443), or killed merely for sport (LE 27:460). Some have suggested that Kantian morality should also oppose modern factory farming.[16]

Yet Kant's humane conclusions about our obligations to animals rest on a theoretical basis that many of his critics find troubling. Kant recognized that animals resemble us in ethically important ways: Like us, animals are

[14] Martin Seligman has long posited that suicidal thinking is a byproduct of learned helplessness. See *Helplessness: On Depression, Development, and Death* (Freeman & Co., 1992). On hopelessness as an indicator of suicidal thinking, see E.D. Klonsky, R. Kotov, S. Bakst, J. Rabinowitz, and E.J. Bromet, "Hopelessness as a predictor of attempted suicide among first admission patients with psychosis: A 10-year cohort study," *Suicide and Life-Threatening Behavior* 41 (2012): 1–10.

[15] See my "A Kantian defense of prudential suicide," *Journal of Moral Philosophy* 7 (2010): 489–515, for a more thorough discussion.

[16] See Lara Denis, "Kant's conception of duties regarding animals: Reconstruction and reconsideration," *History of Philosophy Quarterly* 17 (2000): 417.

susceptible to pleasure and pain and have identifiable interests. However, because animals lack the rational agency necessary for being objects of moral obligation, we have no moral obligations *to* animals as such, according to Kant. In other words, Kant denied that we have *direct* duties to animals, i.e., duties such that if we fail to fulfill them we thereby wrong animals. Our duties to animals are only indirect, duties *with regard to* animals. That is, we have moral obligations not to mistreat animals because mistreating them exemplifies, or encourages us to develop, bad moral character. Animals share in our capacity to suffer, and so to inflict, or to tolerate the infliction of, gratuitous suffering on animals thus "weakens or uproots" a crucial moral sentiment – namely, the disposition to "love something . . . even apart from any intention to use it" (MM 6:443). Since the intention to use another human being wrongs her by treating her as a mere means, emotional dispositions that encourage us to love others (including animals) apart from their usefulness to us thereby discourages such mistreatment and assists us in fulfilling our duty to perfect our own moral nature (G 4:430–431, MM 6:387). Hence, Kant concludes we have a duty to "sympathize actively" in the sufferings of other creatures and to "cultivate the compassionate natural (aesthetic) feelings in us" (MM 6:457). Our indirect duties concerning animals thus rest on the fundamental perfect duty to oneself – that of moral self-perfection.

However, Kant accuses anyone of thinking that we have direct duties to animals – that it is possible to wrong animals themselves – of simple confusion.

> As far as reason alone can judge, a human being has duties only to human beings (himself and others), since his duty to any subject is moral constraint by that subject's will. Hence the constraining (binding) subject must, *first*, be a person; . . . A human being can therefore have no duty to any beings other than human beings; and if he represents to himself that he has such duties... [h]e is led to this misunderstanding by mistaking his duty *with regard to* other beings for a duty *to* those beings. (MM 6:422)

Lacking rational wills, Kant claims, animals are "things," not persons, and respect is owed only to persons, not to things (C2 5:76). Only rational agents can therefore be ends in themselves. In contrast, animals are not categorically different from non-living natural or manufactured objects. Animals have only "relative value" (G 4:428) such that we may make use of them to achieve our ends. So, on Kant's view, animals are not ends-in-themselves. But animals can be (and indeed, ought to be) treated as means either to our rationally chosen ends or to the chief moral end of self-perfection.

Even though Kant's position logically implies much of many of the duties to animals we commonly accept, his position nevertheless seems to rest on a dissatisfying theoretical basis. When we mistreat animals, on Kant's view, it is we who are wronged, not the animals themselves. To the extent that, say, cruelty to animals is wrong on Kant's view, its wrongness has nothing per se to do with the effects of such cruelty on animals themselves. Kant thus denied that non-human animals have what philosophers now call *moral status*. An entity has moral status if and only if its interests (or other facts about it) matter for that entity's own sake such that the entity can be wronged relative to those interests. That normal, adult humans have moral status is not controversial. (However, many debates in environmental, medical, and reproductive ethics rest in part on debates about what else has moral status. Do fetuses or newborns have moral status? This question has been central in debates about the ethics of abortion. What about future generations of humans, plant or animal species, or ecosystems? These have been important questions in population and environmental ethics.)

On Kant's view, while we act wrongly when we mistreat animals, we do not thereby *wrong* the animals we mistreat. We instead wrong ourselves. Yet how could it be true, for instance, that in performing painful experiments on a dog and then killing it, we do nothing wrong *to the dog*? Kantians have tried a number of strategies in response to Kant's position regarding the moral treatment of animals. One possibility is that Kant's own view – that animals lack moral status and so we have only indirect duties to animals – is plausible enough as it is. What difference does it make *why* we should not mistreat animals, if Kant's position implies that we ought not to? Practically speaking, nothing. But I do not find that stance satisfactory. Because animals resemble us in so many morally crucial ways (they are conscious, social, susceptible to pleasure and pain, etc.), it is hard to believe that our duties to them are only indirect, resting solely on how mistreating animals shapes or manifests our moral character. One way to make this point: Imagine the most sociopathic personality possible, an individual so lacking in sympathy for others that engaging in animal cruelty cannot diminish his sympathy further. His cruelty toward animals cannot make his moral character any worse. Kant's position would seem to imply that his cruelty toward animals is morally innocuous. But that, I submit, cannot be right, and so we have reason to seek a better Kantian answer, one that ascribes moral status to animals sufficient to ground direct duties toward them.

A number of Kantians have tried to show how a Kantian theory of morality can make room for direct duties to non-human animals. Some base their argument on the claim that animals have "fragments" of the kind of rational agency humans have.[17] Others propose that because an animal shares with us a "natural good" that matters to that animal, we must see animals and their nature as an end in itself.[18] These efforts have been criticized by others, so

[17] Allen Wood, "Kant on duties regarding nonrational nature I," *Proceedings of the Aristotelian Society* supp. 72.

[18] Christine Korsgaard, "Fellow creatures: Kantian ethics and our duties to animals, " *Tanner Lectures on Human Values*, vols. 25–26, G.B. Peterson (ed.), University of Utah (http://dash.harvard.edu/handle/1/3198692).

I will instead proceed directly to what I believe is the best answer to this worry.[19]

Kant held what I will call a *reductive* theory of moral status. On his view, there is one – and only one – way for something to have moral status and so be owed direct duties. An entity has moral status, according to Kant, if and only if it enjoys rational agency. Kant is not alone among historically influential moral philosophers in subscribing to a reductive theory of moral status. The utilitarian philosopher Jeremy Bentham, for example, held that all and only entities susceptible to pleasure and pain have moral status. Notice that this too is a reductive theory. For while Bentham and Kant disagree about what lends something moral status, they agree that there is only one property that can lend something moral status.

However, it is not obvious why we should assume a reductive view about moral status. There are many ways to be a great painter, many ways to throw a party, many ways to become more physically fit. Why should we not assume that there are many ways to matter morally, many ways to have moral status?

We can begin to see how Kantian morality might accord moral status to animals when we note that Kant himself largely assumed a *simple* position about moral status. That is, he assumes that there is only one moral status: dignity, the moral status possessed by rational agents. He seemed not to have considered the possibility that while rational agents have moral status of one kind, non-rational entities, including non-human animals, could have a moral status of a second kind.[20] Intuitively, this seems like a promising possibility. After all, even if animals have moral status, they do not seem to have the *same* status that human agents have. Because human agents are rational, they have rights that animals do not and cannot have. Animals do not have the right to vote, the right to informed consent about medical treatment, or the right to marry. Yet they seem nevertheless to have a moral status that requires us to do just the kinds of things Kant recommended (not experiment on them needlessly, refraining from overworking them, and so on).

These remarks suggest that Kantian morality might arrive at a more theoretically satisfying view regarding the moral treatment of animals if we adopted a *complex* theory of moral status. On this theory, there are individuals such as human beings, who have moral status of a certain sort because they are rational agents. But there are also individuals such as non-human animals, who have moral status of a different sort because, I suggest, they can experience things as going well or badly for them. I do not have in mind that non-human animals can *cognize* events or states of affairs as good or bad for them. As Kant seemed to

[19] Emer O'hagan, "Animals, agency, and obligation in Kantian ethics," *Social Theory and Practice* 35 (2009): 531–554, summarizes many of these criticisms.

[20] I should note that we should hold out the possibility that as we learn about animal consciousness and cognition, we might have to conclude that some non-human animals are rational agents too.

grasp, animals lack the self-consciousness to form such judgments or to understand themselves as existing over time. But animals clearly have what we might call individual *evaluative perspectives*: Some ways things can go for an animal are better than others, and vice versa, and animals can experience these as such. Dogs, pigeons, and tigers no doubt have evaluative perspectives. There are certain events or facts that make the life of a dog, a pigeon, or a tiger go well for them. Many of the factors that influence evaluative perspectives will be common to many such creatures. For instance, life goes well for all three of these creatures if they are adequately nourished. However, differences in biological species mean that they will not have all of their evaluative perspectives in common. Life goes well for a dog if it lives in a pack, but it goes well for a tiger if it lives a solitary life. So too for things that make these creatures lives go badly. Some will be common to many species, others unique to certain species. All creatures need some protection against predators, but only some benefit from proximity to a seashore.

There are a number of questions we might raise about animals having evaluative perspectives. I have indicated that 'higher' animals have such functions, and it seems clear, in contrast, that many organisms, especially those lacking consciousness, may not. Things can go well or badly in the lives of plants or of bacteria, but such entities do not *experience* their lives as going well or badly. And there may be difficult 'borderline' cases here: Those with deeper zoological knowledge than I will have to settle whether bees or mollusks can experience their lives as going well or badly. However, the fact that some animals have evaluative perspectives offers a ready explanation for what lends them moral status and for why we have direct duties to animals. Simply put, some human actions disregard the fact that those actions are detrimental to animals – that those actions harm animals by making their lives go less well. A grazing animal confined in a small pen for its entire life has a worse life than a similar animal permitted to roam. A highly social animal isolated from other members of its species has a worse life than a similar animal permitted to have companions of its own kind. We thus act in morally objectionable ways when we subject animals to gratuitous suffering (sadistic treatment of animals, for example), when we make use of animals for purely discretionary human purposes (for example, bullfighting), or when we pursue our ends by making use of animals when they could be pursued equally effectively without using animals (experimenting on animals when alternative experimental protocols are available). Kant was therefore correct in thinking that we have a duty not to harm animals, but he misclassifies this duty. Even if Kant was correct in holding that harming animals makes our own moral character worse, such harm is also wrong because animals are entitled to have their evaluative perspectives taken into account in how they are treated.

Notice that this conclusion need not entail a blanket moral prohibition on harming animals. Sometimes it can be morally justified to harm some animals in order to protect other animals from being harmed, as when we intervene in animal populations to achieve better numerical balance between predator and prey species. And it can be morally justified to harm animals when doing so is essential to human well-being (for instance, when attacked by a wild animal or by an animal that carries diseases threatening to humans). Indeed, it is likely to be effectively impossible to engage in agriculture without causing some harm to some animals. These conclusions reflect the fact that on the complex conception of moral status I have outlined, different attitudes are called for with regard to human agents and to non-human animals. For Kant, rationally autonomous beings are entitled to have their rational agency *respected*, treated as an end in itself. This demand, I argued earlier, means that rational agency is not a fungible good, one we should try to promote or maximize. In contrast, animal well-being is a good toward which *promotion* can be the proper attitude. Hence, it is sometimes permissible to diminish the well-being of some animals in order to promote the greater well-being of other creatures.

There remain a number of intricate moral questions about how we promote animal well-being that I will leave aside only because doing so would take us far afield. For instance, does the moral status of animals entail that we are obligated to be vegetarians? Answering this question requires a careful examination of the extent to which meat eating harms animals, how central meat eating is to human well-being, and so on. Practices involving human and animal well-being are among the toughest ethical questions concerning our treatment of animals. Just how much might we have to sacrifice in order to fulfill our duties to animals? I doubt there are easy answers here. But the revised Kantian position I have outlined here, wherein animals have moral status because they have evaluative perspectives whereas humans have moral status because they are rational agents, at least provides us a framework for thinking about this question and helps us to see why it is so challenging. In thinking about conflicts between human rational agents on the one hand and non-human animals and their well-being on the other, trade-offs between the two are complicated. For on the pluralistic Kantian view I have outlined, both humans and non-human animals have moral status, but they have a different kind of status. They matter morally in different ways and for different reasons. This difference explains why answers to quandaries where animal well-being and human interests are at odds do not seem easy to come by: To adjudicate conflicts between animal well-being and human agency requires comparing goods of fundamentally different kinds.

In any event, the conclusion that animals can be owed direct duties because they can possess evaluative perspectives provides a plausible reason for thinking that, irrespective of its impact on our moral character, how we treat animals matters precisely because how we treat them matters *to them*. Their moral status constrains how we ought to treat them. We cannot simply disregard animal well-being, thinking (as Kant did) of non-human animals as nothing more than tools to augment our well-being or to develop our moral character.

Moreover, Kantians do not have to relinquish much of Kant's ethical theory in order to acknowledge direct duties to animals on the basis of their having evaluative perspectives. Kant's picture of *interpersonal* ethics – an ethics governed by the Categorical Imperative, respect for and the manifestation of rational agency, etc. – is not threatened by the picture of *interspecies* ethics I have offered here. Again, nothing in my complex account of moral status suggests that animals should have the right to vote or that we should worry about breaking our promises to them. Humans and animals can both matter morally, even if they matter in different ways. Kant overlooked this possibility, but I hope to have shown how a plausible account of direct duties to animals can be wedded to Kant's interpersonal ethics.

7.4 Conclusion

Critics are right to have reservations about Kant's views regarding sexuality, suicide, and the treatment of non-human animals. Here I have sought to show that with respect to each of these issues, Kant has important insights to offer. In the case of sexuality, Kant recognizes the dangers of sexual objectification and how this threatens to weaken our ability to perceive ourselves and others as full rational agents. With respect to suicide, Kant rightly points out the moral symmetry between suicide and homicide, highlighting how killing human agents fails to treat their rational agency with the respect to which they are entitled. With regard to the treatment of non-human animals, Kant very forcefully articulates the chasm in moral status that separates us as rational agents from non-human animals.

But for each of these issues, Kant obscures these important insights by endorsing assumptions or premises that are implausible, unsupported by his ethical theory, or both. With respect to sexuality, Kant signs on to a very un-Kantian understanding of the 'unnatural' and neglects how the larger context of human relations can make sexual activity less morally problematic than he recognizes. In regard to suicide, Kant adopts an implausibly narrow interpretation of the moral significance of rational agency or autonomy and so overlooks how one form of prudential suicide – nihilistic suicide – could be consistent with Kantian morality. Concerning non-human animals, Kant neglects to consider the possibility of a complex account of moral status, one that ascribes different statuses to animals and to human agents while making room for direct duties to animals.

Kant often allowed his own prejudices or lack of ethical imagination to lead him astray. Yet if my revised Kantian stances on these issues are plausible, then we can salvage the heart of Kantian ethics without endorsing the conclusions Kant himself advocated.

Further Reading

Lara Denis, "Sex and the virtuous Kantian agent," in R. Halwani (ed.), Sex and Ethics (Palgrave Macmillan, 2007), pp. 37–48, provides an excellent overview and defense of Kant's sexual ethics. Allen Wood, Kantian Ethics (Cambridge, 2008), pp. 224–239, offers a compelling take on Kant's sexual morality, drawing on Kant's essay "Conjectural Beginning of Human History." For other perspectives on Kant and marriage, see Kory Schaff, "Kant, political liberalism, and the ethics of same-sex relations," *Journal of Social Philosophy* 32 (2001): 446–462, and Elizabeth Brake, "Justice and virtue in Kant's account of marriage," *Kantian Review* 9 (2005): 58–94. On suicide, my "Kant and the irrationality of suicide," *History of Philosophy Quarterly* 17:2 (2000): 159–176, outlines Kant's main argument for opposing suicide. I try to show how Kantians could defend self-interested suicide under a small number of conditions in "A Kantian defense of prudential suicide," cited above. David Velleman defends a more orthodox Kantian view of the ethics of suicide in "A right of self-termination?," cited above. For a useful discussion of how Kant's views of animals are situated within his larger anthropological and biological theories, see Patrick Kain, "Duties regarding animals," in L. Denis (ed.), Kant's *Metaphysics of Morals*: A Critical Guide (Cambridge, 2010), pp. 210–233. Some other valuable discussions of Kantian views of the moral status of animals include Lara Denis, "Kant's conception of duties regarding animals: Reconstruction and reconsideration," *History of Philosophy Quarterly* 17 (2000): 405–423; Jens Timmerman, "When the tail wags the dog: Animal welfare and indirect duty in Kantian ethics," *Kantian Review* 10 (2005): 124–149; and my own "A direct Kantian duty to animals," *Southern Journal of Philosophy* 52 (2014): 338–358.

8 Reason, Sentiment, and Happiness: Kantian Ethics in a Good Human Life

Reason clearly plays a crucial role in Kant's ethics. First, as we have noted, practical reason, or rational agency, is the fundamental value in Kantian ethics. The two most prominent versions of the Categorical Imperative direct us to value rational agency in two different ways. By conforming our maxims to the Formula of Universal Law, we manifest a kind of consistency in our rational endorsements, and consistency is a central virtue for rational creatures such as ourselves. By acting in accordance with the Formula of Humanity, we respect rational agency in ourselves and in others. Furthermore, Kant saw reason as the source of moral obligation, so that the requirements of morality turn out to be requirements of rationality.

I have sought to make Kant's reason-centered ethics attractive and plausible, articulating what motivated Kant to hold such a view and answering the most common criticisms of that view. Yet many of Kant's critics have grave reservations about the central place Kant gives to reason both in ethics and in human life generally. This chapter will describe three objections of this kind and attempt to answer these objections. The first is that Kantian ethics offers us an ideal of moral agency that is cold, emotionless, and abstract, with no place for warm moral sentiments such as love or sympathy. The second is that Kantian ethics cannot make sense of the special moral significance we ascribe to our relationships with our friends, family, and loved ones. The third is that Kantian ethics divorces morality from happiness, thus raising questions about how living morally fits into a good human life. Each of these objections has some basis in Kant's writings. However, I aim to show that such objections tend to exaggerate or misunderstand the place of reason in Kant's ethics. Moreover, critics issuing these objections do not, in my estimation, adequately appreciate the advantages that a reason-centered approach to ethics has over its rivals.

This chapter also addresses two others elements of Kant's ethics that concern the relationship between morality and happiness. The first is his notion of the Kingdom of Ends. The Kingdom of Ends represents Kant's understanding of how happiness and morality converge in a moral community through the choices and actions of the community's members. The second is his "practical postulates." Kant argues in the Critique of Practical Reason that we ought, for moral purposes, to believe that God exists and that we have immortal souls. If these beliefs are correct, then we can expect what Kant calls the "highest good," the perfect union of moral virtue and happiness, to be realizable, if not in this life at least in the afterlife. I outline Kant's arguments for these practical postulates and suggest that his case for belief in them is less compelling than he thought, particularly if the highest good serves as a goal rather than a guide for moral choice and action.

8.1 Reason, Sentiment, and Motivation

One source of trepidation about Kant's emphasis on reason is that it generates an unrealistic or unattractive picture of moral choice and agency. For Kant, the commands of morality are rational commands. As we noted in Chapter 1, Kant understood the demands of morality as categorical – i.e., as applicable to us independent of our individual desires, or, to use Kant's preferred language, of our inclinations. Kant argues that in order for there to be a universal morality, it would have to be grounded in some feature we share rather than in our inclinations, which vary from individual to individual. Furthermore, even if there were some inclinations shared by all rational agents, to ground morality in any such inclination seems to miss the distinctive force of morality's commands. For instance, we are not excused from a moral demand simply because it does not further the ends we desire. Morality would simply lose the importance we ascribe to it, Kant believed, if it were based in a hypothetical imperative. Only a moral principle that applies to us solely insofar as we are rational agents will adequately capture this importance. Morality must therefore rest on a categorical imperative, a purely rational demand.

Many of Kant's critics have taken his conclusions regarding reason and morality as implying an unattractive picture of moral motivation and of the place of morality in human life. For these critics, Kant's ethics offers us too impersonal or abstract a picture of moral agency and moral choice. By emphasizing the fulfillment of our duty regardless of our particular inclinations or desires, Kant represents morality as a stern, authoritarian taskmaster, a set of demands to be obeyed rather than a desirable ideal to be achieved or pursued with relish. Kantian morality, it would seem, is not genuinely integrated into our lives. Rather, our lives, including what we desire and pursue, must first be judged morally permissible, and then (and only then) can we pursue the lives we find desirable. In the eyes of these critics, Kant's ethics offers a recipe for a schizoid human life, one wherein we must relentlessly submit our choices and actions to the rational tribunal of morality. More specifically, Kant leaves *sentiment* out of morality, thereby marginalizing the non-rational states and attitudes that seem so crucial to morality and to human well-being in general.

As with many objections to Kant's ethics, the objection that Kant leaves no place for sentiment has some basis in fact. The rightness or wrongness of our actions depends on our maxims, according to Kant. By acting on a maxim, we act in pursuit of an end, and so actually achieving that end matters to whether we have acted rightly or done our duty.[1] But the rightness of an action is distinct from its goodness or "moral worth." Kant allows that one can do the right thing without our being motivated in morally admirable ways. He grants that we often act "in conformity with duty" – that is, that our maxims are morally permissible. But in order for our actions to be morally praiseworthy, not merely right, our actions must also be motivated in the right way. In particular, our actions have moral worth when we perform those actions "from duty," and, more specifically, from respect for the moral law (the Categorical Imperative is the moral law expressed as a command) (C2 5:81). Recall our shopkeeper from Chapter 6. He is obligated to charge fair and consistent prices to his customers, even if he could perhaps turn a greater profit by charging higher prices to naïve customers. In charging fair and consistent prices to his customers, the shopkeeper's actions have what Kant called "legality." But whether the shopkeeper's actions also have moral worth will turn on his motives. If he acted on the basis of inclination (because he wants to maintain a good reputation with his customer base, say), then his act is merely legal. But if he acted from respect for morality, then his act also has moral worth.

Many of Kant's critics take this position about moral worth to show that Kant was deeply hostile to certain morally admirable sentiments. Sympathy, love, or any other desire (or inclination) cannot confer moral worth on an action. A moral agent who, for instance, assists a roadside traveler out of pity would be acting rightly, on Kant's view, but because any other motive besides rational esteem for morality lacks moral worth, her actions would not have moral worth. Kant's critics get a great deal of mileage from an infamous passage where he seems to claim that we would be better off, morally speaking, without sympathy and other inclinations. Kant first reiterates his claim that even sympathy cannot confer moral worth on a morally permissible maxim:

> To be beneficent where one can is a duty, and besides there are many souls so sympathetically attuned that, without any other motive of vanity or self-interest they find an inner satisfaction in spreading joy around them and can take delight in the satisfaction of others so far as it is their own work. But I assert that in such a case an action of this kind, however it may conform with duty and however amiable it may be, has nevertheless no true moral worth but is on the same footing with other

[1] Phillip Stratton-Lake, "Being virtuous and the virtues: Two aspects of Kant's doctrine of virtue," in M. Betzler (ed.), *Kant's Virtue Ethics* (deGruyter, 2007), pp. 98–99.

inclinations . . . for the maxim lacks moral content, namely that of doing such actions not from inclinations but *from duty.* (G 4:398)

Kant then asks us to imagine this same sympathetic "philanthropist" robbed of his sympathy:

Suppose, then, that the mind of this philanthropist were overclouded by his own grief, which extinguished all sympathy with the fate of others, and that while he still had the means to benefit others in distress their troubles did not move him because he had enough to do with his own; and suppose that now, when no longer incited to it by any inclination, he nevertheless tears himself out of this deadly insensibility and does the action without any inclination, simply from duty; then the action first has its genuine moral worth. (G 4:398)

Few of us would endorse the picture of moral choice and agency that Kant appears to advocate in this passage: Kant's moral exemplar appears to be a dispassionate servant of morality, devoid of all warm feeling, who does what morality bids him do not because he wants to but because he believes he must. Unlike virtue theorists such as Aristotle, Kant did not seem to suppose that a morally virtuous agent has any particular feelings or sentiments at all. Our greatest moral perfection, Kant claims, is to do our duty "*from duty,*" that is, not simply to abide by the Categorical Imperative but to make abiding by it "not only the rule but also the incentive" of our actions – to do our duty solely *because* it is our duty (MM 6:392). Kantian morality thus functions purely to constrain us. The virtuous person possesses a strength of will, persistently subjecting her choices to moral scrutiny and the court of conscience (MM 6:401, 6:405). The ultimate aim of moral self-cultivation is for us to be ruled by our rational nature, lest our "feelings and inclinations play the master" over us (MM 6:408).

8.2 Duty and Sympathy

Are these critics right? Must Kantians believe that a "grudging or resentfully performed dutiful act" is "morally preferable to a similar act done from affection or with pleasure"?[2] Is an agent obsessed with morality, bereft of sympathy, who joylessly and mechanically fulfills the rational demands morality imposes on her really Kant's moral ideal? Should it really be, as Kant seemed to claim, "the universal wish of every rational being to be wholly free of" all inclinations (G 4:428. See also C2 5:118)?

Again, the criticism that, according to Kantian ethics, "our affective nature is not essential to our moral agency"[3] seems plausible if we take certain

[2] Barbara Herman, "On the value of acting from the motive of duty," in her *Practice of Moral Judgment* (Harvard, 1993), p. 1.

[3] Barbara Herman, "Agency, attachment, and difference," *Ethics* 101 (1991): 778.

statements Kant makes in isolation. However, once we see the larger role that inclinations, and in particular the sentiment of sympathy, have for Kant, this criticism will appear exaggerated, even off base. Moreover, Kant's critics often overlook Kant's positive arguments for grounding morality in reason rather than inclination, arguments that cast doubt on the centrality of inclination or desire to the grounding of morality.

As we noted in Section 3.8, Kant believed that inclinations of "self-love" lead us to carve out moral exceptions for ourselves and are the principal source of wrongful conduct. When we act on a morally impermissible maxim, we act in order to achieve some end we desire or toward which we have some inclination. It would thus be easy to infer that, for Kant, inclinations, including even love and sympathy, are morality's enemy.

That would be a mistaken inference, however. For one, Kant recognized that we are inherently desiring creatures (R 6:58). To think we could expunge all our inclinations, thereby clearing the path for moral virtue, is a vain hope. In fact, it would be difficult to imagine human rational agency at all without inclinations. For inclinations provide the background against which we are able to act morally, or even to act at all. Consider again our shopkeeper, asking whether he ought to charge fair prices to his customers: Initially, he may make his decision on the basis of one of his inclinations, his desire for profit. If so, then what he chooses to do will turn on his beliefs regarding what maximizes profit, deciding either to charge fair prices to his customers believing that this will maximize profit or to charge unfair prices believing this will maximize profit. Of course, Kantians ultimately hope that the shopkeeper will not only perform the right act but do so recognizing that as his duty, so that his action will not only enjoy legality but also moral worth. But the point here is that his moral deliberation does not begin from nothing. His inclinations are where his moral deliberation begins. Similarly, our inclinations reflect our attitudes toward certain ends or states of affairs: how we wish the world would go. As such, they are, we might say, the 'first word' as to what we ought to do, our initial judgment as to what is rational for us to will and to pursue. Importantly for Kant, our inclinations are not the last word about what it is rational for us to do. Because we are rational creatures, we can reflect upon our inclinations and ask both whether we should act on those inclinations and why. Moreover, in claiming that morality assesses our maxims, which in turn contain our ends, Kant in effect claims that morality is predominantly concerned with *how* we pursue our ends, many of which will be based on our inclinations. When, for instance, the shopkeeper is honest about his prices, he is acting in a morally salient and permissible way. But he is also doing something else – namely, pursuing his ends by way of conducting his business. Likewise, in selling a product, securing someone's consent to a form of treatment, etc. – in each of these cases, a person must determine what morality permits her to do in the course of doing something else. And this 'something else' will typically be an act by which a person pursues the ends she values due to her inclinations. Thus, for Kant, acting morally will nearly always be doing something else besides: pursuing ends grounded in our inclinations.

There is thus a legitimate, indeed inescapable, role for inclinations in Kantian morality. We could not rationally deliberate about morality without our inclinations in the background, and a good portion of morality concerns how we pursue the ends our inclinations provide us. Indeed, rather than seeing reason and morality on the one hand and inclination on the other as rivals, Kant understood these as complementary, though with reason and morality playing a leading role. For Kant, we should strive to develop or shape our inclinations and sentiments so that they align with, rather than compete with, the demands of morality. The clearest evidence of this is Kant's surprising claim that we have a moral duty to cultivate our sympathy for others. Our sympathetic tendencies lead us to feel pleasure at others' good fortune and pain at others' misfortune. For Kant, sympathy is one of our natural or 'animal' tendencies, but it can be cultivated or developed. We should not, for instance, avoid confronting human misery of the kind we find in slums or hospitals. Rather, we should seek it out as part of our duty to "sympathize actively" in the fates of others and to develop compassionate feelings in ourselves. This does not mean that we should artificially create misery in others in order to provide ourselves opportunities to develop our active sympathies with them. But we should shun malice, sympathy's opposite, and instead heed the counsel of the Roman playwright Terence: "Because I am human, whatever befalls human beings concerns me as well" (MM 6:460).

Kant is not especially clear about why we have a duty to cultivate sympathy. But we can reconstruct his case for this duty by investigating his remarks on the matter. The duty to cultivate compassion is also, Kant says, a duty to use those feelings as "means to sympathy *based on moral principles*," and, in so doing, exploit our natural proclivity toward sympathy to accomplish what "the representation of duty might not accomplish" (MM 6:457, emphasis added). Kant's suggestion here seems to be that sympathy enables us to do what our abstract understanding of moral duty or moral principle is sometimes insufficient to do. How might sympathy complement or augment our understanding of moral duty or moral principle? Kant does not say this explicitly, but a plausible hypothesis is that having sympathy enables us to identify morally important features of the world, features we then focus upon in our moral deliberations. Sympathy, we might say, makes possible a kind of morally inflected attention to the world around us. The sympathetic person notices the suffering and joy of others, registering these facts not simply in a blasé or indifferent way, but as facts calling for moral attention. The individual who fails to cultivate her sympathetic tendencies – someone who avoids the sites of human misery Kant mentions – is less likely to take the misery of others as a fact meriting her moral attention or concern. Moral feelings such as sympathy and love of one's neighbor are thus "conditions" for the "receptiveness of duty" – i.e., not sources of duty, but psychological attributes that enable us to recognize what our duties are (MM 6:399).

As our discussion of the conscientious Nazi and "false negatives" in Section 6.3 illustrated, some maxims pass Kant's Formula of Universal Law only because they neglect or fail to register morally important facts, and, in particular, the humanity of others and how one's choices or actions fail to respect that humanity. Sympathy is an antidote to this neglect, as it enables a large and important class of morally important facts to draw our attention and thereby enter into our moral deliberation. Were the conscientious Nazi to better cultivate his sympathy, he would see that ethnic and cultural minorities are, like him, human rational agents entitled to respect, and as a result he simply would not entertain the morally impermissible maxim involving the harassment of such groups. These observations illustrate Barbara Herman's point that Kantian ethics – or, more precisely, Kantian agents – need more than moral principles or a list of duties in order to be effective. Our inclinations, all those psychological states of attraction and repulsion, including sympathy and other emotional dispositions, shape what matters to us and hence what we take into account when we make our moral decisions. And often enough, we act wrongly not because our deliberation errs – because our *reasoning* about a moral question goes awry – but because our lack of sympathy prevents certain morally significant facts from being taken into account in our deliberations. To use a mathematical metaphor, we reach the wrong answer not because we have identified the wrong function or rule, but because we have the wrong inputs. Again, our moral deliberation must begin from somewhere, and in particular, it must begin from some pre-deliberative understanding of our moral situation. Kant advocates for a duty to cultivate sympathy because he recognizes the profound role that sympathy has in providing us the correct understanding of our moral situation.

But if the cultivation of sympathy is a duty, why then is Kant critical of the sympathetic philanthropist, moved to help others by the prospect of "an inner satisfaction" that comes from beneficence? The sympathetic philanthropist does what he morally ought to do, and does so from sympathy. Yet her act of beneficence lacks moral worth or "moral content." In part, what worries Kant is the apparently contingent or accidental relationship between sympathy and acting rightly. A sympathetic person will often do what morality asks of her precisely because she is sympathetic. But this will not always be the case. Sympathetic acts can be morally impermissible when they are ill informed or done in haste. Sympathy can be misplaced, as when one consoles a disconsolate person who was just caught cheating or lying. If a person motivated by sympathy reliably acts rightly, it is still true that her acting rightly from this motive is the "product of a fortuitous alignment of motives and circumstances," an alignment that may shift as circumstances change. Being motivated by a sense of duty, on the other hand, makes it the case that when one acts rightly, that is no accident.[4] Sympathy is no better in this respect than other motives or emotional tendencies that lead us to act. Recall our discussion in Section 1.6 of Kant's contrast between the good will and other virtues such as courage (G 4:393). Often the courageous act is the right act. But sometimes that will not be the case, and even when it is the case, it is true only as a matter of coincidence. While courage, sympathy, and the like are, as Kant said, "good and desirable for many purposes," they are indiscriminate and so require principles, and, more specifically, the "basic principles of a good will," in order for us to act rightly.

Ideally, we human agents need both reason and sentiment in order to be virtuous, or even minimally decent, Kantian moral agents. Sympathy and other inclinations have a role in prompting deliberation, providing us with the raw materials with which to engage in moral deliberation. These inclinations are thus indispensable to moral deliberation, and our affective nature – our nature as beings who feel as well as cognize – is far from irrelevant to our moral agency. Our affective nature must be cultivated in order for us to act rightly and to be virtuous. Yet even so, the inclinations must be allied with a good will, a will that recognizes the force of moral requirements. Reason and sentiment are thus cooperative partners in Kantian moral psychology, albeit with reason playing the guiding role.

Lastly, Kant's understanding of virtue, reason, and sentiment does not imply that a morally good person is a morally self-obsessed fetishist about morality, compulsively checking to see if her every action passes moral muster. For Kant, the sense of duty mainly operates in the background of our moral deliberation. The morally decent person has a disposition to subject her maxims of action to moral scrutiny in what Kant thought of as the "court of conscience." But this disposition is not triggered by every act we perform. Rather, a morally mature and morally responsible agent has a well-developed sense of when she needs to subject her choices to moral scrutiny and when not. Marcia Baron helpfully analogizes this disposition to the habits of a safe driver.[5] A safe driver does not subject her every driving choice or action to rational scrutiny, ascertaining whether it is safe to tap the brakes or turn the steering wheel. Rather, she governs her driving choices by well-established patterns of thought and action, and she only explicitly deliberates about her driving choices in atypical circumstances (e.g, snow, heavy traffic). Indeed, it would be essentially

[4] Herman, "On the value of acting from the motive of duty," p. 6.
[5] *Kantian Ethics Almost Without Apology* (Cornell, 1995), p. 131.

impossible to drive safely if every choice one made was subjected to rational scrutiny. Likewise, the morally decent agent need not obsessively subject her every choice to moral scrutiny. She will instead rely on her existing patterns of moral thought and action and resort to explicit moral deliberation only when faced with novel situations or situations of moral conflict. The motive of duty thus influences our choices not one by one, but by serving as a "limiting condition" on what we do from other motives.[6]

The complaint that Kant's ethics gives no role to non-rational sentiments is thus misplaced. While it is true that, for Kant, morality's origin and authority reside in practical reason, it is not true that a morally good agent is one lacking in emotion, sentiment, or desire. In fact, moral deliberation could not take place unless we possessed inclinations and other desiderative states. Moreover, for morally imperfect beings such as ourselves, sentiments such as sympathy, when adequately cultivated and discerning, enable us to take notice of considerations that matter to morality and so should matter to moral deliberation. For Kantians, even if reason has the leading role in morality, reason and sentiment are ultimately complimentary, not antagonistic.

8.3 Partiality and Special Obligations

Kantian ethics is oriented around the notion that we are to treat rational agents with equal respect, and, in particular, to treat each such agent as an end in itself. Several of Kant's critics have alleged that Kantian ethics thereby neglects what is uniquely valuable about each agent. As one critic has put it:

> Although the Kantian formula of persons as ends in themselves is claimed to regard persons as irreplaceable, there is a sense in which Kantian respect does in fact view persons as intersubstitutable, for it is blind to everything about an individual except her rational nature, leaving each of us indistinguishable from every other. Thus, in Kantian-respecting someone, there is a real sense in which we are not paying attention to *her*, for it makes no difference to how we respect her that she is who she is and not some other individual.[7]

If this description of Kantian respect for persons is correct – if Kantian ethics is blind to everything about a person but her rational nature – then it would appear that Kantian ethics has no way of differentiating between strangers on the one hand and all those individuals with whom we have what moral philosophers have come to call *special relationships*. These include our familial relationships and friendships, as well as relationships such as those between co-workers, neighbors, or compatriots. We tend naturally to think that those with

[6] Herman, "On the value of acting from the motive of duty," p. 14.

[7] Robin Dillon, "Respect and care: Toward moral integration," *Canadian Journal of Philosophy* 22 (1992): 121.

whom we have special relationships or attachments have a greater moral claim on us than mere strangers do. We seem to have special obligations to our children, to our parents, or to our friends, obligations we do not have to others. But how can Kantian ethics, with its fixation on rational agency, an attribute shared by intimates and strangers alike, make sense of such special obligations? After all, my friend is no less a rational agent than a person unknown to me.

This worry about special obligations again reflects anxiety about Kantian morality's emphasis on reason. Special relationships are suffused with inclinations and emotions such as love. Yet Kant seems ill positioned to show how any special concern for particular others could be morally justified. How could one's love for a particular person be a source of morally justified concern on a Kantian view? For just as it seemed desirable (from a Kantian moral point of view) to expunge sentiment and inclination from our psychology so that our morally right acts would also have moral worth, so too might it seem desirable to renounce our special relationships so that we achieve the impartial respect for rational nature that Kantian morality requires. Schiller penned lines apparently mocking Kant's heartless attitude toward friendship and other special relationships:

> "Gladly I serve my friends but alas I do it with pleasure.
> Hence I am plagued with doubt that I am a virtuous person."
> "Surely, your only resource is to despise them entirely,
> And then with aversion do what your duty enjoins you."[8]

Those who share the sentiments endorsed in these lines thus fault Kant's ethics for its strict impartiality. Whereas utilitarianism asks us to give each person's well-being equal consideration, Kantianism asks us to give each person's rational agency equal consideration. In so doing, it seems to logically preclude both the kind of special concern we have for certain particular people and the special obligations we bear toward them.

8.4 Finding a Place for Special Relationships in a Kantian Framework

Before considering how special relationships and obligations might be located in a Kantian ethical framework, we must tease out different interpretations of the special relationships objection.

On one interpretation of this objection, our special relationships do not intersect with impartial morality at all. Those with whom we have special relationships are owed special concern, and this special concern is not limited

[8] From Friedrich Schiller, *Xenien* (1797), collected in Goethe, *Werke I*, ed. Erich Trunz (Christian Wegner Verlag, 1949), 221. This translation appears in H.J. Paton, *The Categorical Imperative: A Study in Kant's Moral Philosophy* (Hutchinson & Co., 1947).

or restricted by more general moral demands. This *strong* interpretation of the objection sees our special relationships as giving rise to a moral domain separate from impartial morality, a domain that requires us to attend to the needs and wishes of our friends, loved ones, etc., without regard for the moral demands generated by strangers and those more distant from us.

If this is how the special relationships objection is to be interpreted, then it rests on a deeply implausible understanding of the moral significance of special relationships. Human nature being what it is – namely, too often vain, insecure, or arrogant – our friends and loved ones may very much want to be seen as the centers of our respective moral universes. They may strongly desire that the moral claims of others not interfere with the concern or care we direct at them. But such desires ought to carry very little weight in our moral thinking. The warm feelings we feel toward our friends, relatives, and other intimates are admirable, but they should not render us oblivious to the moral standing and concerns of everyone else. A parent who fails to provide aid when another person's child is threatened with bodily injury because (say) this would momentarily distract him from his children is not being a 'bad parent.' Rather, he is being a morally decent person, a precondition of him being a good parent. Our friends and intimates may thus falsely believe that they are owed not just special concern, but *exclusive* concern. But this is the point of view of someone lacking a mature moral perspective:

> If I cannot attend to a friend because of the demands of some prior obligation, I need not view myself as subordinating friendship to morality, or as valuing friendship less, or differently. The way morality may make demands is part of the structure of a mature friendship; it is why we have reason to believe a true friend will understand.[9]

The strong interpretation wrongly asserts that an adequate concern for our special relationships requires relinquishing our commitment to more impartial moral demands. In discussing friendship, Kant emphasizes that it is founded on mutual love *and* respect (MM 6:469). Our special relationships are nevertheless relationships among rational agents who are no less entitled to respect for their agency as are strangers. Our special relationships are therefore not exempt from moral scrutiny. Kant thus rejects Aristotle's famous dictum that between friends, there is no need for justice.

Fortunately, a more plausible interpretation of the special relationships objection is available. On the *weak* interpretation, we have moral reasons to treat some people partially – that is, to give them greater moral concern than we give to others. We can therefore have special obligations to them that we do not bear to others. There can be apparent conflicts between our special obligations and other impartial moral obligations, and sometimes these conflicts are

[9] Barbara Herman, *Moral Literacy* (Harvard, 2007), p. 22.

correctly resolved in favor of impartial obligations. Nevertheless, that morality has an impartial basis does not preclude our friends and loved ones being entitled to moral concern that exceeds the concern directed to strangers. The question at hand, then, is whether Kantian ethics can allow for special relationships as described in the weak interpretation. In other words, how might Kantian ethics see the fact that X is one's friend or that Y's is one's mother as mattering to our moral obligations? The answer, I believe, rests on how special relationships enable us to develop, extend, and exercise our rational agency.

In a nutshell, Kantian ethics is concerned with the protection, cultivation, and use of our rational agency. We should not lose sight of the fact that we do not come into the world as fully rational agents. Rather, rational agency begins embryonically, and it must be directed and practiced. In order to become rational agents – agents who respond to reasons, incorporate those reasons into our choices and maxims, and subject those maxims to moral scrutiny – we must therefore receive the tutelage of others. While some of those responsible for this tutelage will remain strangers to us, those with whom we have special relationships exert an especially large role in this regard. Through their engagement and supervision, we learn to identify and evaluate our desires, formulate goals, and carry out our plans. Our parents, friends, loved ones, etc., are therefore crucial to our becoming the distinctive rational agents we are. These special relationships also afford us opportunities to act jointly with others. When spouses make plans or when siblings resolve their disputes, they are exercising rational agency, finding reasons that they can share and which will guide their subsequent actions. Even in so simple an interaction as a parent playing pat-a-cake with a child do we witness their mutual engagement as rational actors: The parent raises a hand, the child imitates. The child raises her hand, the parent follows. The child reaches out, proposing that they slap palms. Each makes proposals as to what they ought to do, and each recognizes the other's proposals. This is how they are able to play *together*.

These facts of our special relationships – that they enable us to become rational agents who can choose both for ourselves and with others – generate mutual trust and vulnerability. Special relationships are high risk and high reward. The emotional ties we build with friends, family, and other intimates raise the stakes associated with these relationships, creating expectations for these relationships that we do not have for less intimate relationships. Consequently, these individuals can cause us lasting hurt or injury. Of course, they can also be the source of unusual support or satisfaction (as well as the source of significant demands). As imperfectly rational agents, we humans need domains in which we can become rational agents, as well as domains where we may rely upon certain rational agents to a greater degree than we rely upon others. For perfectly rational beings – like what Kant dubs the "holy will" (G 4:414) – friends, family, and loved ones would not be necessary. But for us, they seem essential to living as fully rational agents. We thus have strong *moral* reasons, reasons stemming from the central Kantian value of rational agency, to treat particular individuals as distinctive sources of obligation and to be treated by particular individuals as distinctive sources of obligation. These reasons are partial, not applicable to every rational agent. And yet these reasons rest on the very same value – rational agency – that grounds the impartial dimension of Kantian morality. Kant himself goes so far as to claim that because friends embody a kind of moral ideal wherein they participate and share sympathetically in one another's happiness, we have a duty to cultivate friendships (MM 6:469).

Again, special obligations do not necessarily take precedence over more general obligations. But we can identify clear space for special obligations in a Kantian moral scheme. The most obvious is our imperfect duty of beneficence, the duty to promote the morally permissible ends of others. Recall that Kantian perfect duties require the performance of particular acts, whereas imperfect duties require the adoption of general ends but provide us latitude in how we go about pursuing those ends. Kant's picture of imperfect duties seems to allow us to pursue the end of promoting the ends of others by considering factors other than those associated with impartial morality. Not only can we take into account factors regarding ourselves (such as our level of resources, etc.), we can also take into account our relationships with others. It would not, in general, be a violation of our imperfect duty of beneficence to give greater preference to our friends, family, and loved ones, and to promote their happiness to a greater extent than we promote the happiness of strangers. Of course, this preference for our special relationships would have a moral limit. For example, as our discussion of the drowning child example in Section 2.5 illustrated, sometimes the needs of strangers are sufficiently great or sufficiently urgent that they should take precedence over the happiness of our loved ones. As one prominent Kantian has put it:

> Kantian ethics has no quarrel with the view that the fact that someone is my good friend, or my child, or simply a person I like is a legitimate reason for doing something for that person that I would not do for just anyone, provided that it is understood that neither subjective preference nor personal ties license me to ignore the needs of others altogether, neglect urgent, grave needs, or ignore other duties, such as duties of gratitude.[10]

Some proponents of the special relationships objection will still contend that Kantianism allowing us to direct added beneficence toward those with whom we stand in special relationships does not really show that Kantian ethics takes adequate stock of these relationships. Our special relationships, such critics contend, do not call for 'doing our duty.' Rather, what we value about such

[10] Marcia Baron, "Virtue ethics, Kantian ethics, and the 'one thought too many' objection,' in M. Betzler (ed.), *Kant's Ethics of Virtues* (DeGruyter, 2008), p. 255.

relationships is the care that we show one another without being prompted by moral considerations. A person who, for instance, helped her friend with an onerous task, believing that her imperfect duty to advance others' ends recommends her doing so, acts from too remote or clinical a motive. We do not want our friends and loved ones to aid us because it is morally right; we want them to aid us because they are our friends and they love us in particular. Special relationships are (or ought to be) characterized by a direct or emotionally unmediated concern for another. To argue, as I have on Kant's behalf, that Kantian ethics allows us to favor our special relationships is to introduce a form of austere moralism into a domain where it simply does not belong. In deciding whether to save one's spouse from peril or to save a stranger, moral deliberation is unnecessary, and, worse still, to deliberate on whether morality permits one to save one's spouse would be to exhibit a failure to value one's spouse properly at all. Such a thought would be, as Bernard Williams famously said, "one thought too many."[11]

To reiterate, it is not a deficiency of Kantian ethics that it encourages us to develop a sense of moral conscience, to ask ourselves whether our choices are morally justified. As suggested in Section 8.2, this does not entail that we ought to be moral obsessives. Rather, we should develop the capacity to identify when we should engage in explicit moral deliberation, including the capacity to identify when our partial moral obligations, those owed to specific individuals with whom we have special relationships, appear to conflict with more impartial moral obligations. Those advancing the special obligations objection sometimes seem to deride Kantian ethics for subjecting those obligations to rational scrutiny. But surely it is mistaken to think those obligations deserve no scrutiny. The picture I have developed here, where the Kantian agent has internalized impartial morality as a limiting condition on her partial obligations and special relationships, gives explicit moral deliberation a place without suggesting that we ought to subject every choice or action to probing moral scrutiny. There is a reasonable middle ground between a wholly unreflective morality and an obsessively reflective morality. Kantian morality, I propose, occupies such a middle ground.

Those same critics may still worry that Kantianism does not really approve of the sentiments of love, attachment, or care that naturally grow out of our special relationships. But this is not the case. Indeed, consider again the imperfect duty of beneficence, which (I argued) incorporates latitude that permits us to accord our special relationships greater moral concern. Note that the duty in question is not to perform beneficent acts, but to establish beneficence as among one's ends. To have an end is to be committed to it, to see it as valuable and hence to be guided in one's choices by that end. In the case of

[11] "Persons, character, and morality," in his *Moral Luck* (Cambridge, 1981), p. 17.

our special relationships, this means that in order to be genuinely beneficent toward our family, loved ones, etc., we must not merely advance their ends and thereby promote their happiness. We must will their happiness *as an end*, promoting it gladly rather than grudgingly. Beneficence thus has an affective or emotional component. To act beneficently toward others requires helping them from a settled recognition that they are worthy of being helped, as well as feeling satisfied in having helped them. Indeed, we can be motivated purely by a commitment to an end of helping *this person*.

Nor does Kantianism ask us to be motivated purely by general considerations when fulfilling our special obligations. In, for instance, keeping a promise one made to a particular person, a morally decent person will of course ask whether that is what she is morally required to do. But this does not preclude her also being motivated by concrete and specific moral considerations: that (for example) breaking the promise would treat this person unfairly or disrespectfully. After all, rational agency does not exist in the abstract. Rational agency is only found in particular rational agents, and in doing as Kantian ethics bids us do – treating their rational agency as an end in itself – we are also engaging with particular rational agents, not rational agency as some sort of timeless or shapeless universal. So too for special relationships and obligations: Their fulfillment stems from a recognition of them as individual human agents with whom we happen to enjoy special bonds.

I suspect that the special obligations objection continues to have traction because of a confusion about the function of moral reasons and moral rules in our moral thinking. Specifically, Kant's critics wrongly suppose that if impartial morality permits a choice, then an agent must make that choice for exclusively impartial reasons. But an individual can perform an action permitted by impartial morality for partial reasons. Compare: The rules of chess permit various maneuvers, for example, castling with one's king and rook. But the fact that the rules permit castling tells us little about the reasons a player might have for castling. Presumably, the player who takes advantage of this rule has a reason for castling – namely, that it increases the likelihood of her winning. But this reason does not stem from the impartial rules of chess. Her reason is instead a partial one, a reason *she* has to perform that maneuver. Likewise, that an agent's particular choice is morally permitted because its maxim can be consistently universalized (or treats humanity as an end in itself) does not entail that an agent's reasons for making that choice are dictated solely by the Categorical Imperative permitting her to act that way. A moral principle directs us toward our duties. But on a theory of ethics such as Kant's, the fulfillment of our duties is nearly always *adverbial*; we fulfill our duties in the course of doing other things and pursuing other ends or interests.[12] Whether our

[12] Rawls, Lectures on the History of Moral Philosophy, p. 178.

actions are morally permissible depend on properties of our maxims, but recall that maxims themselves have ends the agent has willed for herself. In (for example) keeping a promise to another, we pursue our ends (gaining another's trust, say) while also treating that other person's humanity as an end in itself.

Likewise, a person's act can be motivated by partial reasons rooted in a special relationship, and the fact that morality allows her to act on those reasons does not transform them into impartial reasons. Nor does the fact that special relationships are morally permitted lead us to have Williams' "one thought too many": The parent playing pat-a-cake with his child need not be playing *in order to* foster his or his child's rational agency. Their actions are morally permissible, and (I have argued) have a sound basis in rational agency, the core value underlying Kant's ethics. A moral principle such as the Categorical Imperative directs us to choose certain maxims and reject others, not to be motivated in our actions exclusively by whether their associated maxims are morally permissible. Kantian ethics therefore has no complaint with the parent playing for less exalted, more 'personal' reasons: getting exercise, enjoying the child's company, and the like.

The special obligations objection is thus misplaced. Kantianism can acknowledge a domain of direct, personal moral concern that in turn justifies special relationships to our friends, loved ones, and others. Indeed, given how that domain enables us to develop our rational agency and establish relationships of trust, it is not clear that we human agents could be full rational agents without such a domain. This personal concern is not unlimited, but to insist it ought to be unlimited reflects more than a desire for intimacy and love. It reflects an immature desire that our loved ones cordon themselves off from impartial moral considerations altogether.

8.5 Reconciling Happiness and Morality

A final worry about Kantian ethics in this neighborhood concerns how to reconcile happiness and morality. For Kant, the authority morality is supposed to have over us – the reason we should honor morality's demands – is not rooted in our happiness or well-being. Morality's authority stems from the distinctive value of rational agency and the concomitant demand to exhibit and respect that rational agency in our choices. Unlike virtue-based accounts of morality such as Aristotle's, Kant's ethics provides us no assurance that by living a morally defensible life we will also be made happy. On the contrary: Kant seemed to hold that morality and happiness are fundamentally antagonistic. Happiness, in Kant's eyes, is the condition in which "everything goes according to" our "wish or will" (C2 5:124) so that our "needs and inclinations" are satisfied fully (G 4:405). But, as we have seen, Kant thought that the pursuit of our inclinations is the primary explanation for moral wrongdoing – that is, that we are tempted to exempt ourselves from moral requirements when they conflict with our inclinations. Not surprisingly, then, Kant claims that the "metaphysics of morals," the scientific or philosophical investigation of morality's foundations, does not investigate how we can become happy. Rather, it investigates how to have a morally good will (TP 8:278, 8:283), which in turn renders us *worthy* of happiness. (C2 5:130) Virtue is its own reward, goes the common cliché. Kant seems to emphatically agree:

> The highest, unconditional end of pure practical reason . . . consists in this: that virtue be its own end, and despite the benefits it confers on human beings, also its own reward. Virtue so shines as an ideal that it seems, by human standards, to eclipse even holiness, which is never tempted to break the law. (MM 6:396)

But what rewards does Kantian moral virtue actually bring? In her seminal paper "Moral saints," Susan Wolf proposes that a life devoted to Kantian morality would not be a desirable human existence. The most "morally worthy" Kantian agent would be what Wolf dubs a "rational saint." The rational saint "pays little or no attention to his own happiness in light of the overriding importance he gives to the wider concerns of morality. In other words, this person sacrifices his own interests to the interests of others, and feels the sacrifice as such."[13] Wolf is not rejecting the Kantian rational saint as a *moral* ideal. The Kantian rational saint does not represent an attractive *human* ideal, according to Wolf. The saint's devotion to the "wider concerns of morality" will necessarily exert pressure on her pursuing the non-moral concerns that make her happy and make her life distinctive. In contrast to the figure Wolf calls the "Loving Saint" (a kind of exemplary utilitarian moral agent), the Kantian rational saint retains her own desires or inclinations. She simply repudiates the influence these desires or inclinations might have over her choices, and, as a consequence, deprives herself of many of life's enjoyments. Wolf recognizes that Kantian ethics permits us to pursue our inclinations and to realize our well-being within the constraints of moral duty. However, the Kantian rational saint must first determine if these inclinations are morally permissible before she acts on them. Acting on her inclinations must manifest respect for morality's demands. The reasons we have for becoming a skilled furniture maker, rooting for the Knicks, or collecting Mayan art are not moral reasons. But in the very act of asking whether one's inclinations pass moral muster, the Kantian rational saint allows those inclinations to be 'moralized,' thus denying them the rational status that makes those inclinations worthy of pursuit in our own eyes.

We see in this *happiness objection* themes similar to those undergirding the motivational and special relationships objections: that Kantianism draws

[13] "Moral saints," *Journal of Philosophy* 79 (1982): 420.

strong and unflattering contrasts between reason and sentiment, or between the moral domain and the non-moral dimensions of human existence, and seems to lack the resources to integrate these into a recognizable picture of a healthy human existence. If Kant's ethics represents the best example of how to ground morality on rational ideals, then so much the worse for those rational ideals.

8.6 Happy Kantians?

As with the previous two objections, there is some merit to the happiness objection. As we have repeatedly observed, Kant was deeply suspicious of the inclinations the pursuit of which constitutes our happiness. Morality cannot be rooted in happiness. Indeed, "the direct opposite of the principle of morality is the principle of *one's own* happiness made the determining ground of the will" (C2 5:25). And as we have discussed, in order to be good, our happiness must be accompanied by a morally good will.

A first step in rebutting the happiness objection is to point out that, far from suggesting we spurn happiness, Kant in fact held that we have a duty to promote our own happiness.

> Adversity, pain, and want are great temptations to violate one's duty. It might therefore seem that prosperity, strength, health, and well-being in general, which check the influence of these, could also be considered ends that are duties, so that one has a duty to promote one's own happiness and not just the happiness of others. (MM 6:388. See also G 4:399, C2 5:93)

The duty to promote our own happiness is an "indirect" duty – not a duty per se, but a duty the fulfillment of which enables us to fulfill our other moral duties. For Kant, those who are unhappy – undergoing "adversity, pain, and want" – are more likely to be tempted to violate their duties. Hence, they have a duty to promote their own happiness in order to minimize the temptations to immoral action. The end pursued in fulfilling this indirect duty is not a person's own happiness, "but his morality, and happiness is merely a means for removing obstacles to his morality" (MM 6:388). We are to pursue happiness not for its own sake, according to Kant, but in order to preserve our moral integrity.

Proponents of the happiness objection will likely complain that this justification of the duty to pursue our own happiness shows that Kant still did not think much of the value of happiness. After all, Kant's justification of this duty does not imply that happiness is in any way good. Rather, it implies that unhappiness is morally bad, or at least a threat to moral goodness, because it makes being morally good more onerous. Yet at least Kant rejects the thesis that the renunciation of one's own happiness is essential to his moral ideal. To the extent that happiness and morality are at odds in Kantian morality, Kant here proposes that they should at least be harmonized so that the imperatives of happiness do not threaten morality.

Moreover, Kant's conception of the value of happiness – and of its relationship to morality – is more subtle than it appears. He was fond of using courtroom metaphors to describe how we internally appraise our own conduct. For example, Kant calls "conscience" an "inner judge," a kind of internal court wherein our actions are subject to "acquittal or condemnation" before the tribunal of our own practical reason (MM 6:400–401. See also MM 6:428–441 and C2 5:98). This judicial metaphor can help us understand the place Kant ascribes to our own happiness in moral deliberation. In actual courts, judges rely upon standards regarding *admissible evidence*. For example, in the United States, hearsay (wherein a witness lacks direct knowledge of some claim but was told of its truth by someone else) is generally inadmissible. The judge (or the jury) must ignore any evidence resting on hearsay. Such evidence is treated as irrelevant to the legal matter at hand. Kant seemed to understand the role of one's own happiness in the court of moral conscience in a similar way. When considering the morality of her actions, a person is not to "renounce claims to happiness" (C2 5:93). When "complying with his duty," she cannot renounce happiness, for it belongs to our nature as human beings to be devoted to our own happiness. A person must instead "take no account of" or "abstract altogether" from considerations of happiness (TP 8:278). Note that this does not mean that happiness has no value or should not be taken into account in other forms of deliberation or decision making. It entails only that, in our own moral deliberation, our own happiness (though not necessarily the happiness of others) is an inadmissible kind of reason or consideration.

It might still seem, though, that Kant thought of happiness as an aim or concern that corrupts human morality and human reason. However, Kant's picture is in some regards just the opposite: Reason corrupts happiness. Allen Wood has emphasized[14] that, for Kant, the inclinations that constitute our happiness are good. However, these inclinations become sources of wrongdoing only when, through our social interaction with other human beings, they generate competitiveness, jealousy, and other vices. Our "animality" gives us desires for self-preservation, self-propagation, and community with others. Our social interactions can transform these benign desires into "diabolical vices" because those interactions invite us to think of happiness not in its own terms but in comparison with the happiness of others:

> only in comparison with others does one judge oneself happy or unhappy. Out of this self-love originates the inclination to *gain worth in the opinion of others* ... from this arises gradually an unjust desire to acquire superiority for oneself over others. Upon this, namely, upon *jealousy* and *rivalry* can be grafted the greatest vices of secret or open

[14] Allen Wood, *Kantian Ethics* (Cambridge, 2008), p. 4.

> hostility to all whom we consider alien to us. . . . nature itself wanted to use the idea of such a competitiveness (which in itself does not exclude reciprocal love) as only an incentive to culture. Hence the vices that are grafted upon this inclination can also be named vices of *culture* . . . e.g., *envy, ingratitude, joy in others' misfortunes.* (R 6:27)

For Kant, life with others shapes our desires, sometimes in malign ways, leading us to inclinations rooted not in our genuine needs but in pathological longings to outdo or surpass others. We thus end up using our rational capacities to pursue status or power over others. When the vices of rivalry and competition spread, we mutually corrupt one another, as each seeks not his true needs but to accumulate or achieve more than another. Kant thus saw that we human beings need one another, but the very need that drives us together also has the potential to engender inequality and injustice. Kantian morality, a morality that asks us to treat each rational agent with equal respect, is the antidote to this "unsocial sociability." Once again, we see a familiar Kantian theme about happiness: Our inclinations are in themselves benign. They pose a threat to morality only because we rationally determine to act on them instead of recognizing the authority of morality's demands.

Finally, Wolf argued that being a Kantian moral saint would not be a desirable way to live. That may be so. But it is worth noting that, for Kant, a saintly life, one directed to acting morally above all else, is certainly not morally required. Morality acts as a constraint on the pursuit of our happiness, but morality itself need not be the most central concern of human life. Kant would agree with Wolf that a decent moral agent is not one "dominated by" the motivation to live a morally defensible life.[15] Kant's ethics thus leaves clear space for us to pursue our happiness simply *because* it is our happiness. Kant's picture is not that reason always prevails over happiness. For sometimes reason itself leads us to pursue our happiness in unhealthy and unethical ways. Reason and happiness must instead form a happy marriage, one in which each plays its proper role in enabling us to choose a life for ourselves that is both fulfilling and just.

8.7 Happiness and Morality in Kant's Kingdom of Ends

The previous section established that Kantian ethics does not disallow us pursuing our happiness. In fact, it commends us pursuing our happiness, within the limits established by impartial morality, for the very reason that our satisfying the inclinations that constitute our happiness is thereby good.

Still, some critics may be left unconvinced. That Kantianism permits, in a limited way, the pursuit of our own happiness merely shows that it is *possible*

[15] "Moral saints," pp. 430–433.

to be a decent moral agent from a Kantian perspective while not being utterly miserable. But how happy is a decent Kantian moral agent *likely* to be? Perhaps the conscientious Kantian agent will still lead a life that is far less happy than the life she would lead were she to neglect her moral duties. So even if Kantianism *allows* us to pursue our happiness, individuals may reasonably ask whether being a Kantian moral agent is on balance worth it.

No doubt Kantian morality understands the relationship between happiness and morality as contingent. There is no assurance that an individual who is conscientious about fulfilling her duties (as Kantianism understands them) will live a satisfying life. And it must be conceded that in conflicts between happiness and morality, Kant believed that morality should prevail. Indeed, this is the point of Kant's claim that the supreme principle of morality is a categorical imperative: The demands of morality apply to us regardless of our ends and inclinations, and hence do not vary depending on how fulfilling those demands will (or will not) promote our happiness.

It would thus be misleading to claim that Kantian ethics *guarantees* the congruence of morality and happiness. Nevertheless, there is an aspect of Kantian ethics that we have not yet discussed, his notion of a *Kingdom of Ends*, that highlights an underappreciated element of Kantian ethics – namely, that individual happiness is to a large measure a moral and *social* achievement.

Kant's Kingdom of Ends is his way of representing his ethics in terms of a large scale social ideal. Note that the two formulations of the Categorical Imperative we have addressed, the Formula of Universal Law and the Formula of Humanity, are principles that direct us to think about ethics primarily in terms of our own individual maxims or actions. Kant defines a kingdom as a "systematic union of various rational beings through common laws." A Kingdom *of Ends* is a union of the ends of all of those rational beings "in systematic connection." Kant is characteristically obscure here. What he seems to mean by a Kingdom of Ends is a social order in which all rational beings are guided by principles that direct them to treat one another as rational beings – more specifically, a principle wherein each is treated as a means to the ends of others but also as end in himself or herself (G 4:433). One salient feature of the Kingdom of Ends is that it will preclude conflict among the ends that different individuals have. The Kingdom of Ends is one where a person's pursuit of an end that cannot be shared with others is disallowed (as we saw in our earlier analysis of the Formula of Universal Law in Chapter 2). This does not entail that every end that any individual has will be fulfilled. For one, the Kingdom of Ends cannot overcome the fact that different individuals have different, and sometimes incompatible, ends. For example, rival businesses may compete for the same set of customers. Yet such competition is permissible in Kant's Kingdom of Ends so long as it serves some larger end shared by all (for example, competition encourages fair pricing, innovation).

But the Kingdom of Ends is not simply a social order in which individuals' ends are transparent and consistent with the ends of all. It is a social order in which individuals' ends harmonize with each other. The ends of the various individuals form a system

> when these ends are not only mutually consistent, but also harmonious and mutually supportive. ... The laws of a realm of ends are such that universally following them would result in the agreement and mutual furthering of the ends of all rational beings in a single unified teleological system.[16]

The Kingdom of Ends is thus not simply an order in which all those ends that can be shared by all are tolerated. Nor is it merely true that each individual's ends are given equal consideration. It is a more robust ideal than this: Each member of the Kingdom of Ends brings to that kingdom her personal ends. The Kingdom of Ends is a social order in which the morally permissible ends of *each* member are promoted by *every* member. The result, in Kant's eyes, is the maximally harmonious relationship among individuals and their respective ends.

Kant deploys the concept of the Kingdom of Ends as the basis for another formulation of the Categorical Imperative: that we must always "act in accordance with the maxims of a member giving universal laws for a merely possible kingdom of ends" (G 4:439). Roughly, we should only act as if our maxims were to function as principles for the Kingdom of Ends. Kant admits that the Kingdom of Ends is not achievable and so functions as a moral ideal (G 4:433). For our purposes, the crucial question is, to the extent that our shared social life instantiates Kant's Kingdom of Ends, how happy would its members be? The answer, I believe, is very happy indeed. Imagine a moral community in which each member is respected as a rational agent and treated as an end in him or herself. Each member fulfills her perfect moral duties and is deeply and continually committed to the ends prescribed by her imperfect duties. Each individual would strenuously develop her talents, thereby increasing the chance that her ends and the ends of others can be realized. Each individual would also be committed to beneficence, to promote the ends of others. In such a community, each person's ends – which together constitute her happiness – would thus be promoted to the maximal degree permissible with treating each person as an end in him or herself. Each individual would not be perfectly happy, of course. But they would be as happy as the demands of morality allow them to be, for they would have as many partners in the pursuit of their happiness as there would be members of the Kingdom of Ends.[17]

[16] Allen Wood, *Kant's Ethical Thought* (Cambridge, 1999), p. 166.
[17] Rawls, Lectures on the History of Moral Philosophy, pp. 232, 312–313.

Again, Kant posits the Kingdom of Ends not as an achievable reality but as an ideal worth approximating. The Kingdom of Ends is that "set (or sets) of possible ends which would be satisfied if all men did their duty and God and nature were cooperative."[18] And of course, God and nature may not be perfectly cooperative with our ends. Not all of our ends would be realized even in the Kingdom of Ends. But the Kingdom of Ends is as close as we can come to what Kant thought of as the "highest good": the coexistence of complete moral virtue with complete happiness (C2 5:111).

What I wish to underscore is that the extensive realization of our ends, and the happiness that thereby accrues to individuals in the Kingdom of Ends, is not achieved by each individual pursuing his or her ends in isolation from other individuals. To a large degree, an individual's happiness hinges on the moral principles that structure the social order in which she lives. Her happiness (or unhappiness) obviously depends to some degree on her own efforts, skills, and acumen. But if Kant is correct about happiness in his Kingdom of Ends, then he holds a view about the origin of happiness that those living in highly individualistic cultures often overlook: The happiness of any one individual is a social, indeed a moral, achievement. Again, the morally decent individual does not have reason to believe that her happiness is assured, according to Kantian morality. Individual morality need not be its own reward. However, if Kant is correct and happiness is in no small measure a social achievement, then a morally decent individual can reasonably hope that her community will contain other similarly decent individuals, thus bringing the Kingdom of Ends closer to fruition and enhancing the prospects that she (and others) can live happy and satisfying lives. In this respect, the social world represented by the Kingdom of Ends is a "world of self-rewarding morality."[19]

8.8 Kant's Practical Postulates

The Kingdom of Ends, I have proposed, presents us a with very compelling ideal, a social order in which happiness is as abundant and as widely distributed as the demands of morality permit. But Kant himself hoped for an even closer relationship between virtue and happiness. This is evident from his treatment of the aforementioned highest good and what he called the "practical postulates."

To speak of a "highest good," Kant says, is ambiguous. It can mean the "supreme" or unconditioned good, which Kant identifies as "virtue" (C2 5:110).

[18] Thomas E. Hill, "The kingdom of ends," in his *Dignity and Practical Reason in Kant's Moral Theory* (Cornell, 1992), p. 59.

[19] Rawls, Lectures on the History of Moral Philosophy, pp. 312–313.

As we saw in Section 1.6, one avenue through which Kant arrives at the Categorical Imperative is by trying to identify the principle that would guide the choices of a morally good will. Such a will would be guided not by its inclinations – that is, by the pursuit of happiness – but by respect for the moral law and respect for the humanity of those subject to that law. In being so guided, the good will exhibits virtue, the "moral strength of a human being's will in fulfilling his duty" (MM 6:405). Virtue in turn makes a person *worthy* of being happy. In contrast to the supreme good, what Kant calls the "whole and complete good" is realized when happiness is added to virtue in equitable proportion. "In the judgment of an impartial reason, which regards a person in the world generally as an end in itself," there is something deficient about a person seeking happiness and, thanks to her moral virtue, being worthy of it but not achieving it. "Inasmuch as virtue and happiness together constitute possession of the highest good in a person, and happiness distributed in exact proportion to morality (as the worth of a person and his worthiness to be happy) constitutes the *highest good* of a possible, the latter means the whole, the complete good." (C2 5:110–111) What is the role of the highest good in Kant's ethics, and in our ethical thinking generally? As Kant sees it, we are not to aim to promote or realize the highest good directly. The "moral law," Kant declares, "is the sole determining ground of the pure will." If the highest good can be achieved, it will be achieved not by pursuing it directly, but by means of developing moral virtue and acting as the Categorical Imperative demands (C2 5:109, 5:119). Nevertheless, the highest good is "the necessary highest end of a morally determined will and is a true object of that will" (C2 5:115). We ought therefore to will the highest good and see its promotion as a duty of ours (C2 5:125). As we have seen in our discussions of the Formula of Universal Law (Section 3.6), Kant holds that a condition on the rationality of pursuing an end is that the realization of that end be possible. So too for the highest good; because "we ought to strive to promote the highest good," the "possibility of this highest good" must be presupposed (C2 5:125).

The trouble is that we have every reason to believe that the highest good is *not* achievable in the world as we know it. A person's happiness is the condition in which "everything goes to his wish and will" (C2 5:124). Unfortunately, nature and morality often do not cooperate or 'harmonize' so that the degree of happiness a person enjoys corresponds with her level of moral virtue. It is an upsetting fact that the morally vicious often get their way, manipulating the world and other people so that everything goes according to their "wish and will." (No doubt you can conjure up images of persons with immense wealth, power, or fame who seem to have the entire world at their beck and call.) Conversely, the morally virtuous sometimes end up miserable, the world seemingly conspiring to work against their "wish and will." (Think here of Job, from the Biblical Old Testament.) There is, Kant says, not the "least ground" for supposing "a necessary connection between the morality and the proportionate happiness of a being belonging to the world as part of it and hence dependent upon it" (C2 5:124). After all, the requirements of morality and the imperatives of happiness often not only fail to coincide – they sometimes stand in opposition to one another (C2 5:112). Indeed, Kant goes so far as to conclude that the highest good, "happiness in exact conformity with moral worth is not to be expected and is to be held *impossible*" in the world as we experience it (C2 5:145, emphasis added).

Kant thus seems to have argued himself into a dilemma: We must, for moral reasons, presuppose that the highest good is possible. Yet based on our own moral experience, we have abundant evidence against its possibility.

Kant's practical postulates are his way of extricating himself from this dilemma. If, as Kant claims, the highest good is not possible in our earthly world – we should not expect the morally virtuous to flourish, nor should we expect the morally vicious to be miserable – then perhaps the highest good is possible over a longer run. Given enough time, though, happiness might well be apportioned to moral virtue. And given that we are, in Kant's eyes, rationally committed to the prospect of the highest good, we must therefore be committed to whatever conditions make it possible. We must therefore presuppose "the *existence* and personality of the same rational being continuing *endlessly* (which is called the immortality of the soul)" (C2 5:122). Note, though, that even if we are immortal, that by itself would not ensure the possibility of realizing the highest good: Each of us could continue to exist forever without virtue and happiness being distributed in accordance with the ideal of the highest good. In order to ensure that the highest good is possible, we must further presuppose the "existence of a cause" capable of bringing about the just distribution of happiness in accordance with moral virtue (C2 5:124). We must therefore 'postulate' the existence of God, a "moral author" of the world able to bring about the "exact conformity" of happiness with moral virtue (C2 5:145). In addition to our wills being free to act on moral demands independently of our inclinations (see Section 5.1 for details), individual immortality and the existence of God are what Kant calls "postulates of pure practical reason" – claims that we are entitled to make not because we possess evidence in their favor, but for "practical purposes" (C2 5:133). Because we are rationally committed to the highest good, we are rationally committed to the conditions necessary for realizing the highest good. The soul's immortality and God's existence are among these conditions. Therefore, Kant reasons, we are rationally committed to the soul's immortality and God's existence.

We will consider whether Kant is correct in arguing that we are committed to these practical postulates in a moment. But we should first be clear on what entitles us to believe in these postulates. Kant repeatedly insists that the postulates in question are *practical*. We are entitled to believe them because of our commitment to morality, and in particular, to the highest good. But this does not entitle us to speculate regarding the specifics of God's nature or our own immortal existence. Granted, God must have the properties that make it possible for God to advance the highest good: In order to be able to ensure that happiness is apportioned to moral virtue, God must possess certain perfections, including being all-knowing, all-powerful, etc. (C2 5:140). But God's existence and our immortality are not put forth by Kant as "theoretical dogmas" or "speculative cognitions" (C2 5:132). They are instead beliefs to which we are rationally drawn by our practical needs, and, in particular, by our moral allegiance to duty and the highest good (C2 5:133). All we are entitled to by dint of Kant's practical postulates is belief in a very minimal God and a very minimal afterlife. Kant therefore does not intend these postulates to lend support to any particular system of religious belief (C2 5:126).

Should those attracted to Kant's ethics be similarly attracted to his practical postulates? Is Kant right that the postulates necessarily arise from our "moral disposition," so that belief in them can "waver ... but can never fall into unbelief" (C2 5:146)? There are, I think, three reasons to be skeptical on this front.

The first is that believing the practical postulates also requires accepting other controversial claims from Kant's metaphysics. As we noted in Section 5.2, Kant argues in his great work of metaphysics, the Critique of Pure Reason, that we have no basis for concluding that God or an immortal soul exists, but also no basis for concluding these do not exist. Establishing whether these claims are true or false necessarily takes us beyond the boundaries of experience, where (Kant maintained) we cannot establish well-founded rational conclusions. From the standpoint of what Kant called "theoretical" reason, God's existence and the soul's immortality are undecidable questions, but it is precisely because they are undecidable that we are permitted to adopt beliefs about them that answer to our moral needs. So long as God's existence and the soul's immortality involve "no intrinsic impossibility" or contradiction, we are permitted to settle the question of their existence on practical, rather than theoretical, grounds (C2 5:4).

The worry is that we might not agree with Kant that theoretical reason leaves these questions available for practical reason to address. Even if Kant is correct that God's existence and the soul's immortality are not inherently contradictory, we might think that Kant is simply wrong to think that the difficulties of mustering evidence for or against these theses means that they cannot be rationally appraised. Generally, when we lack specific positive evidence for a thesis, we do not take this to show that this thesis is equally likely to be true or false. We instead situate that thesis in the context of other things we know or have evidence for. Suppose we consider the thesis that life on Earth began when an alien race colonized the planet's oceans 10 billion years ago. I readily admit that we lack specific evidence to disprove this possibility, but that hardly seems enough to justify being agnostic about it. The alien colonization thesis does not fit the rest of what we know about life on Earth, the possibility of intelligent extraterrestrial species, etc., and so should be treated with great skepticism. Similarly, that we humans are immortal and that there exists an all-powerful God who ensures that virtue is rewarded with happiness may not accord well with what we know about human beings and the laws of nature. And with respect to God's existence, we might reason that the very divergence between virtue and happiness Kant invokes to defend his practical postulates speaks *against* the existence of such a God: As proponents of the well-known philosophical 'problem of evil' may ask, if a benevolent and all-powerful God can ensure that virtue is rewarded with happiness in the afterlife, why does that same God not ensure that virtue is rewarded with happiness in *this* life? For critics with these worries, Kant's practical postulates will seem like wishful thinking, even if, strictly speaking, he is correct that we do not have decisive evidence to refute said postulates. In other words, in order for there to be room for Kant's practical postulates, we must embrace Kant's controversial agnosticism about God's existence and the soul's immortality, and for some, this agnosticism is difficult to swallow.

Second, Kant's practical postulates appears to rest on a suspect version of what is known as *pragmatic reasoning*. Pragmatic reasoning aims to decide what we should believe not on the basis of evidence, but on the basis of the benefits of believing. Here's a well-known example from the American philosopher William James:

> Suppose, for example, that I am climbing in the Alps, and have had the ill-luck to work myself into a position from which the only escape is by a terrible leap. Being without similar experience, I have no evidence of my ability to perform it successfully; but hope and confidence in myself make me sure I shall not miss my aim, and nerve my feet to execute what without those subjective emotions would perhaps have been impossible. But suppose that, on the contrary, the emotions of fear and mistrust preponderate; or suppose that . . . I feel it would be sinful to act upon an assumption unverified by previous experience, – why, then I shall hesitate so long that at last, exhausted and trembling, and launching myself in a moment of despair, I miss my foothold and roll into the abyss. In this case (and it is one of an immense class) the part of wisdom clearly is to believe what one desires; for the belief is one of the indispensable preliminary conditions of the realization of its object. *There are then cases where faith creates its own verification*. Believe, and you shall be right, for you shall save yourself; doubt, and you shall again be right, for you shall perish. The only difference is that to believe is greatly to your advantage.[20]

Note that James' mountain climber lacks evidence that he is in fact able to leap the abyss. But the climber ascertains that he will benefit from believing that he

[20] *The Will to Believe and Other Essays in Popular Philosophy* (Longmans, Green, and Co., 1912), pp. 96–97.

can make the leap. His reasoning is therefore pragmatic, rather than evidence-based: He believes he will succeed because he expects to benefit from the belief, not because the available evidence suggests the belief is true.

The reasoning Kant uses in support of his practical postulates has a similarly pragmatic feel. Though Kant does not quite come out and say this, he seemed to worry that our commitment to the highest good – and our commitment to pursuing moral virtue, the basic condition of the highest good – might waver if we believed that the highest good was ultimately beyond our reach. That the highest good could not be achieved exerts pressure on our allegiance to morality: If we cannot expect virtue to be rewarded with happiness, then virtue must be its own reward – a noble ideal, but one that many people will find hard to live by. Best from a moral perspective, then, to believe the highest good is achievable, which in turn (Kant argues) requires believing in God's existence and the soul's immortality.

The challenge here is that it is not obvious that Kant is correct that the weight of the benefits speaks in favor of believing his practical postulates. Suppose we grant to Kant both that some people will be more committed to the highest good if they believe it is achievable and that their belief in its being achievable will be bolstered if they also believe Kant's practical postulates. Those claims are not enough to justify Kant's practical postulates from a practical point of view, however. For we must also consider whether and how such belief might be detrimental to us. For some, believing that the highest good is achievable only during our immortal afterlives might encourage moral complacency or make the pursuit of the Kingdom of Ends less urgent. After all, if God will *eventually* bring virtue and happiness into harmony, why (aside from our own self-interest) is it especially imperative that we try to develop our moral character? Our confidence that the highest good is achievable has a flipside: In relying on God to ensure its achievability, we may rely less on ourselves and our own efforts to achieve it. On the whole, then, it seems as likely that widespread belief in the practical postulates will make Kant's Kingdom of Ends and the highest good a more remote possibility than a more immediate possibility.[21]

Finally, we might question how Kant understands the highest good as a moral ideal. Again, he reasons that our commitment to the highest good brings in tow belief in the practical postulates as the necessary conditions for its realization. But must a moral ideal be achievable in order for it to be rational to commit to pursuing that ideal? Christians are sometimes admonished to live a Christ-like life. But according to Christian theology, because Jesus was of

[21] This criticism seems also to apply to the cognitive bias psychologists have dubbed the "just world hypothesis" (See A. Furnham, "Belief in a just world: research progress over the past decade," *Personality and Individual Differences* 34 (2003): 795–817).

divine origin, no human being can literally be like him. For Christians, Jesus presents an unachievable ideal. But that fact alone hardly seems to speak against *trying* to live a Christ-like life. This example illustrates that moral ideals can serve two functions: They can serve as *guides* to how to live, or they can serve as *goals* for how to live. Kant usually interprets the highest good as a goal for individuals and for moral communities. But it does not seem unreasonable to see the highest good as a guide for our individual and collective moral lives – as a state of affairs to be striven for, even if it cannot be fully achieved. (Kant himself seems to express sympathy for the highest good as a guide rather than a goal at MM 6:354.) Yet if the highest good is a guide rather than a goal, then we need not assume it is achievable, either in this life or in the afterlife. And if we need not assume it is achievable, then Kant's case for his practical postulates essentially evaporates: Belief in God and in personal immortality would not be necessary conditions of achieving an ideal we pursue without supposing that it can be fully achieved.

Kant's practical postulates are an outgrowth of two instincts: a sincere allegiance to grand moral ideals such as the highest good, along with a world-weary skepticism about those ideals being within our reach. The postulates are an attempt to reconcile these instincts. They cannot, in my estimation, be judged an entirely successful reconciliation. Conceding the desirability of the highest ideal as a moral ideal, it is doubtful that we must treat it as a goal rather than as a guide; even if we treat it as a goal, it is doubtful that this goal is best served by belief in Kant's postulates; and even if it is best served by such a belief, that belief may prove hard to conjoin with apparently powerful non-moral (i.e., metaphysical) considerations that speak against the existence of God and of the immortal soul.

8.9 Conclusion

Kant was a moral philosopher who took the authority of morality seriously and urged his readers to do likewise. He was given to enthusiastic, even fanciful, wonder about moral duty and its reign over our inclinations:

> *Duty*! Sublime and mighty name that embraces nothing charming or insinuating but requires submission, and yet does not seek to move the will by threatening anything that would arouse natural aversion or terror in the mind but only holds forth a law that of itself finds entry into the mind and yet gains reluctant reverence (though not always obedience), a law before which all inclinations are dumb, even though they secretly work against it. (C2 5:86)

Such remarks understandably tempt readers to interpret Kant's ethics as (a) positing a unbridgeable dualism between reason on the one hand and sentiment or inclination on the other, and (b) associating morality with the former and seeing the latter as either morally significant or even at odds with morality. That interpretation is mistaken. Indeed, this dualism of reason and sentiment has a stronger grip on these opponents than on Kant himself. As a result, they overlook how Kantian ethics, despite locating morality's source in our practical rationality, nevertheless ascribes sentiment and inclination indispensable roles in moral deliberation and discernment. Kantian ethics does not give sentiments, personal attachments, and happiness moral carte blanche. But nor does it consign these to the margins of human life either. There is no reason why living as Kantian morality prescribes should result in our being alienated from ourselves, from others, or from our emotional lives.

Further Reading

For additional depictions of Kantian ethics (or Kant himself) as cold, aloof, or unconcerned with the particulars of human relations, see Rae Langton, "Duty and desolation," *Philosophy* 67 (1992): 481–505, and Ermanno Bencivenga, "Kant's sadism," *Philosophy and Literature* 20 (1996): 39–46. Stratton-Lake, Kant, Duty, and Moral Worth (Routledge, 2001) defends a similar view about moral worth and the motive of duty as I have here. Marcia Baron's Kantian Ethics Almost Without Apology (Cornell, 1995) is a thorough and influential treatment of the place of duty in Kant's ethics. Richard Henson, "What Kant might have said: Moral worth and the overdetermination of dutiful action," *Philosophical Review* 88 (1979): 39–54, offers valuable metaphors for how Kantians might think about the conflict between moral and non-moral motives. Sally Sedgwick, "Can Kant's ethics survive the feminist critique?" *Pacific Philosophical Quarterly* 71 (1990): 60–79, raises several of the worries addressed in this chapter from a feminist perspective. Marcia Baron, "Virtue ethics, Kantian ethics, and the 'one thought too many' objection," in M. Betzler (ed.), Kant's Ethics of Virtues (de Gruyter, 2008), is a thorough discussion of the worry that Kant's ethics is too "impartialist" to allow for special concern or special obligations. On the concern that Kantian ethics does not respect individuals as such, see Robin Dillon, "Respect and care: Toward moral integration," *Canadian Journal of Philosophy* 22 (1992): 105–132. Critiques of the place of reason in ethics include Michael Stocker, "The schizophrenia of modern ethical theories," *Journal of Philosophy* 73 (1976): 453–466; Bernard Williams, "Persons, character, and morality," in his Problems of the Self (Cambridge, 1976) and Wolf's "Moral saints," 419–439. On the highest good, see Stephen Engstrom, "The concept of the highest good in Kant's moral theory," *Philosophy and Phenomenological Research* 52 (1992): 747–780, and Paul Guyer, "From a practical point of view: Kant's conception of a postulate of pure practical reason," in *Kant on Freedom, Law, and Happiness* (Cambridge, 2000), pp. 333–371.

9 Conclusion

As stated at the outset, this book has sought to provide an opinionated analytical introduction to Kant's ethics. As the readings listed at the end of the chapters suggest, much more has been written about all of the topics addressed in this book. My aim has not been to present Kant's ethics so as to render reading other secondary literature superfluous. Rather, my aim has been to introduce Kant's ethics to the reader in part so that those wishing to consult other secondary literature can do so without becoming unduly disoriented or discouraged.

At the same time, this book has been analytical in that it aims to help readers appreciate the insight that Kant brought to philosophical ethics. Newcomers to Kant's ethics usually end up identifying Kant's 'greatest hits': the Formula of Universal Law, the Formula of Humanity, his appeal to dignity. Like any skilled philosopher, Kant did not pull his conclusions from thin air, but grasping how Kant motivates these ideas and how they are interrelated is much tougher. My hope is thus that readers have left with a richer sense of Kant's ethical thinking in its totality. In repeated confrontations with Kant's ethical writings, I continue to be struck by how, even as Kant's thinking matured or shifted, certain themes recur. Perhaps the most recurrent, and in my mind the most compelling, is the picture of morality as a cooperative enterprise undertaken by mutually respectful rational equals who seek to live together on shared, transparent terms – terms that enable them to act rationally, both individually and collaboratively, in the pursuit of diverse ways of life.

Finally, this has been an *opinionated* introduction. I have not been studiously neutral on questions of how best to interpret Kant's ethics. My interpretations have been guided not only by Kant's texts but also by my own judgment as to which interpretations are most philosophically credible, taken both in isolation and in light of Kant's other intellectual commitments. In some cases I have suggested that Kant defended claims that fit poorly with his other commitments (various claims he makes about practical issues such as those addressed in Chapter 7 are the most prominent example). Other times his thinking needed to be supplemented in order to solve problems generated by his existing ethical commitments (for instance, the need to consider maxims that fail to take humanity properly into account, as discussed in Chapter 6). There are also subjects where Kant's own approach seems unsatisfying but may be the best on offer. (I would put his treatment of freedom of the will, addressed in Chapter 5, in that category.)

No doubt other scholars can raise legitimate questions about the interpretations I have offered and the positions I contend represent the best Kant (or Kantian ethics). But again, my aim has not been to forestall readers' interest in consulting other interpretations of Kant's ethics. Quite the contrary. Kant was one of the chief architects of the intellectual movements loosely collected under the heading of the 'European Enlightenment.' He famously advocated three principles to guide enlightened thinking. First, we are to think for ourselves and not permit others to do our thinking for us. Second, we are to think from the perspective of everyone else, disinterestedly and with a conscious effort to forego egoistic or self-serving bias. Finally, we are to strive for consistency in our thinking and acting, applying the same rigorous standards to all. In light of these principles of enlightened thinking, it would be deeply un-Kantian of me not to recommend that readers look elsewhere for additional knowledge of Kant's ethics.

Much of this book has been defensive, oriented around addressing Kant's many critics. This is an important undertaking; a philosophical theory is only as plausible as the strong objection it can withstand. However, adopting this defensive posture runs the risk that we lose sight of the appeal of Kant's ethics in the first place. To that end, let us wrap up with a picture of what a conscientious Kantian moral agent looks like – of what it would be like to live as Kant's ethics recommends – in the hope that this serve as a vivid brief in favor of the Kantian moral perspective.

First, a conscientious Kantian moral agent will have a definite self-conception. She will view herself and her choices as deserving of others' respect. She serves as an end in itself, not simply as a means to others' ends – or merely a means to her own. While not arrogant, neither is she servile or unduly modest. At the same time, she extends this same respect to other rational agents, seeing herself as only one rational agent among many. In line with Kant's Formula of Universal Law, she is concerned to act on principles that others can share with her.

The conscientious Kantian will also strive to cultivate moral virtue. But virtue for her is not a state of knowledge (as it was for Plato), nor a state of character moderate in its emotions and choices (as it was for Aristotle), nor an emotional disposition such as sympathy (as it was for David Hume or other 'sentimentalists' in ethics). The conscientious Kantian is not contemptuous of sympathy or other virtues, however. She appreciates their importance in enabling her to perceive the moral landscape aright and to put her own moral convictions into action. But she also sees that in the absence of defensible moral principles to accompany them, these attributes of character can lead her moral judgment astray. For a conscientious Kantian, moral virtue instead consists in strength of moral will: a willingness to subject her maxims and choices to moral scrutiny, as well as a steadfastness in acting only on morally permissible maxims, even in the face of self-interested inclinations to the contrary. As a result of these efforts, the conscientious Kantian is "at peace with herself, calm and tranquil, and yet always prepared to stand down the potential threat to good conduct that her propensity to evil could pose."[1]

That said, the conscientious Kantian is not fixated on fulfilling morality's demands. She has enough confidence to recognize that her own beliefs regarding morality are mostly on the right track – that, by and large, if she refrains from deceit, coercion, promise breaking, manipulation, etc., she will satisfy her perfect duties, and she satisfies her imperfect duties by cultivating her own character and skills while seeking to promote the happiness of others. The conscientious Kantian therefore does not deliberate about every morally significant choice. Her good moral habits enable her to make wise moral choices for the most part, and deliberation is seen as necessary mainly in hard cases or when moral duties appear to conflict. For her, morality is therefore a feature of a life devoted to other worthwhile ends or pursuits, not its sole preoccupation.

The conscientious Kantian's moral outlook is universal and egalitarian. All rational agents are entitled to respect and to an equal degree. The conscientious Kantian is not a jerk, someone who cannot appreciate the perspectives of others and so sees them as tools to be manipulated or worked around.[2] Nor is she an asshole, someone who, from a sense of entitlement, helps herself to special advantages without regard for the concerns of others.[3]

The conscientious Kantian also carves out a separate sphere of moral concern for her family members, friends, colleagues, and the like. For her, these individuals are a source of certain central desires and affections. Beyond this, these relationships function as a laboratory or crucible for developing and exercising her moral agency and the agency of others: By affording them the opportunity to cooperate, plan, and act with one another in intimate and interdependent ways, these special relationships foster the rational agency and moral interrelatedness particular to Kant's Kingdom of Ends.

These special relationships are also a distinctive sort of happiness for the conscientious Kantian individual. She does not expect the world to bend to her will. She recognizes that being good and being happy do not necessarily coincide, and while morality's demands are occasionally onerous, whatever

[1] Anne Margaret Baxley, *Kant's Theory of Virtue: The Value of Autocracy* (Cambridge, 2010), p. 81.

[2] Eric Schwitzgeibel, "A theory of jerks," *Aeon*, June 4, 2014 (http://aeon.co/magazine/philosophy/if-youre-surrounded-by-idiots-guess-whos-the-jerk/).

[3] Aaron James, *Assholes: A Theory* (Anchor, 2014).

resentment they may cause her is short-lived. The inclinations the pursuit of which form the basis of her happiness sometimes interfere with what morality seeks from her. She therefore seeks to govern these inclinations without eliminating them. All the same, she understands that her happiness (and the happiness of others) are the products of both individual and collective action, and she has reason to hope that her own well-being, and the well-being of others, can grow over time. Her happiness is in turn augmented by a certain sense of earned pride in whatever level of moral virtue she has achieved. She has achieved the "contentment with oneself" that Kant understands as a kind of satisfaction associated with the awareness of one's own virtue (C2 5:117).

Above all else, a conscientious Kantian moral agent will be hardheaded but guardedly optimistic about her own capacity for moral choice and moral virtue: She will subject herself to high moral standards but be generous in interpreting the choices and actions of others. She believes that moral improvement, both for individuals and groups, is possible – but not inevitable.

Index